# Wounded Images

"This is a vivid and challenging text that calls upon readers to re-examine and reconstruct the fundamental building blocks of theology through a powerful, poetic encounter with God's wounded image in the literature of Jean Rhys. This meeting with brokenness is both tragic and renewing; it demolishes old paradigms and unfolds to reveal the surprising form of a tender and transformative hope."

—**Heather Walton**, professor of theology and creative practice,
University of Glasgow

"Kristine Whaley offers a nuanced, sensitive, and sophisticated account of a relational theology of the *imago Dei* that insists on taking account of, and remaining accountable to, the experiences of the most marginalized. *Wounded Images* draws together a wealth of material, from a wide-ranging analysis of twentieth- and twenty-first-century theology to a deep consideration of the methodology of theological engagements with literature, to detailed, original readings of the theological implications of Jean Rhys's literary works."

—**Elizabeth Anderson**, senior lecturer in English, University of Aberdeen

"This careful critique of the *imago Dei* focuses on the limitations of traditional hierarchical and oppressive imaginings of God as power. The theme of wounding and trauma is established as a personal and present concern, not an abstract notion that affects others outside of scholarly work. The call to tell, and listen to, stories from the margins and situations of trauma is compelling and makes this book of interest to a reader of theology as lived experience, as well as the academic working in the interdisciplinary field of marginal theologies and literature, and the work of Jean Rhys."

—**Fiona Darroch**, lecturer in religion, University of Stirling

"This book is deeply theological, beginning with Karl Barth and Paul Tillich followed by more contemporary feminist theologians, yet also rooted in the wounded female characters of Jean Rhys' fiction. It weaves complex strands of argument to suggest how God connects to us through the wounds. There are no easy solutions, but the end is not despair, rather a reminder that even the oppressed and broken are made in the image of God who is bound to us in love."

—**David Jasper**, professor emeritus of literature and theology,
University of Glasgow

# Wounded Images

Revisioning the *Imago Dei* through a Reading
of Jean Rhys's Interwar Novels

Kristine M. Whaley

☙PICKWICK *Publications* · Eugene, Oregon

WOUNDED IMAGES

Revisioning the *Imago Dei* through a Reading of Jean Rhys's Interwar Novels

Copyright © 2024 Kristine M. Whaley. All rights reserved. Except for brief quotations in critical publications or reviews, no part of this book may be reproduced in any manner without prior written permission from the publisher. Write: Permissions, Wipf and Stock Publishers, 199 W. 8th Ave., Suite 3, Eugene, OR 97401.

Pickwick Publications
An Imprint of Wipf and Stock Publishers
199 W. 8th Ave., Suite 3
Eugene, OR 97401

www.wipfandstock.com

PAPERBACK ISBN: 979-8-3852-0302-4
HARDCOVER ISBN: 979-8-3852-0303-1
EBOOK ISBN: 979-8-3852-0304-8

Cataloguing-in-Publication data:

Names: Whaley, Kristine M., author.

Title: Wounded images : revisioning the imago dei through a reading of Jean Rhys's interwar novels / by Kristine M. Whaley.

Description: Eugene, OR: Pickwick Publications, 2024. | Includes bibliographical references.

Identifiers: ISBN 979-8-3852-0302-4 (paperback). | ISBN 979-8-3852-0303-1 (hardcover). | ISBN 979-8-3852-0304-8 (ebook).

Subjects: LCSH: Rhys, Jean. | Imago dei. | Theology in literature. | Religion and literature. | Feminist theology. | Womanist theology.

Classification: BX260 W48 2024 (print). | BX260 (epub).

VERSION NUMBER 03/20/24

Scripture quotations marked (NIV) ared taken from The Holy Bible, New International Version® NIV® Copyright © 1973, 1978, 1984, 2011 by Biblica, Inc. Used with permission. All rights reserved worldwide.

Scripture quotations marked (ESV) are taken from The Holy Bible, English Standard Version (ESV), which is adapted from the Revised Standard Version of the Bible, copyright Division of Christian Education of the National Council of the Churches of Christ in the U.S.A. All rights reserved.

For my parents

# Contents

*Acknowledgments* | ix

Prologue | 1

**Part One: Deconstructing Foundations**

1. The Image of God Explored: Examining Twentieth-Century Theological Foundations | 13
2. The Image of God for the Oppressed: Focusing on Lived Truths | 43

**Part Two: A Turn to Literature**

3. Literature as a Challenge to Theology: Forming a Methodology | 69
4. Destruction and Desire: Jean Rhys Novels and a Beginning Theory of the *Imago Dei* | 93
5. Wounds and Connection: Reflection on Isolation and Relationships in Rhys | 125

**Part Three: Reconstructing a Theory of the Imago Dei**

6. Reframing Definitions: Trauma and Immanence | 151
7. Transcendence Redefined: Kathryn Tanner's Radical, Empowering God | 177

Epilogue | 199

*Bibliography* | 205

# Acknowledgments

A GREAT NUMBER OF people supported me during the writing of this, and in several stages of my academic journey. My parents have gone above and beyond to support me, and I am forever grateful to have such loving and inspiring people to raise me. My family continues to be an incredible group of people to always have in my corner. I hope they know I'm in theirs, too. My friends, many of whom have read versions of this, listened to me weep over it, and who have encouraged me to keep going.

I am especially grateful for the support and encouragement I've received from Heather Walton, my doctoral supervisor. I have heard it said that having a good supervisor can make or break your experience, and I had the best of them. Thank you for pushing me, and for believing in me.

# Prologue

I SIT ON THE train from Glasgow to Liverpool, headed for a solo two-day trip in order to allow myself both peace and joy during an annual weekend I have been observing for the past three years. This anniversary of loss is honored as I allow myself to wallow for two days without work, without people trying to cheer me, and without the guilt I often feel for not being better.

Grief has taught me a lot in these last few years, and while I often lament having to compound it through working on a book about trauma, I also realize it has helped me. I wonder what I would be like, or rather, how much more guilty and sad I would be if I did not have this project to help me process. It was not planned. I chose the topic before the tragic events, but the bulk of the work happened after. And as is common with work like this, the research and the personal have bled into one another.

So I sit, looking out the window of the train. Watching this still new-to-me country slide by as I think. I am so glad I can take the train to a new-to-me city, spend some time making fresh memories even as I am focused on old ones. And as I think about how much I am looking forward to seeing Liverpool, to checking another box on my wish list, I also think about how much the me of three or four years ago would not understand about this weekend. I would never have gone alone before. I love being around people—I am an extrovert; I long to have a person with me at all times. I am also a bit anxious and doing new things alone is often scary. Or it used to be. Now, most of my life is spent doing new things on my own, so I have gotten used to it, good at it even. I enjoy dinner at restaurants on my own or going to the movies by myself. It's more than growing older. It's a developed comfortableness with a life unwanted.

As it is commonly, the events leading up to the sudden death of my brother-in-law are all now layered upon themselves, and I had to heal from a myriad of things at once. Loss of an important community, of my beloved dog, of the stability of a full-time job had all preceded Kevin's heart attack but just barely. The months between November and February were difficult, and then unbearable. I had only just decided to take the risk of moving to Scotland to pursue my doctorate full time when Kevin died, and I worried about leaving my family during this time. Losing so much threw me into a depression I had never experienced before. Yet, it was in this depression that I moved to Scotland, somewhat purposefully getting away in the hopes that I could heal.

And so, this anniversary weekend is when I mourn many things. Who I was. Who I thought I was going to be. My deeply loved dog, Lizzy. Kevin, who had been married to my sister for twenty-three years, since I was eleven, and was really another brother. I mourned the life I had once loved and which now seemed like a terrible memory. I had been working at a small Christian school, which had begun as a wonderful community of diverse theological thought. I had found a community to inspire me to pursue my own theological research. Yet, due to significant differences of opinion at the administrative level, the department I admired was quickly dismantled and replaced with a strict sense of complementarian theology. Clearly, this left me ostracized, and I was faced with the choice to stay at a lower position and give up my doctoral studies, or to leave. After deciding to leave, I realized that in the midst of systemic, organized misogyny, I had been unable to do anything other than survive. In leaving, I realized that for me survival actually meant escape, even though I originally saw it as losing. This shift in understanding my "calling" had also added to the intense grief and mourning. Instead of overcoming circumstances, meeting my goals, and feeling like one made in the image of God, I felt beaten and desperate. I found myself unable to perform simple tasks, the trauma of the situation affecting even the most mundane areas of my life. The wounds left by the layers of trauma exposed even more, less-obvious wounds which I had been hiding for years.

This weekend anniversary helps me to remember all of this. I remember it as grief but also as redemption. Because what I have learned from the trauma itself and the years that followed is that healing doesn't look like I thought it would. Healing has looked like many moments of solitude, a thing I never thought I'd long for. It has looked like change—of scenery, of friends, of day-to-day life. Healing looks like weekend trips to a new city alone, just so that I can allow myself to cry as much as I want or laugh as much as I want. As I sit on that train, I just keep thinking about how exciting it will be to do *whatever I want*. There are things I want to see, but I keep the list short in case I decide something else has caught my eye. I will take pictures, but I won't send them until I'm back in Glasgow. This weekend is for me. It is for the me from before, who is not the me now, nor the me I will become.

And this is what healing has meant to me. That there is freedom, both in allowing myself to mourn and weep and allowing myself to hope. I do not need to be anything else, because what really has happened in my healing is that I have stopped running. I have finally realized what my counsellor meant when she told me I needed to believe that God loved the me I was, rather than the me I was trying to be. I have stopped trying to become something and have decided to let that version of me arrive at her leisure.

## A Journey

I begin this book with a reflective prologue because as I have worked through this research, I have become aware of my need to both locate myself in the research and also outside of it. I obviously have personal ties to the topic of this work, yet I have also become aware of the danger of not acknowledging my own limitation in studying trauma. As philosopher Lorraine Code states in her chapter of *Feminist Epistemologies*, belief in a "view from nowhere . . . presupposes a universal, homogenous, and essential 'human nature' that allows knowers to be substitutable for one another."[1] The idea of a universal human experience is not only provably inaccurate, but unhelpful, particularly in my research. Instead, as Code argues for, I sought not only to understand my own experience and viewpoint, but to then break that down by knowing the lives and experiences of others. The structure of this book follows that process—therefore, I must first understand and explain my own standpoint.

I began to think about what it meant to be made in the *imago Dei* when I first encountered the predominant theories about the concept in

---

1. Alcoff and Potter, *Feminist Epistemologies*, 16.

seminary. I had struggled throughout my life to feel as if I fit in, and so grasping at this doctrine was another search for my sense of self. I had been raised in an Evangelical home, attending primarily Evangelical churches. I had never heard other than Evangelical theological theories about things like the atonement, free will, or the *imago Dei*. So, I was inspired learning from twentieth century theologian Karl Barth. His insistence on God as the sole actor in our redemption always gave me relief.[2] To think that I did not have to be perfect to be loved by God was refreshing. His theory of reconciliation as our salvation also provided me a much-needed shift in thinking. However, even in the theology he gave me, I was still unsatisfied with his anthropology. Still feeling out of place in seminary, particularly as I was only one of two women in the program, I hoped that regardless of my success, fulfilment, or ability to become, I was still one of these images, and I could not find this in Barth. I wanted to remove the image from any kind of requirement on me or my abilities, and to believe instead that I could merely survive. Most importantly, I began to believe that to be in God's image did not have to mean fulfilling other people's expectations of myself, but instead would be something that I could believe at my lowest moments. This belief could bring me out of the darkness and carry me through the places I could not walk.

I began to study more diverse theology, as well. Global theology, liberation and process theology, and particularly feminist theology all opened my eyes to ways I had believed theological theories simply because of my background rather than because they were correct or most generally logical. As I read through various literature, I kept coming back to the ways women, and other marginalized people, are unable to simply overcome the obstacles, oppressions, or traumas that prevent them from recognizing the image in themselves. Therefore, not only is it important that I recognize where I stand in this research, but it is essential that I decenter myself. In order to allow diverse experiences to inform my research, I have to "interactively"[3] know others. As philosopher Sandra Harding explains the need for me to see how marginalized people experience

---

2. "Hence it follows that the work of God in the working of the creature, and His revelation in the revealing of the creature, can never be ascribed to the creature, but only and always to God Himself. That which works is His co-operating love. That which speaks is His co-operating Word. And for that working and speaking the creature on its side has no capacity. It is not, then, the creature which works in God's working, but God Himself who works on and in His own working. God alone is and remains eternal love" (Barth, *Church Dogmatics* III/3, 111).

3. Alcoff and Potter, *Feminist Epistemologies*, 20.

trauma. She states: "Knowledge claims are always socially situated, and the failure by dominant groups critically and systematically to interrogate their advanced social situation and the effect of such advantages on their beliefs leaves their social situation a scientifically and epistemologically disadvantaged one for generating knowledge."[4]

While theology has helped broaden and deepen my understanding of God and the world, I have always found literature (particularly from the period between the World Wars) to teach me in profound ways. It has been a helpful tool in understanding the larger world, as well as locating how I experience it. I am especially drawn to books that allow us to see complex characters not as role models, but instead as demonstrations of truths about life. As a teenager, I discovered amongst my mother's books *The Great Gatsby*. I was enraptured by the book and the world it created, so I read everything that F. Scott Fitzgerald wrote. I loved his ability to construct such a beautiful world that was simultaneously so deeply broken. I saw Gatsby as a tragic figure who was unable to really know himself. His self-hatred was the primary theme that I perceived through the novel, but I also recognized Fitzgerald's return to it throughout his other works. He wrote of men desperately trying to be something better, hoping that the money and fame and prestige and company would all fix the wounds of their pasts. I admired the lack of happy endings, too. In particular, in the short story, "Babylon Revisited," we see the effects of what Fitzgerald believes is a poisonous drive of the American Dream. Having lost his wife and lost custody of his daughter, Charlie Wales tries to fix his life. Yet no one believes he is better, and he ends the story still alone and sorrowful. Charlie, disconnected from community, does not find redemption for his trauma and wounds.

It is in Fitzgerald's attempts to demonstrate the fruitlessness of this type of achievement that I began to connect trauma to my dissatisfaction in *imago Dei* theories. I realized that I had been trying to become not just a theologian, but one without an adjective. Instead of a relational theology, done in conversation and in community, I thought it better to seek an unbiased doctrine—something which I now understand is impossible, no matter who attempts it. I wanted to shed essential aspects of my life because they seemed like obstacles. Like Gatsby, I was trying to recreate myself as someone I imagined I should be but who did not really exist. However, I realized, my *imago Dei* could not be in a belief that I had to

---

4. Alcoff and Potter, *Feminist Epistemologies*, 54.

deny parts of myself; by doing that I would have been all surface and no substance, no truth, just like Gatsby's elaborate façade. I am a woman. I am white. I have lived, and I have the scars and memories that come along with that. These parts of me are the lenses through which I see and am seen. My place in the world matters. As philosopher Giorgio Agamben said, "it is only through recognition by others that man can constitute himself a person."[5] It is not that others put an identity on me, but that I know myself through the recognition of others. I know myself both in how I am similar to and different from people around me. I know things about myself because of how I relate to other people, how I react to them, and how I am affected by them. Agamben goes on to explain that we mask ourselves, trying to be seen in certain ways, but this is not truly being known. He says, "What we must search for is simply the figure of the living being, for that face beyond the mask . . ."[6] I need to know myself, but also others, as we are actually. Not in what we strive to be.

Therefore, it became necessary to examine the *imago Dei* in terms of characters who I had initially thought were not like me. Or, rather, were more like me than I wanted to believe. I wanted to see what could happen if the hero of the story did not overcome, did not learn to love herself. Could I believe that someone who failed was, exactly as they are, also made in God's image? And what would this do to my understanding of God? How can a flawed, wounded person image a perfect God? And if they could, could I?

The novels of Jean Rhys are similar to Fitzgerald's in time period, geographical location (for some), and beautiful prose. Again, you see a world artfully described that removes the mask of achievement. Her characters, in various ways, attempt to hide, fix, or change who they are in order to become who they wish they were. Rhys's incredible, ahead-of-her-time understanding of intersectional oppression makes clear that the women have had little choice in their circumstances. The women of Rhys's novels have been abused, oppressed, and neglected. They do not always make good decisions, but they are not the privileged men of Fitzgerald's stories, throwing away or wasting opportunity. You feel for these women, but you also get angry at them. You wish you could help them, and you wish they would help themselves. You want someone to be nice to them, and you want them to stop being so mean to some people and trusting of

---

5. Agamben, *Nudities*, 46.
6. Agamben, *Nudities*, 54.

the wrong people. The women are complicated, but Rhys does not help them out of their trouble. Rhys's novels also do not have happy endings, but rather complex demonstrations of how multiple layers of suffering leave people without the possibility of so-called happiness.

In examining different theories of the *imago Dei*, various understandings and conceptions of God, and diving deeply into the complicated world of Jean Rhys, I have discovered a way to understand the image of God that is always present in the wounds, the hurt, and the joys we carry with us. I can now see that I was never supposed to strive to become God, but instead to allow an intertwined relationship with myself, God, and the world in order to redeem the wounds I have. I do not try to go back to a clean slate, a version of myself that did not suffer, nor do I pretend these wounds are gone or were somehow actually good things. I see that I may suffer again, but these sufferings and my failings do not remove my *imago Dei*. If I want to believe, as Christian theology teaches, that everyone is made in the image of God, I must start with understanding how the image is present even when we do not see it or feel it. When we cannot acknowledge our own achievements, or when we merely survive the life we are in, we must be able to simultaneously acknowledge God with us. I cannot ask any longer how I am meant to become the image of God, but instead say that I am in every stage of life part of the *imago Dei* and allow that to transform how I move in the world.

## Structure

This book, then, is much like my train journey. Though this journey has personal impact, it is also one I find vital for theological work. It is necessary that theology is able to specifically identify the *imago Dei* in a broken, traumatized humanity. In not clearly demonstrating how the image is reflected in those who most need to be seen as part of the image, we have allowed the theory to be exclusionary and to perpetuate oppression.

My work is in three main sections. The first section, comprised of chapters one and two, will work through various helpful and foundational theories. Chapter 1 briefly examines the works of Karl Barth and Paul Tillich before moving into an overview of early feminist theologians' responses to them. In examining Barth and Tillich, I wish to first understand why they were so helpful in my initial theological reconstruction. The focus Barth has on relationship and the work of God has been very influential in my personal theology, and I need to begin there in order to give a proper foundation to my own work. Tillich, similarly, allowed my early theological convictions to incorporate my experiences. His method of correlation was the first experience I had of seeing theology interact practically with life. However, as I demonstrate through feminist responses to them, their work was still lacking in many ways. In understanding how Valerie Saiving, Judith Plaskow, Mary Daly, and Rosemary Radford Ruether interacted with these men and other contemporary theologians, I am able to begin explaining the challenges that I still face.

Chapter 2 is an examination of Black and womanist theology, particularly the work of Katie Geneva Cannon. The challenges Black theology offers to the work of those in Chapter One are essential to expand theology in order that it not be seen as predominantly white, especially in its application. Cannon's theology is foundational, and her method allows it to become practical and active. Through this chapter, I have able to again identify how strength and the ability to overcome have been too predominant in most *imago Dei* understanding.

In the second section I turn to literature as a theological resource. I will explain and defend my methodology in chapter 3, looking at both the ways Cannon has combined literature and theology well, and the ways in which I think it can be critiqued and developed. In understanding the arguments of philosophers like Martha Nussbaum and Anneleise van Heijst, I develop a method of examining literature that challenges my theology and prepares me to rebuild it with important questions in mind. Therefore, as I explain, I work to remove the desire to ignore or inappropriately heal trauma and oppression, and to allow the work of Jean Rhys to challenge how I will reconstruct my *imago Dei* theory. This leads me to chapters 4 and 5, where I analyze the four interwar novels of Rhys, seeing what traits her characters share and how they might inform my theology. In Rhys, I do not get answers, but instead I am able to narrow my focus. Her characters, amateur sex workers—women who are excluded from society who also begin to exclude themselves—offer challenges to my implicit bias toward those who help themselves. As Fitzgerald's work is often credited for critiquing the American Dream, Rhys's work truly critiques the social hierarchies we often do not question. She is not simply arguing for equality between genders, but she layers various obstacles for her characters to give us an understanding of how economic, national, and gendered bias works together to exclude the most vulnerable populations. Her women are outcasts even from the groups they (seemingly) should be part of, but they are also not mere victims. In not only showing how the women have been abused, she explains how they then turn on others. In different ways, they each try to make someone even lower than themselves so that they can feel "better than." It is this principle that ultimately breaks apart the former *imago Dei* theologies I held, forcing me to reconstruct my theory based on my encounter with Rhys's fictional world.

The final section is the reconstruction of my *imago Dei* theory. Examining first theologies of trauma, in chapter 6, I see how various theologians have emphasized the need to acknowledge and redeem trauma. These theologians, particularly Shelley Rambo and Catherine Keller, also explain the need to see God actively working in the world. In this chapter, I develop not only a better understanding of trauma, but also the immanence of God. Because of a renewed understanding of immanence, I also look at the focus of God as primary actor, seeing how allowing God to be active and present also removes the need for us to overcome those things that demean us in order to reflect the image of God. Yet, because of the challenges raised by Keller's panentheism (in which I critique her understanding of God's agency in transformation of people's lives), I also need to examine my understanding of who God is.

This leads to chapter 7, where I explore Kathryn Tanner's radical definitions of transcendence and immanence. By seeing how redefining these terms has allowed Tanner to reconcile aspects of Barth's theology of transcendence with her political theology requiring activism, I can also reconcile my belief in God as an active and unique being within the world with the trauma that I must acknowledge. Redefining transcendence then allows me to understand God as essentially connected to human trauma and wounds, leading me to a new definition of the *imago Dei*. This new understanding allows a paradox of hope and trauma, aligning the image with the grief of the broken.

Working on this project has been therapeutic for me to reconstruct my theological understandings. Yet it has also forced me to see the various ways I was both abusing myself and others. I realize that my trauma does not stop me from also inflicting harm, but that it also can allow me to connect with others in their own trauma. There is importance in how I understand what trauma can restore.

This train trip to Liverpool is not long. A couple of hours, and I am in a new city. I'm here to explore a place I've heard so much about. I'm here, alone on Valentine's Day no less, to spend a night in a hotel room with takeaway and wine while I cry about loss. I'm also here to gain things. As I ride a tour bus around, I make friends with a couple visiting from the States. They complement me on my bravery. I smile and thank them, laughing inside at how a previous version of me would have been aghast to see this trip. It is a quick journey, but one I am grateful to take. Much like this journey I've been on for years, it introduces me to new people and hope and, as I stand in the pouring rain looking out at the sea, I am filled with love.

# PART ONE

## Deconstructing Foundations

# 1

# The Image of God Explored

Examining Twentieth-Century
Theological Foundations

## Introduction

IN ORDER TO CRITIQUE and restructure an understanding of the *imago Dei* that speaks to the concerns of women like myself, as well as those of others who are further marginalized by oppressive cultural and theological understandings, I will begin in this chapter by examining the work of those theologians who first challenged my previous understandings of the *imago Dei*. As I learned about the influential work of twentieth century neo-orthodox theology, particularly the work of Karl Barth, I began to see the way in which God and humanity relate in new and more practical ways. Further, the methodology of Paul Tillich allowed me to see that rather than believing the *imago Dei* to be a theoretical concept not easily grasped, it could radically impact my daily life. Therefore, in this chapter I will look first at the work of Karl Barth, and the very practical aspects of his theology. Secondly, I will examine the work of Paul Tillich, whose work both directly addresses some of Barth's conclusions and is often used in formulating responses to Barth by feminist and liberation theologians. Finally, I will briefly discuss some early feminist developments and critiques of the work of these and other influential male theologians. These mirror the questions I wish to pose and also show me the direction in which I need to travel in order to address the challenges that motivate this research.

What follows is therefore not a comprehensive or in-depth discussion of these figures, but instead the beginning of road map I am constructing to explore the *imago Dei* in its complexity. Understanding the foundation upon which I began this exploration is vital and these first steps will continue to impact upon more comprehensive analyses as I move through the various ways in which contemporary theological work has expanded upon this important doctrine.

## Exploring Barth's Theory of the *Imago Dei*

Karl Barth's influence in systematic theology marks arguably one of the most important shifts in theology in the contemporary age. References to his work appear in a wide range of theological texts, from systematic to practical. Some of these contain critiques of his patriarchal approach, as well as noting other areas of concern. These are significant but it is also important to highlight the important contribution his theology made at a particularly crucial time. Working directly against what he saw as theology "compromised in the face of the ideology of war,"[1] a compromise he believed had discredited liberal theology during the years leading up to the First World War,[2] Barth sought to demonstrate the ways theological work could address social issues while maintaining a commitment to orthodox principles. Thus, Barth did not divorce his theology from his context, but instead worked directly in response to the horrors of the wars and the Holocaust and steadfastly critiqued the ways Christian theology was being used to justify oppression and genocide.[3] Particularly important in Barth's work is the focus on God's work in the world, which Barth sees as specifically accomplished in the Incarnation of Christ. In order to understand his *imago Dei* theory, I will thus begin with his work

---

1. Grenz and Olson, *20th Century Theology*, 67.

2. "He was scandalized to find that nearly all of his liberal professors publicly supported Kaiser Wilhelm II's war effort." Smith, *Theology of the Third Article*, 17.

3. "Liberal theology left no resources for self-critique in that it located the life and power of God in the fulfillment of idiosyncratic human goods. Now patriotism, collective achievement, and racial purity were endowed with divine significance and made relevant to salvation . . . Against this, Barth took a definite theological posture, which endured throughout his life's work." Smith, *Third Article*, 17.

on Christology, and then on the nature of God, focusing particularly on how these impact his theory of humanity.

It is through the Incarnation that God's reconciliation work is completed, fulfilling the will of God. As Barth said, "All things in heaven and earth are the objects of the divine purpose. But this purpose is not disclosed in all things; it is disclosed only in man. [sic][4] The cosmos surrounding man is not alien to God."[5] Barth believed, primarily, that the purpose of God is to restore Creation. He sees this focus on reconciliation as central to understanding God's freedom and love. Because God freely choses to love Creation, and therefore reconcile with it, "this desire and decision for union with creatures in Jesus Christ was . . . the ground and basis of the creation of the world itself."[6] This restoration was always intended to be undertaken through the Incarnation, and in fact, creation was set in motion for "no other reason than to enter into covenant fellowship with it . . . "[7] This restoration is achieved through Christ and reconciles God and humanity. Therefore, for Barth, God's purpose and work in the world is embodied in Christ. He says:

> [Jesus] is the creaturely being who as such embodies the sovereignty of God, or conversely the sovereignty of God which as such actualizes this creaturely being. He is the creaturely being whose existence consists in His fulfillment of the will of God. And finally He is the creaturely being who as such not only exists from God and in God but absolutely for God instead of for Himself.[8]

As stated, God works purposefully toward the restoration and reconciliation of Creation, which as embodied by Christ is then passed to humanity in order to continue that work. He says, "For the Creator Himself has turned to His creature not only in general but most particularly."[9] Relationship with this creature is, then, of primary importance, and "He

---

4. It had been custom for "man" to indicate "human," and while some take the time to "translate" this term according to our current standards, I believe it is important to leave the words as they stand. Even as "man" was supposed to stand for all humans, this is clearly a symbol of women's separation from God. Discussions revolve around "man and God," rather than "woman and God."

5. Barth, *Church Dogmatics* III/2, 16.

6. Grenz, *20th Century Theology*, 74.

7. Grenz, *20th Century Theology*, 74.

8. Barth, *Church Dogmatics* III/2, 133.

9. Barth, *Church Dogmatics* III/2, 3.

who is the Creator of man is also the Creator of the cosmos, and His purpose towards the latter, although hidden as such, is none other than His revealed purpose for us."[10] This purpose of restoration is not solely God's, as it has now become humanity's purpose as well. However, the brokenness of humanity leaves us unable to accomplish this task. Barth argues it is always in and through Christ as God and Man that the divide is restored. Barth says, "Even the fact that man is the creation of God, standing as such in a special relation to God, is a fact that is not accessible to human thought and perception otherwise than through the Word of God [Christ]."[11] Christ is the enactor, allowing humanity to be able to see God and participate in relationship with God.

In this, we see that for Barth, God's omnipotence is all-encompassing. God acts and in so doing, enables humanity to act. By bringing humanity into the work of God, again focused on the restoration of Creation, Barth states that all work done is located within this encompassing will of the One God. This means "God is one and indivisible in His working . . . [the Trinity] does not imply the existence of separate and divine departments and branches of authority."[12] Barth's belief that the Triune God acts as One in purpose is thus transposed to the human as also acting in this one purpose. He continues: "This is the fundamental consideration on the basis of which we regard it as legitimate and necessary to enquire specifically about the command of God the Creator at the conclusion of the doctrine of creation . . . For the work of creation itself is not separate, nor is it a mere part of the one whole command, but the one whole command in this particular form."[13] God's work, done through the activity of the Trinity and then passed on to humanity, is always focused on this primary goal of restored relationship. In centralizing this goal, Barth is then able to see each action of humanity as either for reconciliation or against it (and thus against God). Yet it is also important to continually stress the significance Barth places on all salvific activity being primarily the work of God. No reconciling activity can happen apart from God.[14]

10. Barth, *Church Dogmatics* III/2, 18.
11. Barth, *Church Dogmatics* III/2, 25.
12. Barth, *Church Dogmatics* III/4, 33.
13. Barth, *Church Dogmatics* III/4, 35.
14. "Hence it follows that the work of God in the working of the creature, and His revelation in the revealing of the creature, can never be ascribed to the creature, but only and always to God Himself. That which works is His co-operating love. That which speaks is His co-operating Word. And for that working and speaking the creature on its side has no capacity. It is not, then, the creature which works in God's working, but

## The Nature of Humanity and Sin

As humans are unable to act according to God's will without God first reconciling with us, the understanding of human activity must first be centered, again, on Christ. The Incarnation is the definitive reconciling act, and so humanity, in replicating Christ's action, must itself be understood through Christ. This is the important shift Barth makes to shape the concept of the "Human" through prioritizing Christ. Rather than centering the discussion of humanity upon people, Barth says, "It is from within this context that theological anthropology must interpret man. But in so doing it interprets man himself in his inner reality."[15] When Barth then uses this framework to discuss the Christian's call to be Christ to the world, this means human activity continues the activity of Christ. The reconciling work that humans do is participation in the continued reconciliation of the Incarnation. Barth says of humanity:

> They are not simply and directly the covenant-partners of God as His creature; they are destined to become this. And this means concretely that they are destined to participate in the benefits of the fellow-humanity of that One, to be delivered by Him . . . From the very first, even in their creatureliness, they stand in the light which is shed by Him. But if they are in His light, they cannot be dark in themselves, but bright with His light.[16]

However, human beings are not God and sin disrupts their participation in God's reconciling work. Sin, in Barth's view, is the replacement of God with self. He explains that "Sin in its totality is always pride."[17] As with his other doctrines, Barth understands sin Christologically. Sin manifests itself as the human acting in place of God and participating in evil that opposes the work of God in Christ. Going against the work of Christ can be seen as attempting to usurp the hierarchy of God over humanity or, simply stated, attempting to be powerful outside of God's will. Any such human action then represents a failure in fulfilling who we were created to be, because it is done apart from reconciliation with God. Actions that perpetuate the destruction of Creation, like sloth or deceit, can only be overcome by the work of Christ in reconciling with Creation.

---

God Himself who works on and in His own working. God alone is and remains eternal love" (Barth, *Church Dogmatics* III/3, 111).

15. Barth, *Church Dogmatics* III/4, 25.
16. Barth, *Church Dogmatics* III/4, 225.
17. Barth, *Church Dogmatics* IV/1, 414.

In Barth's context, we can see the work of the Nazi party as a model for what it means to act directly against God. The destruction of other human lives, deceit about God and God's purpose, and the attempt to elevate some new view of the right ordering of creation directly contradict Christ himself. In analyzing Barth's view of sin, Aaron T. Smith says, "Sin is perpetual criminal offense, unjustified reversal of life and death, the relationship in which we stand with God . . . It is robbing God of his due majesty and glory by placing ourselves first and him second."[18] Understanding how Barth perceives the doctrine of humanity as having practical consequences for how life should be lived in the world enables us appreciate the importance he places on rightly conforming our theological approach to God's revelation. To understand God in any way apart from the specific life and work of Christ is, in Barth's view, not only not to know God but also to work against God's reconciling purposes in the world.

## The Nature of God

In this context, Barth's work on the Trinity, and especially the Spirit, can give practical insights into God's continuing work of restoration after the Incarnation. Barth's analogy of the Trinity as Revealer, Revelation, and Revealedness[19] indicate a unity in action. As Arvin M. Gouw explains, "In the revelation-based trinity, the unity of God lies in the essence of God. But in the reconciliation-based trinity, the unity of God lies in the bond of the Holy Spirit."[20] As stated, the Triune God works as a unified whole in the act of reconciliation, but Barth locates our bond to that act in the process of Christ as Revelation and the Spirit as bonding us to that Revelation. The Spirit, now the direct presence of God in the world, works through humanity in a cooperative mission to continue the purpose of God.

In his book on Barth's pneumatology, Smith says, "As Spirit *of the Word*, God exists and is known in the time of his acts, in his history

---

18. Smith, *Third Article*, 26.

19. This analogy can be seen in many explanations of Barth's trinitarian doctrine, but can also be seen in *Church Dogmatics* III/4, 32. As I earlier quoted, he states, "God is one and indivisible in His working. That He is Creator, Reconciler and Redeemer does not imply the existence of separate divine departments and branches of authority . . . Always in the ethical event God commands and man acts in all three spheres at once."

20. Gouw, "Transcendence and Immanence of the Trinity in Barth and Lossky," 28.

with humankind."[21] (emphasis original) God's acts are now linked to the Church's acts as the Church acts in accordance with God's will and nature, seen through Christ. Barth sees this as a progression of activity in the world, moving from the first person of God to the third that is connected to us. He explains that this progression highlights the relationship between God and humans as well, saying, "it leaves the Creator and the creature and their mutual relationship within the bracket of the *credo*."[22] This credo, the Christian belief about God, states that God freely created out of God's own loving desire to be in relationship with Creation. Again, I quote Barth:

> It is the noetic basis of creation. When and as we know what free and absolutely basic and controlling grace is—the grace of God revealed to us in Jesus Christ as the remission of sins and the resurrection of the dead, as the kingdom of God—only then do we know, but then we know for certain, what creation is, who the Creator is confronting man, and what it means to be the creature of this Creator . . . "[23]

It is from the beginning demonstrative of the character of God, in the actions of creation and Incarnation, to be reconciled with and in restored relationship with humanity.

Yet while God works toward reconciliation, humans in their brokenness (sin) are still distinct from God. They are, he emphasizes, "the creature man, who would not exist without God, who exists only by His will, who has contributed nothing to Him . . . "[24] This distinction reminds us of the broken aspects of humanity—pride and disunity, which keep humanity from fully participating in the reconciliation of Christ. Therefore, demonstrating Christ's reconciling relationship between God and the world also highlights distinction between humans, and shows that relationship among humanity is a practical outworking of this doctrine. In explaining this, Barth employs an understanding of relationship based upon the I-Thou encounter.[25] This event is firstly one through which Jesus brings humans into their true humanity. Jesus

21. Smith, *Third Article*, 165.
22. Barth, *Church Dogmatics* III/4, 39.
23. Barth, *Church Dogmatics* III/4, 39.
24. Barth, *Church Dogmatics* III/4, 39.
25. Barth was influenced by Martin Buber's book *I and Thou*, published in 1923, which explains Buber's understanding of humanity's relationship with God. Barth, and others, used this concept in developing his own understanding as I discuss here.

takes the confession of "I am" and then requires us to respond to that. As Barth says, "In thinking and pronouncing this word [I], I do not remain in isolation."[26] As Jesus says "I," we relate to Him and then say "I," relating to others. Furthermore, our response is as the "Thou." We are both "Thou" to Jesus and to each other.

The Spirit reforms us to a humanity reflecting Christ. To be truly human is, as previously stated, to be like Christ. Smith explains, "It is the life and action of the Spirit to overcome our reality with God's, to be the self-determinative capacity of God for us."[27] It is therefore, as Lisa P. Stephenson points out, an *imago trinitatis* that humans display. She says, "Therefore, humans display the *imago Dei* in a twofold sense: by being created as a 'Thou' whom God as an 'I' can confront and . . . existing in an I-Thou relationship to one another."[28] Barth's focus in this area is consistently on two things: that humans display the *imago Dei* in relation to both God and each other, and that God is the primary agent enabling humans to do this. Stephenson explains that there are four principles to Barth's appropriation of model of the I-Thou relationship as it applies to mutual relationships within humanity. She defines these as:

1. Begin with one person looking the other in the eye.

2. There is to be mutual speaking and hearing between the two persons. Although openness within an encounter is vital and lays the groundwork for humans, they must go beyond being open and move into the experience of speech.

3. Mutual assistance is provided between the two persons.

4. This conception resists the precedence of individuality and points persons toward the other. It rejects the Cartesian "I think, therefore I am" philosophy in which it is possible to be an "I" without a "Thou." In addition, this conception of the *imago Dei* embraces the totality of the human person. The image is not to be found only in one aspect of a person (e.g. soul, reason), but includes all aspects [of selfhood].[29]

---

26. Barth, *Church Dogmatics* III/4, 244.
27. Barth, *Church Dogmatics* III/4, 33.
28. Stephenson, "Directed, Ordered and Related," 439.
29. Stephenson, "Directed, Ordered and Related," 447–48.

## The Image of God

This brief review of Barth's theology demonstrates the holistic understanding that underpins Barth's relational model of the *imago Dei*. It implies much more than a mere concession that humans image God by being in relationship with each other or even with God. The relationship required demands more than an ideal form of love. Instead, Barth stresses that this loving relationship is working toward a shared purpose. We do not simply love each other in the theoretical sense, but rather we must also practically impact upon each other and recognize how we each interact in order to reconcile with God. Once again, it is important to be aware of Barth's context, and his concern that proper theology leads to better society (as evidenced particularly in his opposition to the German Christian Church of Nazism[30]).

### *Relationship as Liberation*

The focus Barth places on Christ's work and his centering human action on the purposes of God has been significant in some forms of liberation theology.[31] In her essay on this topic, Jane A. Barter says, "The idea of liberation cannot, according to Barth, be grounded in theories of the self or society; but instead, must be given its content in the concrete historical encounter of God with humanity in Jesus Christ."[32] This establishes the purpose of reconciliation as paramount, in light of God's reconciliation with all of humanity. It then works to prevent human motives or selfishness from damaging the work of liberation, and thus can keep liberation open to all people. This liberative work does not mean the person will be freed from oppression, but that the oppressed can be confident in being liberated to both self-actualization and participation in the divine purpose. She explains, "In Christ, the Christian is liberated *to* service of God *and* neighbour."[33] The person is able to act in the mission of reconciliation and extend this mission of reconciled relationship to others. In both Barter's and Stephenson's assessments, Barth's relational *imago Dei*

---

30. "Barth's theology is able to take a prophetic stance toward the world, a strength that clearly demonstrated in his early denunciation of Nazism as a form of idolatry . . ." Grenz, *20th Century Theology*, 75.

31. See my later discussion of James Cone, chapter 2.

32. Barter, "Theology of Liberation," 160.

33. Barter, "Theology of Liberation," 160.

allows people to work toward better and mutual I-Thou relationships, which would theoretically reduce oppression. Liberation in context of reconciliation allows for the restoration of both the oppressed and the oppressor, ideally. The overthrow of these oppressive relationships would be achieved with a perfected living out of the I-Thou relationship. This mode of living would mirror the Trinity, bringing humans closer to living in accordance with God's purposes for creation. He explains: "In its basic form humanity is fellow-humanity. Everything else which is to be described as human nature and essence stands under this sign to the extent that it is human. It if is not fellow-human, if it is not in some way an approximation to being in the encounter of I and Thou, it is not human."[34] Through this understanding, our human relationships must more closely replicate the mutuality of the Trinity, and thus become more focused on reconciliation. As Barth emphasizes of the Trinity, "The *perichoresis* of God's three modes of being does not destroy their independence."[35] Emphasizing the unity and independence of the Trinity again, Barth allows for their differing actions toward the same will. While Barth sees each member's action as unique, the outcome (restoration) is the same. Humanity, then, should likewise act toward this same goal, even as individual works and circumstances differ. God's outward empowering work restores creation, giving it the ability to return this love to God and to Creation as a whole.

### Relationship as Hierarchy

This argument for a reconciling and restorative relationships between humans appears ideal and has been elaborated upon by many theologians. It is particularly influential in liberation or practical theologies. However, while Barth's argument for the *imago Dei* rests initially on action and restorative relationship, there are significant problems in how he actually applies this to real relationships between people. Specifically, Barth still holds to a divinely ordered and implicitly hierarchical understanding of gender relations. Stephenson points out that, "Barth believes that when the female follows the male initiative, the female actualizes the fellowship

---

34. Barth, *Church Dogmatics* III/2, 285.
35. Barth, *Church Dogmatics* III/4, 33.

that they both participate in together."³⁶ This model of hierarchy is, as Stephenson notes, intended to promote:

> mutual initiative and mutual response between the male and female, [but] Barth's model of an ordered, interpersonal relation between male and female does not exhibit mutual initiative and response between the two sexes and thus does not reflect the quality and character of the internal interpersonal relation of the Godhead.³⁷

The outworking of Barth's relational model depends on his argument that relations reflect the created order. Barth sees the *imago Dei* as being hierarchical largely because this relational model is taken to be a mirroring of the Trinity³⁸; including an inherent imbalance in power dynamics between men and women that are seen as directly contributing to the purposes of God. Stephenson explains, "The male is not a person because he is first, or superordinate, or the leader. The female is not a person because she is second, or subordinate, or the follower."³⁹ Instead, it is within the interaction they have with each other that personhood is achieved. Having come first, men initiate, and thus hold the role of initiator in the relationship between man and woman. This reflects the Triune order for Barth. The Father sends, Christ reveals God, and the Spirit bonds. Man, Barth maintains, "is ordered, related and directed to her very differently from what she is to him."⁴⁰ Though Barth claims equality for women ontologically, they are relationally to respond to men, as Christ and the Spirit relationally respond to the Father. Gouw explains, "As an outflowing of this divine essence, the trinity exists as three persons in the divine energies, yet the Father is the source of this outflowing, maintaining the monarchy of the Father."⁴¹ Barth mirrors this functional hierarchy in men and women, saying, "If order does not prevail in the being and fellowship of man and woman . . . the only alternative is disorder . . . A precedes B, and B follows A. Order means succession. It means preceding and following. It means super- and sub-ordination."⁴² Barth believes that this inequality

---

36. Stephenson, "Directed, Order and Related," 441.
37. Stephenson, "Directed, Order and Related," 444.
38. It is best to look at Barth's "revelation" analogy of the Trinity, as seen in n25.
39. Stephenson, "Directed, Order and Related," 446.
40. Barth, *Church Dogmatics* III/4, 164.
41. Gouw, "Transcendence and Immanence," 30.
42. Barth, *Church Dogmatics* III/4, 170.

really displays equality, because "it affects equally all whom it concerns."[43] However, he proceeds to say that man is "taking the lead as the inspirer, leader and initiator"[44] and any rebellion from the woman on this is akin to disorder, which as previously stated is sin. This understanding of both God and humanity leaves a very real, and demonstrably problematic, order of power—it is not true equality but instead circumstantial equality. Men hold power in the initiation, as God is ultimately the only powerful being in the God-human relationship. This contrast of power must be acknowledged and, as I will explain, many have seen this inequality as ultimately detrimental to the Barthian *imago Dei* theory.

It cannot be ignored that in this model, there exists an obstacle between women and God. In emphasizing the leadership position of men, obedience is then the function of women, whether they are ontologically equal or not. While many have tried to deny this has practical consequences in women's lives,[45] the damage this can cause has been researched and documented.[46] The practical outcome of Barth's theology represents a real problem, no matter how he strives to claim equality for the sexes. If women are subordinate in function, they are surely in some manner also subordinate in ontology—just as humans are ontologically subordinate to God. Barth argues that man leads woman in doing the work of God, but also argues that we are fully human in our participation in God's work. This is a clear statement about the divide between women and God.

## Paul Tillich's Advocacy of Courage

A contemporary of Karl Barth, Paul Tillich did most of his substantial work after leaving Germany due to his opposition to Hitler's regime. Because of his critical opinions and radical teaching, he had been released from his professorship at the University of Marburg but was then

---

43. Barth, *Church Dogmatics* III/4, 170.

44. Barth, *Church Dogmatics* III/4, 170.

45. I cite Smith's defense of Barth, "However, the language of 'command and reception,' or 'super-ordination and subordination' should be taken neither to indicate a form of ontological deficiency in the Godhead nor to justify, on such a basis, male-female hierarchy in humanity" (Smith, *Third Article*, 3). This may be comforting to some of Barth's followers, but a theoretical equality that is not functional is no better than an ontological hierarchy.

46. Please see an academic study of abuse: Westenberg, "'When She Calls for Help'—Domestic Violence in Christian Families," 71.

invited to teach at Union Theological Seminary. Due to his circumstances, his most influential works were published both in English and German. Like Barth, Tillich is to be numbered amongst those striving for social change through theological work. Yet though they have obvious similarities, Barth and Tillich disagreed on foundational doctrines, particularly the Otherness of God. Unlike Barth, Tillich saw God as essentially connected to humanity, and thus rejects the notion of a contrasting power dynamic between God and humans that Barth upholds. Furthermore, Tillich's model of theology, based on the method of correlation, begins in a very different way from Barth's. Rather than seeing the world first through Christ, Tillich believed it was necessary to begin with the questions the world articulates in cultural forms and address these through theological answers. This existentialist approach to theology then centered his work on being. He sought to explore both the beingness of humanity, but also of God. It is through these connections that Tillich's *imago Dei* theory is developed.

Tillich states, "Theology, as a function of the Christian church, must serve the needs of the church."[47] This opening sentence of his *Systematic Theology* frames the work as focused on the need to serve the church by speaking of God comprehensively to "every new generation."[48] As he explains his focus in the "Introduction," in which he cites works from Barth to Martin Luther, the challenge is bring together an "emphasis on the eternal truth over against the human situation and its demands."[49] In contrast to Barth, however, Tillich is determined to remain attentive to humanity through this linking of divine disclosure and contemporary human concerns. He describes his method of correlation as the defining gesture of theology: "Theology formulates the questions implied in human existence, and theology formulates the answers implied in divine self-manifestation under the guidance of the questions implied in human existence. This is a circle which drives man to a point where question and answer are not separated."[50] This move "evoked the protest of theologians such as Karl Barth, who were afraid that any kind of divine-human correlation makes God partly dependent on man."[51] Because human questions and divine answers are no longer separated

47. Tillich, *Systematic Theology*, 1:2.
48. Tillich, *Systematic Theology*, 1:2.
49. Tillich, *Systematic Theology*, 1:5.
50. Tillich, *Systematic Theology*, 1:5.
51. Tillich, *Systematic Theology*, 1:68.

in Tillich's thinking the formation of the God-human relationship does not rely on the clear division Barth insists upon between God and humanity. They are in a correlative relationship, which "means something real for both sides."[52] While Tillich implies a correlative theological approach can encompass a plethora of questions, he still determines, "The basic theological question is the question of God."[53] This is not in opposition to other questions, though, but rather frames the basic question of being. As he links question and answer, Tillich affirms, "God is the answer to the question implied in being."[54] This prompts the movement towards asking "What is being-itself?"[55] Tillich's answer to this is God. God is not simply the "highest being" or "a being alongside others" but instead "it is possible to say that He is the power of being in everything and above everything, the infinite power of being."[56] This relocates the notion of power, as well. Rather than the Barthian insistence that God is the primary actor, the only source of power, it locates power as a mediated relation between God and creation.

## The Nature of God

God is the power that gives being to Creation but is not opposed to it. There is no contradiction, no divide, between God and Creation. Thus, Tillich argues that God can be known through symbolic understanding,[57] and we must focus on the significance of that symbolism. As Tillich continues to examine the nature of God, his work on the Spirit and the Trinitarian principles further explores the work of God in the world. He begins by considering God as Spirit, "the most embracing, direct, and unrestricted symbol for the divine life."[58] Spirit, for Tillich, is the unity of the body and mind, not a part but instead the "all-embracing function in

---

52. Tillich, *Systematic Theology*, 1:69.
53. Tillich, *Systematic Theology*, 1:181.
54. Tillich, *Systematic Theology*, 1:181.
55. Tillich, *Systematic Theology*, 1:181.
56. Tillich, *Systematic Theology*, 1:261.
57. As he argues in his essay, Tillich, "Theology and Symbolism" (107–8), "Theology is the conceptual interpretation, explanation and criticism of the symbols in which a special encounter between God and man has found expression." Therefore, God is understood through experiences or analogies through which we glean information, rather than facts known in a scientific fashion.
58. Tillich, *Systematic Theology*, 1:276.

which all elements of the structure of being participate."[59] Therefore, the Godhead does not have a "person" who is Spirit, but rather is holistically Spirit. This does not mean Tillich denies the Trinity, but instead sees the Trinitarian principles as movements of God within Godself. He explains the first principle as the basis of the Godhead, or "the inexhaustible ground of being in which everything has its origin."[60] The second principle cannot be reduced to *logos* but is instead the creativity of the Godhead. In this, he arrives at the understanding that the third principle, the Spirit, unites the two principles and "is in a way the whole."[61] The Spirit allows the Godhead to be effective in majesty and creativity. It is through this empowering view of God that Tillich desires humans to determine their place in Creation. As the question-answer circle is posed, humans understand their own being through the understanding of God's being. In seeing God as Spirit, Tillich states that it is Spirit that gives life, creation is grounded in God as Being-Itself and so also grounded in the processes of God's existence.

It is important to note that in declaring God as Being-Itself, Tillich is directly rejecting a common interpretation of the doctrine of transcendence—that God is other than or infinitely separated from Creation.[62] This rejection is in accordance with his rejection of the idea of absolute difference and separation between God and humanity. This motif then extends to a general rejection of difference and/or separation in humanity itself, other to emphasize the pitfalls of stressing distinctions between people or allowing difference to assume undue importance. However, this is less helpful than it may seem in dealing with oppression or marginalized groups. Erasing differences, no matter how well intentioned, may prevent us from grappling with the oppressive features of differential social realities and nor does it allow for the goods of human difference to be affirmed. I will continue to examine this later in this chapter.

---

59. Tillich, *Systematic Theology*, 1:277.
60. Tillich, *Systematic Theology*, 1:278.
61. Tillich, *Systematic Theology*, 1:278.
62. As I discussed with Barth, understanding God's transcendence meant seeing God as wholly other. While also stressing a cooperation with the doctrine of immanence, it was vital for Barth to keep God "other" than creation. This separation is then not meant to say God is apart from Creation, but instead implies a qualitative understanding of God's difference from Creation.

## The Nature of Humanity and Sin

Tillich's work on being did not end with *Systematic Theology*. His work *The Courage to Be* (1952) was published a year later and continued exploring the idea of "nonbeing." In his biography of Tillich, Andrew S. Finstuen explains, "In contrast to the collectivist and individualist solutions to the human situation, Tillich advanced an explicitly Protestant form of courage in response to the three threats of nonbeing."[63] These threats of nonbeing are what Tillich termed "anxieties." Rather than circumstantial fears or references to mental health, Tillich specifically defines anxieties as deeply rooted existential fears. Therefore, anxiety appears "in three forms" which are connected to "fate and death . . . emptiness and loss of meaning . . . [and] that of guilt and condemnation."[64] Anxiety in these forms is thus common to all people and not linked to a lack of resilience or specific fear inducing circumstances. Fear of death, for example, is not the fear of a sudden or imminent threat, but the general fear of death that defines existence. The three fears together combine into the general fear of nonbeing—the person will either cease to be literally or symbolically, through loneliness or ostracization. Here I note similarities to the I–Thou model discussed previously in that understandings of human brokenness are centered on isolation and nonparticipation in the I–Thou relationship.

Tillich's discussion of these anxieties relates to his understanding of the doctrine of sin. Rather than linking sin to specific actions, Tillich likens it to separation from God. In *Systematic Theology* he says, "The state of existence is the state of estrangement. Man is estranged from the ground of his being, from other beings, and from himself."[65] In his essay on Tillich's doctrine of humanity, David E. Roberts writes, "Sin disrupts essential unity between man and God. It is the attempt to center life, power, and meaning in one's own finite self."[66] Tillich argues that humanity, in the desire to find worth and self-sufficiency, separates from the life which God gives, and seeks instead to assert being in an overly individualistic manner. Sin is not manifest in specific choices or deeds but, "is an expression of man's estrangement from God, from men, from

---

63. Finstuen, *Original Sin and Everyday Protestants*, 169.
64. Tillich, *Courage to Be*, 41.
65. Tillich, *Systematic Theology*, 2:51.
66. Roberts, "Tillich's Doctrine of Man," 127.

himself."⁶⁷ In *Courage To Be*, he explains that this estrangement is then felt in the "anxiety of meaninglessness."⁶⁸

As anxiety is revealed through a person's struggle with the fear of nonbeing, the fear of ostracization from society, whichever way this is manifested, also continues to affect the person's ability to connect. He explains that this disconnection produces a continuous searching, "one is driven from devotion to one object to devotion to another and again on to another . . . Everything is tried and nothing satisfies."⁶⁹ Finally, the person's anxiety, in its most extreme form, gives in to despair. Roberts continues:

> Man's inability to overcome the estrangements which characterize sin produces despair. As Kierkegaard saw, despair has two elements: first, self-hatred, including the will to self-annihilation; and secondly, the feeling that man cannot escape from himself, accompanied by the extreme measures he takes to try to escape (such as flight into mental illness, mental disease, intoxication, accidents).⁷⁰

Following Søren Kierkegaard's understanding of despair, Tillich argues that anxiety must turn to courage rather than despair, for the only other option to dealing with despair is neurosis. "Neurosis is the way of avoiding nonbeing by avoiding being,"⁷¹ as he explains, and this avoidance of being leads to affirming something which the person is not. This avoidance of being stops the person from making "responsible decisions" or "any kind of moral action."⁷² While Tillich attempts to separate the concept of nonbeing from this pathological anxiety, or neurosis, he clearly states that the person is now self-destructive, increasingly far from restoring their essential being and relationship with God (Being-Itself). As this anxiety continues, Tillich says, "the warnings of fear no longer have an effect" and "life vanishes."⁷³ This is how Tillich understands sin as leading to death. It is not the physical

---

67. Tillich, *Systematic Theology*, 2:53.
68. Tillich, *Courage to Be*, 47.
69. Tillich, *Courage to Be*, 47–48.
70. Roberts, "Tillich's Doctrine of Man," 128.
71. Tillich, *Courage to Be*, 66.
72. Tillich, *Courage to Be*, 75.
73. Tillich, *Courage to Be*, 79.

cause but rather, "One desires annihilation in order to escape death in its nature, not only as end, but also as guilt."[74]

To be inwardly focused is also to disconnect from God (Being-Itself), which disconnects us from others (beings), and thus we to cease to be. To overcome this sin, the person must restore relation with God. They must overcome alienation by recognition of connection to God, to creation, and turn towards an outward focus. Yet, even within the state of disconnection there is a sense of God. As George Pattison explains: "Tillich nevertheless resists what he calls the heterodox view that the substance of human life is as such originally fallen, since, even in the state of separation, there remains a consciousness of God. Paradoxically, therefore, the reality of sin becomes evidence for God!"[75] God draws near, because as Tillich argues, estrangement from God actually generates evidence of God. Even as we pull away, we are always aware of God and that we are denying our true essence.

## The Image of God

Therefore, anxiety cannot merely remain anxiety, but must move toward courage. As Tillich begins to define courage in *The Courage to Be*, he says it is recognition of self regardless of oppression. "Courage is the affirmation of one's essential nature, one's inner aim or entelechy, but it is an affirmation which has in itself the character 'in spite of.'"[76] This idea of *in spite of* holds much weight for the whole of Tillich's argument. "*In spite of*" is the use of the anxiety of non-being to reclaim being, the overthrowing of outside forces or inside voices trying to alienate us from our nature and beginning to become in active and thoughtful ways. The person who reclaims this, who allows their anxiety of non-being to shift into becoming, then fully embraces their stature as human. They are no longer restrained by oppression. The anxiety of non-being is defeated. Pattison reminds us that this is always done in conjunction with and in connection to God—although once again this is connection to our true selves as well. Pattison says:

> No matter how deeply separated we may have become from our essential being and no matter how fragmented and conflicted

74. Tillich, *Systematic Theology*, 2:78.
75. Pattison, *Paul Tillich's Philosophical Theology*, 16.
76. Tillich, *Courage to Be*, 4.

our lives may have become, we retain an implicit sense for what would make us whole. The isolated individual wants love, the empty formalist craves depth and content, the chaotic child unconsciously yearns for boundaries, and so on. Nevertheless, in the situation of estrangement, we cannot give ourselves what we need. In art or utopian imagery we can envisage how a fulfilled life might look but mostly, it seems, we cannot attain it.[77]

As stated in Tillich's conceptual frame anxiety is necessary for us to be able to turn toward courage, and as we experience anxiety, we develop courage. Anxiety is necessary for us to understand our ability to partake in the relationship with Being-Itself and to return to our true essence. Tillich claims this is done through vitality. Vitality, which he calls "power of life," means that humans "can transcend any situation in any direction."[78] Humans, when encountering situations, are able to overcome the difficulties of the situation and be "beyond" them. Tillich says this is through being linked to the essence of being, to have courage *in spite of* the situation one is faced with. As he states, "He can transcend any given situation in any direction and this possibility drives him to create beyond himself. Vitality is the power of creating beyond oneself without losing oneself."[79] He uses this concept of "in spite of" repeatedly to show that the circumstances will continue to oppress, to divert the person from overcoming, but that the possibility to overcome lies within the person's connection to Being-Itself and their true being. Regardless of the situation, for Tillich, anxiety can properly lead to the courage to overcome.

Tillich's definition of courage needs to be interrogated further here. Courage is not a lack of fear, but the conscious decision to overcome the anxiety of nonbeing. Tillich is not speaking of courage in the face of specific circumstances; he discusses how the desire to reclaim being propels the person to see any oppression or any situation as unable to destroy their essential being. The person then feels connected to society, or their own community, and thus does not see the situation as ultimately threatening to this part of their being. Vitality has given way to courage. He says: "Courage as a human act, as a matter of valuation, is an ethical concept. Courage as the universal and essential self-affirmation of one's being is an ontological concept. The courage to be is the ethical act in which man affirms his own being in spite of those elements

---

77. Pattison, *Paul Tillich's Philosophical Theology,* 23.
78. Tillich, *Courage to Be,* 81.
79. Tillich, *Courage to Be,* 81.

of his existence which conflict with his essential self-affirmation."[80] This idea of courage as reclamation of self, in whatever form this takes for the individual person, becomes particularly meaningful when brought back into conjunction with his method of correlation. Tillich's method removes the barrier between religious and secular life, allowing the two to be deeply integrated with each other. However, there is still a tension in this situation, as Tillich points to the tension of being both in the world and outside of it. David E. Roberts explains:

"Being a self means that man is both over against the world, as a subject, and in the world, as an object. He is so separated form everything as to be able to look at it and act upon it; he so belongs to the world that he is an episode in the process. But each factor determines the other."[81] This leads us to understanding Tillich's relational model of the *imago Dei*. As Barth worked to emphasize the *imago Dei* as action mirroring the Triune God, Tillich also links relationship (with each other or with God) to action. Once a person has the courage to participate in the being and Being-Itself, the person creates past their given situation.

## Courage for the Marginalized?

Tillich's work on the issue of becoming, and his understanding of the *imago Dei*, directly includes and supports the experience of the marginalized—those experiencing a variety of oppressions and sufferings. *The Courage to Be* discusses how humanity can overcome various difficulties, diverse anxieties, giving hope to those who do not currently see themselves in the *imago Dei*. All of this is both important and helpful, especially in terms of allowing women and other similarly marginalized peoples to claim full participation in the image, or truly, in the identity of being human.

To ask questions about life is the starting point for Tillich, and this is precisely why his contribution has been so significant to the work of feminist theology. As Krista Hughes says, "the self ought to be reconsidered altogether: as that which is internally constituted by its relations with others."[82] Like Tillich, Hughes is seeking to demonstrate that people are both separate and connected to the world around

80. Tillich, *Courage to Be*, 3.
81. Roberts, "Tillich's Doctrine of Man," 115.
82. Hughes, "Commentary and Study Questions," 98.

them. People are shaped by their experiences, and so those experiences, cultures, or other people must be included when examining the self. Theological work with standpoint epistemology focuses on this same need,[83] to constitute the self in relation with others. As many feminist theologians demonstrate, understanding anxieties and their movement toward courage are not merely theoretical concepts, but in fact have very practical implications for women's lives.

## Feminist Theology's Response

In this frame Tillich's work has an empowering aspect. Nevertheless, just as Barth's interpretation of the *imago Dei* is inherently restrictive due to its retention of notions of ordered hierarchy, Tillich's *imago Dei* is restrictive in its assumption of universal human experience. Both, truly, are issues of power. While Barth is clearly allowing unequal power to exist within humanity, Tillich does not adequately address the fact that unequal power is a reality in the world. To fully understand the implications of this issue within theology, I turn to the formative works of Valerie Saiving, Judith Plaskow, Mary Daly, and Rosemary Radford Ruether. As they address prominent understandings developed by various male theologians, they develop theology more attuned to the lives of the marginalized.

### Valerie Saiving: The Reclamation of "Selfishness"

In 1960, Valerie Saiving published "The Human Situation: A Feminine View" in *The Journal of Religion*. This is widely regarded as marking the emergence of feminist theology in the contemporary context. In this essay, Saiving criticized the dominant white male views of sin and personhood, focusing primarily on their representation in the theological thinking of Reinhold Niebuhr. Her work became a critical reference point for emerging feminist theologians directly influencing several key thinkers including Mary Daly and Judith Plaskow[84].

In "The Human Situation," Saiving begins by addressing specifically the problem of assuming universal experience. She says, "This alone

---

83. See Prologue.

84. The work of these women is widely regarded as the birth of feminist theology as an academic discipline. See Grenz and Olson, *20th-Century Theology* as an example of this view.

should put us on guard, especially since contemporary theologians constantly remind us that one of man's strongest temptations is to identify his own limited perspective with universal truth."[85] Because she begins with skepticism that a man's theology is universal, she can consider the concept of anxiety from a distance. Seeing that anxiety is characterized by "fear for the survival of the self and its values"[86] it follows that the anxiety of man is pride. As she points out, "Man knows he is merely a part of the whole, but he tries to convince himself and others that he is the whole."[87]

Women have a different experience, though, according to Saiving. Looking specifically at the anthropological work of two women, Ruth Benedict and Margaret Mead, she highlights the different societal roles women undertake. In the dominant view, as exemplified in Barth, men are to take the lead and women are to follow. While men are taught to develop individuality to differentiate themselves, a woman "will, in a broad sense, merely take her mother's place."[88] Saiving says that a man "must prove himself" while for a woman "all she needs to do to realize her full femininity is to wait."[89] This waiting takes several forms in the woman's life. First, she waits for her body to begin menstruation, the first step into womanhood. Then she waits to become pregnant, something Saiving says is a passive role for women. The man impregnates the woman, even if it is within a consensual relationship. She waits to breastfeed, to serve her family, and then to see this complete in menopause.

Yet all of this was changing, in Saiving's view, because of cultural transformations. Now that (white) women were not entirely overwhelmed with domestic labor, there were opportunities for them to exercise greater agency and explore the active development of their achievements. As women began to have careers, to work outside the home, to progress in these "masculine" ways, Saiving says the anxieties of women must be specifically addressed. For Saiving, it is clear that women differ from men, but that this does not equal subordination. She says, "They want . . . to be both women and full human beings."[90] Niebuhr's concept of sin as pride, that she is directly addressing here, does not thus equate to women. Women are instead trying to discover

85. Saiving, "Human Situation," 100.
86. Saiving, "Human Situation," 101
87. Saiving, "Human Situation," 101.
88. Saiving, "Human Situation," 103.
89. Saiving, "Human Situation," 103.
90. Saiving, "Human Situation," 103.

how to be fully human, because, as Saiving argues, women's sin is selflessness. She locates women's sin in trivializing themselves and their work, and in looking to "others for one's own self-definition."[91] For Saiving, it is important for both men and women to overcome their respective sins in order to work in the cooperative way Barth and Tillich desire. Women will not return to the place of follower, she proclaims, and this is a good thing. She argued that in doing this, society would recapture the love, freely given by God and then mirrored by humanity, that many theologians (including Barth) see as redemptive/restorative.[92]

## Judith Plaskow: Essential Selfhood

Saiving's work directly influenced the Jewish theologian Judith Plaskow. Her book, *Sex, Sin and Grace: Women's Experience and the Theologies of Reinhold Niebuhr and Paul Tillich* (1975), is introduced with a review of Saiving's essay. Using Saiving as a starting point, she examines Niebuhr's and Tillich's theologies of sin and grace. Like Saiving, she sees women's experience in society as characterized by passivity. She says, "Women have passively conformed to expectations of them," but at the same time have "enrich[ed] it."[93] In examining this experience, she posits that a main problem within women's lives is "that women do not shape their own experience, but allow their life choices to be made for them by others."[94]

After establishing her analysis of women's experience in society, Plaskow turns to Niebuhr's understanding of sin. Like Saiving, she views it as inadequate. However, Plaskow does not remain satisfied with Saiving's analysis either. Instead, she sees sin as linked to finitude. She says:

> Human nature as finite freedom poses a danger but it also imposes a responsibility. Human beings can ignore their finitude, but they can also fail to live up to the obligations of their freedom. The refusal of self-transcendence ought to be, if one uses Niebuhr's categories, no less a sin than pride—a sin against oneself, against other persons, and against God. If pride is the attempt to usurp the place of God, sensuality is the denial of creation in his image.[95]

91. Saiving, "Human Situation," 109.
92. Saiving, "Human Situation," 111.
93. Plaskow, *Sex, Sin and Grace*, 29.
94. Plaskow, *Sex, Sin and Grace*, 32.
95. Plaskow, *Sex, Sin and Grace*, 68.

Further, Plaskow does not see a viable solution in Tillich's doctrine of sin. While it seems to be able to transcend the male specific views of Niebuhr, she sees it as having ultimately the same consequences. The problem with Tillich's method is specifically in his understanding of self. She says, "Tillich establishes selfhood, in the ontological sense, as a primal reality."[96] This cannot work, as Saiving has already demonstrated. "Essential selfhood . . . does not in itself exist," she explains.[97] While aspects of Tillich's work can be used to understand women's experience, it is grounded in the assumptions of a male experience. Plaskow states, "Just as he does not provide the philosophical basis for understanding sins of self-negation in the doctrine of sin, so he does not clearly explain how such sins are affected by the dynamics of acceptance."[98]

Plaskow concludes her book with an optimistic view of experience. Rather than being concerned with developing a universal viewpoint, she welcomes the diversity. She says, "If there is no universal experience, there are significant human experiences which many groups share and which may be illuminated through concern with particular experience . . . Human particularity represents not just limit but also possibility."[99]

## Mary Daly: God and Women

Tillich's influence is especially obvious in Mary Daly's *Beyond God the Father: Toward a Philosophy of Women's Liberation* (1973). Daly begins her book with a radical revisioning of God, which is largely inspired by the failings she sees in theologians like Barth. She believes that Barth, Niebuhr, and others "spend energy answering questions that women are not really asking."[100] Rather than focusing on what women need and want, these theologians are merely placating them by attempts to argue that the assertions of Paul on women and other "problematic" areas of the Bible are not to be read as misogynistic. This is unacceptable. However, in her re-examination of Christian theology, she finds much common ground with Tillich, and especially his work in *The Courage to Be*.

---

96. Plaskow, *Sex, Sin and Grace*, 112.
97. Plaskow, *Sex, Sin and Grace*, 112.
98. Plaskow, *Sex, Sin and Grace*, 147.
99. Plaskow, *Sex, Sin and Grace*, 174.
100. Daly, *Beyond God the Father*, 5.

Daly begins her critique with the traditional concept of God as a being. If God is a being, separate from the created world, then God still "functions to legitimate the existing social, economic, and political status quo, in which women and other victimized groups are subordinate."[101] Daly believes that some (men) in the human race will appear to most resemble God if God is a specific being, and that this will necessarily entail the separation of other people from God—as well as continuing patterns of male domination. As Daly famously said, "If God is male, then the male is God."[102] Moreover, to see God in the traditional sense of a being is to see God as over and against creation, detached from it and thus idealizing a harmful detachment from the created order. She says, "it is damaging and implicitly compatible with sexism if it encourages detachment from the reality of the human struggle against oppression in its concrete manifestations."[103] Daly believes that specific forms of oppression must be addressed, and so in discussing both God and being, as Laurel C. Schneider says, "She finds it essential to place non-being squarely within the experience of structural evil and the oppression of women under patriarchy."[104] However, women have the potentiality to create, in the image of God, a new world. Daly argues that women can overcome nonbeing by overthrowing the patriarchal structure that is currently crushing them.

Daly's next step in re-examining the language used to define God is to move past Tillich's argument for God as Being-Itself. While Tillich argues for God as the power of being, Daly takes this image further in describing God as action. Through emphasizing the active nature of *Being-Itself*, God becomes "Verb" rather than "Noun."[105] God is no longer simply *Being-Itself*, or the power of being, but instead God is the active verb of "Be-ing."[106] Daly says, "Women who are experiencing the shock of nonbeing and the surge of self-affirmation against this are inclined to perceive transcendence as the Verb in which we participate—live, move, and have our being."[107]

---

101. Daly, *Beyond God the Father*, 19.
102. Daly, *Beyond God the Father*, 19.
103. Daly, *Beyond God the Father*, 20.
104. Schneider, "From New Beginning to Meta-Being," 427.
105. Daly, *Beyond God the Father*, 33.
106. Daly, *Beyond God the Father*, 36.
107. Daly, *Beyond God the Father*, 34.

Second, with specific reference to women's situation, she critiques Tillich's understanding of courage. She has rightly addressed a main difficulty within it in that it "lacks specific grounding in the concrete experiences of the oppressed."[108] This leads her to question the practical outworkings of his theological argument. Detached from the specifics of oppression, or rather, the specifics of sexism, it must remain a detached and purposeless theology. Tillich's work does not specifically address sexism, and so cannot further human overcoming as Daly believes we must. Instead, we should talk of God by encouraging humanity to move toward the "androgynous mode of living, toward transcendence."[109] While all humanity is threatened by nonbeing, as Tillich claims, Daly believes that the consequence of this falls most heavily upon women in a patriarchal society. It is therefore crucial that they respond with courage, As she states, "I am suggesting that at this point in history women are in a unique sense called to be the bearers of existential courage in society."[110] As Tillich argued for three phases or types of anxiety, Daly says that women have an added anxiety that is especially difficult to overcome—the anxiety manifest in guilt at rejecting social norms. She explains, "The anxiety of guilt over refusing to do what society demands, a guilt which can hold one in its grip long after it has been recognized as false."[111] Yet when a woman is able to deal with this added anxiety, and to overcome it, this allows her to reach "higher levels of intellectual discovery or creativity,"[112] which is the great courage Daly promotes.

Despite her strong critique Daly continues to use the language of Tillich in her analysis. She continues to argue for the *courage to be* in the face of anxiety of nonbeing, just as Tillich does, and to even accept both a greater awareness of the self and the whole of society as the outcome. However, the woman has a special responsibility to reject incorporation into this society, striving to create a new one in which she is no longer oppressed. It is vital to remember that Daly argues that humans' ability to transcend is how they can reflect the image of God. She says, "It is the creative potential itself in human beings that is the image of God."[113]

---

108. Daly, *Beyond God the Father*, 34.
109. Daly, *Beyond God the Father*, 21.
110. Daly, *Beyond God the Father*, 23.
111. Daly, *Beyond God the Father*, 24.
112. Daly, *Beyond God the Father*, 23.
113. Daly, *Beyond God the Father*, 29.

While Daly's work represents a vital reshaping of Tillich's approach that engages with the transformative role that women can play there are aspects of her work that are still open to question and critique. In seeking to move beyond male understandings of God she also moves entirely beyond the male-centered religious traditions of Western culture.[114] This means abandoning this sacred inheritance entirely. The move to recreate society apart from religion is not one supported by all feminist theologians. In their own critiques of Barth, Tillich, of Daly's contemporaries, chose to remain within the religion that had formed their understandings of the sacred.[115] For example, in her essay on Daly, Judith Plaskow explains that while Daly chose to leave Christianity, her decision to stay within Judaism was influenced by Daly's encouragement to remain and "highlight and expose areas of oppression."[116]

### Rosemary Radford Ruether: God in Relationship

Rosemary Radford Ruether is a leading Catholic feminist theologian who has worked prominently in the areas of liberation theology and ecofeminist theology. Her commitment to the Catholic church is apparent in her work, which often focusses upon how churches can work to "achieve justice."[117] She is also an important voice in my work here, as she remained committed to Christianity even in working to deconstruct much of its patriarchal heritage.

Ruether, like other second-wave feminists, was concerned with the masculine language surrounding talk of God. Like Elisabeth Schüssler Fiorenza, a New Testament scholar and another early feminist theologian, she worked with a "hermeneutics of suspicion," in interpreting sacred texts and traditions. This reveals that much of the language of the Bible is patriarchal and thus must be re-examined and redefined in order to allow for the full participation of women in humanity. Her early work particularly focused on the "existing social hierarchy and system of power"

---

114. In *Beyond God and Father*, Daly argues that women remaining in the Christian church is akin to accepting oppression. She became increasingly vocal about her rejection of Christianity.

115. Notable feminist theologians who remained are Elisabeth Schüssler Fiorenza and Rosemary Radford Ruether, whom I will discuss here.

116. Plaskow, "Lessons from Mary Daly," 102.

117. Clifford, *Introducing Feminist Theology*, 94.

that had been justified through this problematic language.[118] Like Daly, she believed that referring to God in masculine terms was exclusionary of women, but moreover she believed it did not fully encompass the character of God. Instead, she discussed God's being as an "empowering matrix."[119] By defining God in this manner, Ruether believed it demonstrated the all-encompassing nature of God. God is "beneath and around us as an encompassing source of life and renewal."[120]

Ruether's reason for avoiding gendered analogies for God, or, like her fellow feminist theologians deciding to use feminine language particularly, is primarily motivated by her concern not to limit God. She argued against the limitations gendered forms place upon God, the disconnect from continuing faith in Christianity which some feminist talk of God assumed (particularly the goddess language popular with some feminists like Carol Christ), and her continuing belief in the ineffability of God. She explains: "Christian theology has always recognized, theoretically, that all language for God is analogical or metaphorical, not literal . . . To take one image drawn from one gender and in one sociological context as the normative possessors of the image of God and the representatives of God on earth. This is idolatry."[121] In essence, Ruether was taking Barth's "otherness" doctrine to its own conclusions, arguing that even his insistence on the male pronouns for God and the hierarchy model he proposed was imposing too much knowledge upon God. In an edited volume representing the early days of Reuther's work, Pamela Cooper-White says, "Theologically, at least one wing of the liberal feminist method could be seen . . . in the appropriation of the thought and method of major nineteenth- and twentieth-century theologians, such as Karl Barth . . . "[122] This appropriation, Cooper-White argues, allowed continued attempts to achieve equality with men. However, Ruether's theology proves her desire is to not simply gain equality with men, but rather to mend broken relationships women have with God. Ruether rejected the hierarchy Barth and others had continued. As Clifford explains, "This hierarchy creates an unnecessary distance between women and the God to whom they pray that can present difficulties for women in their spirituality."[123]

118. Ruether, "Development of My Theology," 2.
119. Ruether, *Disputed Questions*, 24.
120. Ruether, *Sexism and God-talk*, 47.
121. Ruether, "Feminist Theology and Spirituality," 16.
122. Cooper-White, "Early 1990s: Whose CWR? Whose Feminism?" 19.
123. Clifford, *Introducing Feminist Theology*, 96.

Important in understanding Ruether's theology is her desire to not only elevate women, but to affirm their place in their faith traditions. Unlike Daly and others who left Christianity and turned their backs on traditional forms of religion, Ruether believed women could affirm Christianity and work within the tradition to dismantle sexism. In her work, there is a critique of the past, a seeking of alternatives supported by biblical or extra-biblical traditions, and finally a construction of a theology that affirms "women's personhood, her equality in the image of God, her equal redeemability, her participation in prophecy, teaching, and leadership."[124] Ultimately, Ruether believed that by focusing on more authentic understandings of God would contribute to the end of sexist oppression of women. She says: "The patriarchal distortion of all tradition throws feminist theology back upon the primary intuitions of religious experience itself: namely, the belief in a divine foundation of reality which is ultimately good, which does not wish evil or create evil, but affirms and upholds our autonomous personhood as women, in whose image we are made."[125] Reuther is thus advocating that women should question the motives of previous interpretations, translations, doctrines, and teachings of faith and begin to build a theology that more genuinely reflects and responds to the nature of God. If God is loving, good, and upholds life, then theology must affirm those characteristics. Ruether argues that these understandings of God do not align with the hierarchical and power-focused theologies previously constructed. Most importantly, Ruether's theology enforces an equal standing within the *imago Dei* that directly speaks to the experiences, including the diverse kinds of experiences, of women.

## Conclusion

In this chapter, I have been able to distinguish aspects of *imago Dei* theologies that remain helpful, while identifying areas in which they remain lacking. In analyzing Barth and Tillich, I continue to maintain their importance in affirming principles such as God's participation in the world, the deep connection the world has with God, and the need to recognize the power that can come from this. Continuing to the feminist theologies, I have emphasized that this power of God is meant for the marginalized

---

124. Ruether, "Feminist Theology in the Academy," 59.
125. Ruether, "Feminist Theology in the Academy," 59.

in particular—God empowers the powerless, and is active and present to everyone, not just the privileged. Recognizing that too much desire for individual power leads to oppression of the "other," I can continue to challenge my own theology to be one of reconciliation.

While each of the theologies I have examined above have expanded understandings of both God and humanity in relationship with God—to varying degrees of inclusiveness—I am also keenly aware of the social privilege each standpoint implicitly maintains. These theologies have contributed much of value in enabling understandings the *imago Dei* that relate to my own experiences and those of many other women like me. However, I realize that I must also understand how these types of theologies function within a context of systematic marginalization. While I certainly respond to the work of the feminist theologians who have articulated responses to Barth and Tillich similar to those outlined above, I am still left with a sense of unease. As I asked in relation to Tillich's existentialism, I do not see how someone who is experiencing violent or life-threatening suffering is helped by being admonished to overcome anxiety. I cannot assume that my growing ability to see myself in relationship to God applies in the experience of those who have not had the same support and opportunities I have benefited from. Here, I truly must begin to decenter my own standpoint and allow other views to challenge how I recognize God and understand the *imago Dei* manifest in human persons.

# 2

# The Image of God for the Oppressed

Focusing on Lived Truths

## Introduction

AS OUTLINED IN CHAPTER 1, I am searching for a more transformative and inclusive understanding of the *imago Dei* than those which have prevailed in the past. Barth's Christocentric theology vivifies the image in terms of reconciliation. God is reconciled to humanity through Christ, and the image of God is restored in us by participation in this relationship. This reconciliation is displayed by imitating Christ's actions during his life and through restored relationships with others. For Tillich, the image is a source of existential courage. We connect to our anxiety and use it to develop the courage which will in turn enable us to partake in Being-Itself (God) and transcend our circumstances.

While these theological models have helpful aspects, I was unsatisfied because neither addressed my context as a woman nor the feminist critique of theologies based on male-centered perspectives. Specifically, I had experienced profound personal devaluation because of my gender and neither of these theories addressed the way in which women, in particular, struggle to affirm the *imago Dei* in relation to their own identities. Thus, I was encouraged by the work of those feminist theologians who have directly responded to the dominant theological traditions I have represented through Barth and Tillich. Pioneering feminist theologians, inspired by Valerie Saiving, voiced the need for women to reclaim their own value in the face of societal oppression. Furthermore, through Saiving's rejection of the universalizing notion of sin as pride (identified as a facet of male experience in particular) I came to understand how doctrinal perspectives can be challenged and revised through engaging with the diversity of human experiences.

In truth, however, the theology being developed by these white feminist theologians still focused largely on universalizing categorizations of experiences and existential conditions. As has been widely discussed the feminist theologians of the second wave did not adequately take into account the different types of oppressions women of color faced.[1] Moreover, during the period in which these feminist voices emerged Civil Rights movements and liberation theologies were advocating more radical forms of engagement equipped to speak to real experiences of marginalized groups and promote transformation. As Womanist theologian Keri Day explains in her chapter "Doctrine of God in African American Theology,"[2] "Concepts of God could either cultivate the conditions for the possibility of human equality, justice, and transcendence or frustrate these attempts altogether."[3] I am aware of and acknowledge the many missteps white feminists have taken in this regard. As theologian Mary Hunt states, "White feminists have made and continue to make a lot of mistakes. Experiences of race, nationality, gender, class, sexual orientation, and access to resources create conditions of inequality that persist over generations."[4]

As stated, in research that seeks a more inclusive and liberatory vision of the *imago Dei*, I must challenge my own privileged location and listen to those who are speaking from the margins. In this chapter, I therefore begin with a review of insights from Black Theology that contribute to my project. I begin with James Cone's engagement with and critique of Barth; a critique that raises challenges to my own theological presuppositions. Following this, I will move to examine work of Womanist theologians, focusing on the influential theologian and ethicist Katie Geneva Cannon. Through Cannon's distinct theological method, my understanding of the *imago Dei* is not only enlarged but becomes more focused. Cannon's theology challenges my understanding both by raising questions I need to address and by giving me further tools to

---

1. As I reference in The Need for Womanism in chapter 2 of this book.
2. Pinn and Cannon, *Oxford Handbook of African American Theology*.
3. Day, "Doctrine of God in African American Theology," 140.
4. Hunt, "Katie Geneva Cannon Incarnate," 109.

reconstruct my own theological perspective. Her development of the doctrine of *imago Dei* links theological examination, historical contexts, and practical applications to demonstrate the real implications this doctrine has upon cultures. In her theology, I am able to see how she can continually re-examine her own bias and desires in order to strive for the most ethical theological anthropology possible. Furthermore, she is able to see common ground in otherwise differing theologies, explaining how they can all inform her own understanding.

Through this exploration of Black and Womanist theology, I will seek to expand both my perception of the doctrines of the *imago Dei* and understanding of God, clearly aligning them with the practical and social activism the theologians in chapter 1 of this book were also advocating. By embracing the work of Black and Womanist theologians, not only can interpretations of these doctrines become more inclusive, but issues of theological methodology will emerge with greater clarity.

## Black Theology and the Doctrine of God

Womanist theologian Keri Day's analysis of an African American doctrine of God demonstrates that theology in African American contexts is "in part . . . against a white theological backdrop that did not take racial equality and justice seriously in its constructions of God."[5] Therefore an important aspect of Black theology is the response it makes to white theology, the oppression suffered under white supremacy, and the ways in which these two things are related. As a result, Black theologians often begin theological analysis with a re-examination of the image of God in theology.[6] As stated previously, Mary Daly argued in a different context, "If God is male then the male is God."[7] If images of God are modelled on the figures of powerful white men who control, judge, and exercise authority then we are at risk of losing the image of God who shares the

---

5. Day, *Oxford Handbook of African American Theology*, 140.

6. Day says, "African American theology, in large part, is shaped by the historical inhumanity of racial oppression and hegemony in America . . . Enslaved Africans recognized that one's theological anthropology (being the nature of humanity in relation to God) was directly connected to one's construction of God. Because the humanity of slaves was rendered inferior through early white Christian formulations, their constructions of God were also deeply and profoundly racist. Yet slaves rejected such ideas, maintaining that they were made in the image of God, who acknowledged their humanity" (*Oxford Handbook of African American Theology*, 140).

7. Daly, *Beyond God the Father*, 5.

suffering of those who are oppressed. Furthermore, the beliefs humanity holds about God are enacted in the way we approach human relationships. As Day says, "Enslaved Africans recognized that one's theological anthropology (being the nature of humanity in relation to God) was directly connected to one's construction of God."[8] And so, it is fundamental to Black Theology to begin with challenges and revisions of the doctrine of God. After doing this, I will be able to present a better understanding of the *imago Dei* prevalent in Black Theology.

Theological work has been highly significant for Black activists and religious thinkers in the United States. As James Cone and Gayraud S. Wilmore state, "Our interpretation of history, its tragedies and its triumphs, has come out of our encounter with God, and our understanding of God has come out of our historical struggle."[9] For Black theology, God's interaction with the world and presence in the world are vital. Unlike Barth's understanding, here God's immanent involvement with creation had to be emphasized in order to affirm the worth of Christianity to people whose lives were structured by systemic injustice. Stanley Grenz explains, "If God is real, then this God must be involved in the struggles of the present to bring about liberation from oppression."[10] While Barth argued for the importance of God's separation from the world in order to avoid adjusting our theology to popular cultural norms, as he accused the Nazi party of doing, Black theology recognized the importance of God's activity in the world. Without an understanding of God's connection and presence in this current time, it was understood, Christianity would become merely a theoretical belief system without saving potential.

The influential forebear of Black Theology Howard Thurman[11] argued that "the divine personhood of God grounds and makes possible the absolute value and worth of all human persons."[12] Thurman's understanding was particularly focused on the idea of love in community. In his mystical theology each person was endowed with a "Divine Spark" which connected them to God.[13] The Fall, or sin, is understood as a separation from God due to selfish desires. As a person returns to God,

---

8. Day, *Oxford Handbook of African American Theology*, 140.
9. Cone and Wilmore, *Black Theology*, 3.
10. Grenz and Olson, *20th Century Theology*, 201.
11. Thurman, an early figure in Black theology, developed a theology of radical nonviolence that would later influence the work of Martin Luther King Jr.
12. Cone, *Black Theology*, 2.
13. Cone, *Black Theology*, 3.

their spark gradually unites them with God and transforms them into people who seek loving connection with others. In Thurman's thinking, the more loving and more focused upon others a person becomes, the more they are connected to God.

Thurman's theology here is not completely dissimilar to Barth's, though. As in Barth's "I–Thou" understanding of the image of God, Thurman emphasized that the consequence of knowing God would be reflected in our interactions with other humans. Thurman says, "To speak of the love for humanity is meaningless. There is no such thing as humanity. What we call humanity has a name, was born, lives on a street, gets hungry, needs all the particular things we need."[14] Loving others means loving them in their particular place, understanding the particular person, and being concerned with their particular needs. However, Thurman's approach is more particular than Barth's as he calls for an active stance against distinct oppressions such as systemic racism and the violence it generates. Thurman's theology clearly embraces an activist stance but from the 1970s onwards many African American theologians wished to go further than him in challenging what came to be described as "soft" theological discussions.[15] As Day describes, there were increasing calls for black liberation theologies[16] that proclaimed that understandings of God must speak directly to social structures and challenge the evils of systemic oppression. A leading figure in this development was the theologian James Cone.

## James Cone: Theology Is Anthropology

For Cone, theology is always human-talk about God.[17] It is impossible to separate the forms this talk takes from concrete human situations—historically, culturally, and experientially. The tendency of white theology to assume a "universal" viewpoint is, Cone and other liberation theologians would argue, naïve at best and deceitful at worst. As he stated, people's theology "cannot be divorced from their place and time in a definite history and culture."[18] Cone accepts Ludwig Feuerbach's

---

14. As cited in Cone, *Black Theology*, 14.
15. Day, "Doctrine of God in African American Theology," 142.
16. Day, "Doctrine of God in African American Theology," 142.
17. Day, "Doctrine of God in African American Theology," 142.
18. Cone, *God of the Oppressed*, 37.

dictum: "Theology is anthropology"[19] in the sense that it is always rooted in the world we find ourselves in and constructs horizons to support our human longings. Through Cone's anthropological theology, God is imaged as actively siding with the oppressed, requiring a committed stance against oppression and systemic injustice, and suffering with the "poor and weak of society."[20]

But Cone's thinking on these issues does not entail an entire repudiation of former theological thinking on the *imago Dei*. Importantly, Cone began his theological work studying Karl Barth. Cone's doctoral dissertation, "The Doctrine of Man in the Theology of Karl Barth," was an examination of Barth's theological anthropology, from which Cone was able to build a framework for his own Black theological thinking. In interrogating the development of Barth's theological anthropology Cone writes,

> In liberal Christianity, it is not God who determines the religious relationship; it is [thinking] man [who relies on reason to know God]. We must not forget that Barth began his career as a liberal theologian. The first World War [however] shattered his hope of the Kingdom of God on earth. In due time Barth was led from his anthropocentric conception of Christianity to a thorough-going theocentric conception.[21]

Understanding Barth's historical context is vital to understanding the evolution of Barth's work, and Cone points out the way this context shaped Barth's conception of God's otherness. Barth's influence on Cone's future work here is clear. Barth, along with his dialectical contemporaries, sought to understand Christianity's place in the developing crises of World Wars I and II and in particular address the theological responsibility for the nationalistic, racist ideologies of these wars.[22] Cone's theology, like Barth's, is contextually located understanding of "what we have understood God to be doing . . ."[23] These theologies are, intrinsically, methods of working against injustice.[24] However, as J. Kameron Carter says, "Cone was not

---

19. Day, "Doctrine of God in African American Theology," 142.
20. Day, "Doctrine of God in African American Theology," 142.
21. Cone, "Doctrine of Man in the Theology of Karl Barth," 3.
22. Carter, "Humanity in African American Theology," 178.
23. Wilmore and Cone, *Black Theology*, 3.
24. Maat, "Looking Back at the Evolution of James Cone's Theological Anthropology," 596.

seeking to do 'white theology' in (Barthian) blackface."²⁵ His was not a mere adaptation of dialectical theology in African American context, but instead, a utilization of the tools of white Western theology in order to push theological examination further, and to more actively locate that examination in the context of African Americans. His desire to develop a theology for the Black Power movement allowed him to examine Barth's theology and turn it "into a critique of white theology."²⁶

## From God to Humanity

My exploration has thus far been focused on the image of God in human lives within a Christian perspective, and this work is primarily undertaken in light of Christ. This is particularly the case in Black theology. In his essay "Black theology and human purpose," theologian and ethicist Riggins R. Earl, Jr. states, "In black theology, the notion of human purpose is closely tied to a perception of Jesus. In this sense, human purpose (or theological anthropology) is connected to Christology (or the life and import of Jesus the Christ). It is the human being, Jesus, who models human purpose."²⁷

Rather than notions of overcoming (as with Tillich's courage) and empowered imitation (as with Barth's Christology), Black theology is specifically looking toward Jesus to understand human nature and purpose. In a significant move, the ministry of Jesus and his sacrifice are used to question traditional understandings of self-denial that are commonplace in white theologies.²⁸ Earl argues that we must rethink self-denial in connection to people who are not willfully sacrificial but who are forced to make sacrifices because of structural oppression.

---

25. Carter, "Humanity in African American Theology," 178.
26. Carter, "Humanity in African American Theology," 178.
27. Earl, "Black Theology and Human Purpose," 126.

28. This focus on denial can be seen in theologies such as Calvin (total depravity's taint of the human will), Augustine (original sin as distorted will/love), Luther (sin as inward focus), and as I discussed in chapter 1, Niebuhr's focus on pride as sin. In each of these, the overcoming of sin is demonstrated by a concern for others, a focus on God's will rather than one's own, and attempts at humility. As you can also see in Barth, the focus is on God's saving work in spite of our failing and a change in us to be like Christ. While this can be a hopeful and helpful theology, it can also affirm the self-denial that feminist theologians, and as I now discuss, black theologians are critiquing. In their critiques, they demonstrate how a total focus on self-denial can damage those already oppressed.

Specifically, it must be understood that African Americans were not willfully practicing self-denial by being slaves to others. This type of enforced loss of self conflicts with what Earl understands as ethical becoming. He says, "Philosophically and socially, the idea of self-denial must be viewed as the primal ethical act that is foundational to the self's developmental sense of agential identity and accountability."[29] Self-denial, then, must be a voluntary act demonstrating the person's agency in choosing to serve the other, not a forced servitude.

Furthermore, self-denial is not to be practiced with disregard to the self. Earl connects his theology to that of Dietrich Bonhoeffer, one of the few white theologians he believes demonstrates an understanding of different types of denial. He argues that Bonhoeffer rejects understandings of self-denial as a type of "suicide."[30] Instead Bonhoeffer states that, "To deny oneself is to be aware only of Christ and no more of self, to see only him who goes before and no more the road which is too hard for us. Once more all that self-denial can say is, 'He leads the way, keep close to him.'"[31] This type of self-denial is a movement of the self to become like Christ, to be near to Christ, and it enables us to endure suffering because Christ leads the way.

In recognizing these important distinctions between modes of self-denial, Black theologians work to understand the humanity of those whose selfhood is forcibly destroyed by an oppressor. Cone images this recognition as welcoming the advent of a "Black Messiah" who helps Black people to deny the false white Messiah they have been offered and recognize God's salvific solidarity with their struggles.[32] Cone and other Black theologians argue that this Black Messiah has liberative potential for Black people, and that this form of Christocentric theology allows Black people to regain their agency and sense of humanity—*even as they continue to be oppressed at the present time.* There is hope for the future for, as Cone emphasizes, Jesus was resurrected as the sign of God's resurrecting power.

29. Earl, "Black Theology and Human Purpose," 127.
30. Earl, "Black Theology and Human Purpose," 127.
31. As cited in Earl, "Black Theology," 128.
32. "Black theology emerged because of the continued failure of white religionists and theologians to relate the Gospel to the pain and suffering of African Americans . . . It asks, for example, What do Jesus Christ and the Gospel mean to people with their backs pressed against the wall? What does it mean to say that the Source of all persons is the one God; that all have the image of God etched into their being; that all persons are equal before God and loved equally by God?" (Burrow, *James H. Cone and Black Liberation Theology*, 25.)

The kingdom is this resurrection. Therefore, "Jesus is now my story, which sustains and holds me together in struggle."[33]

Developing Cone's theme further, Earl connects the narrative of Jesus to the work of leaders of the Civil Rights movement, including Martin Luther King, Jr. In his civil disobedience Cone believed King demonstrated how Black people can share in Jesus's redemptive work. Earl states: "James Cone correctly saw that, especially as embodied in King, obedience to the way of the Cross of Jesus, which symbolizes self-denial, leads to self-actualization. For King and Cone, self-denial commanded by Jesus empowers the oppressed to assert human purpose in a nonpassive, self-agential manner."[34] In this frame, action taken by the oppressed to regain agency is discipleship to Jesus. To do work to free others from similar oppression is the way of the Cross.

In his examination of liberation theology, philosopher and theologian Cornel West argues that in this practical application of liberation theology, serious and comprehensive understandings of the various strains of these theologies is required. He argues that "the major intellectual task of liberation theologians is to continue to re-examine and reshape the traditional doctrines of the church . . ."[35] In keeping with this, Black theology is also required to continue examining itself over and over. Importantly, Black theology must examine its treatment of Black women and their role in liberation theology. As Cone states, "Although Black women represent more than one-half of the population in the Black community and 75 percent in the Black Church, their experience has not been visibly present in the development of Black Theology."[36] The feminism that had arisen in the 1960s and 70s, as I discussed in chapter 1, was implicitly focused on the privileged status of white women. Similarly, the work of Saiving and Plaskow and other feminist theologians was unable to be inclusive in extending the *imago Dei* to comprehend Black women's particular circumstances. Saiving and Plaskow focus on women's need to recover from the sin of selflessness, yet they still focus on issues truly only applicable to privileged women—such as the right to enter the workforce voluntarily. Saiving, particularly, locates hope in the movement of women from the "traditional" role of housewife to have their own meaningful careers. This perspective, based upon white

33. Cone, *God of the Oppressed*, 98.
34. Cone, *God of the Oppressed*, 98.
35. West, *Cornel West Reader*, 397.
36. Wilmore and Cone, *Black Theology*, 279.

women's experience, does not consider the fact that most Black women were already working outside the home; not because of their desire to achieve autonomous selfhood but because of economic necessity.

Black theology, as it emerged, while arguing for the liberation of Black people, was also unable to address the specific to the circumstances of Black women. As Cone admits, "It was not until I was challenged by Black and other Third World women that I became aware that the significance of feminism was not exhausted by the White women's movement."[37] In acknowledging that Black women were being ignored by both liberation theologies, Cone insists that the work of Black women theologians is vital "to do justice to this issue."[38]

### The Need for Womanism

Liberation for all women needs to include diverse experiences of what reclamation of self might look like. This liberation cannot be assumed to apply in exactly the same form to all women, and therefore must be embodied in various and differing contexts. Black theology and Feminist theology offered insufficient resources to comprehend the multi-layered oppression of Black women. Being oppressed in terms of both their blackness and their gender, even within the Black community itself, necessitated the production of theological thinking that would specifically address their concerns. As theological reflection must be practiced with the particularity of human experience in mind, it became clear that feminist theology had to be challenged. Much as Cone used some of the tools of white theology to construct his own work, womanism both uses the resources of Black and feminist theology and creates its own vivid, new theological vision. This, as theologian Cheryl Kirk-Duggan explains, is womanist theology:

> Womanist theology emerged as a corrective discipline during the 1980s, concerned about the plight of black women in the United States, of global African diasporan women, ultimately the wholeness of all persons across gender, race, class, age, and ability.[39]

---

37. Wilmore and Cone, *Black Theology*, 279–80.

38. Wilmore and Cone, *Black Theology*, 282.

39. Kirk-Duggan, "Womanist Theology as a Corrective to African American Theology," 267.

This intersectional theology draws inspiration from the work of Alice Walker, as Black women voiced their own experiences. Kirk-Duggan cites the origins of this as being:

> [W]hen scholar-activist Katie G. Cannon adapted Walker's definition as an analytical rubric. She recognized that neither traditional feminist theology, which problematized gender, nor traditional black theology, which problematized race, provided all the categories needed for her world, which included poor black women, "the least of these."[40]

This need for womanism is explained further by Katie Cannon:

> The womanist writing consciousness does not obscure or deny the existence of tridimensional oppression but rather through full, sharp awareness of race, sex, and class oppression we present the liberating possibilities that also exist . . . Whether we begin with paradigms created by mentors of European and Euro-American ancestry or with theoretical constructs emerging from the oral traditions in the African Diaspora or with a dialectical, syncretistic interplay between the two, we must answer the inescapable questions of appropriation and reciprocity.[41]

Cannon's acknowledgement of the complex relationship between theologies is also seen in the way other womanists respond to and discuss certain feminist texts. In response to early white feminist texts, theologian J. Cameron Carter explains that Black women "have been positioned in such a way as to receive actual and figurative violence against and domination of their bodies not just by white males but by men of any race with white women's participation."[42] As I outlined in the previous chapter, feminist theology struggled to grasp the way Black women had been positioned as prime representative of abjected, sinful bodies against men's (primarily white men's) disembodied goodness. Womanists made clear that while white women are seen as embodied (and thus tied to the "flesh" in a way white men are not), they still are granted some agency. If they perform in appropriate ways—wife, mother, homemaker, modest, chaste, etc.—they can overcome their fleshly nature. They are, in some respects at least, able to express choices through their bodies. Black women, however, have not

---

40. Kirk-Duggan, "Womanist Theology as a Corrective to African American Theology," 267.

41. Katie Cannon, *Katie's Canon*, 135.

42. Carter, "Humanity in African American Theology," 180.

in many historical and contemporary contexts been able to make their own decisions concerning whether to marry and when to stay at home raising their babies etc.[43] They have been often subjected to the violence of rape without legal redress and in terms of this they stand in a fundamentally different relationship to their bodies. As Carter explains,

> But if this is a statement of white women's existence in relationship to man (she is *for* [the white] man), its deepest presumption is that (white) woman does indeed *possess* a body. She is man's complement. But this is precisely what the colonial experience—and related to this, modern slavery—refused to black and similarly positioned (indigenous) women. In their situation, just as lands were deemed unknown and empty (*terra nullius/terra incognita*), the people of those lands (and in the case of slaves, those brought into those lands to work it) were deemed unknown and empty. They were not just reducible to their bodies as their original possessions (as in the case of white women). They lacked even this; possession of the body for them was not a possibility.[44]

In advocating revised understandings of personhood for Black women, Delores Williams continues to explore the identification with Jesus that is so important within Black Christianity, maintaining that the main focus of this should be on Jesus's life and ministry, rather than his suffering and death. She argues that redemption comes through participation in the liberative ministry of Jesus, which entails the work toward "self-actualization, self-control, and self-care" as well as ministry to others.[45] She thus moves the focus from Jesus's suffering to his call to discipleship, and argues that in the experience of Black people, caring for themselves is a valid response to that calling. It also has kingdom significance. The survival and progress of Black people resisting the oppression of slavery and its legacy in a racist social order broadens human purpose and unites them in Christ's mission.

Womanist theologian M. Shawn Copeland similarly calls for a Christ-centered embodied theology that can bring freedom to Black people. In her text, *Enfleshing Freedom: Body, Race, and Being*, she lays out five points she believes connect their bodies to what becomes an

---

43. Florida and Mellander, "Geography of Inequality," 90.
44. Carter, "Humanity," 181.
45. Earl, "Black Theology," 138.

empowering interpretation of the doctrine of the *imago Dei*. These points are:

> That the body is a site and mediation of divine revelation; that the body shapes human existence as relational and social; that the creativity of the Triune God is manifested in differences of gender, race, and sexuality; that solidarity is a set of body practices; and that the Eucharist orders and transforms our bodies as the body of Christ.[46]

These five points direct her theological anthropology to bring about a freedom that does not require situational change, overcoming, or reconciliation with oppressors to become actualized. Instead, the *imago Dei* is already seen in the lived, embodied existence of people. For Black people, Copeland says slavery "deformed these convictions."[47] It attempted to destroy potential in black people and to "displace God" within them.[48] In order to redeem the *imago Dei* in Black people she calls for them "to love their flesh, to love their bodies, to love themselves and one another into wholeness"[49] in the present and in future hope.

This call for self-love is prevalent in Black theology. It is not the kind of love much white theology calls for: the disconnected "love your neighbor" mandate that requires me to abrogate my personhood. Instead, it envisages a dignity of self-love even in the presence of oppression. This dignity is formed from the lived practice of respectful love in a community of oppressed people who, whilst unable to practice self-determination, nevertheless continue to deny the oppressors claims they are lesser beings. To fully understand the nature of this dignity, I turn now to Katie Geneva Cannon and her presentation of dignity as a kind of "quiet grace."[50]

## Katie Geneva Cannon: Restoring the *Imago Dei*

In a tribute to the life and work of Cannon, Beverly Rose Wallace explains "Dr Katie Cannon described herself as a womanist liberation

---

46. Copeland, *Enfleshing Freedom*, 2.
47. Copeland, *Enfleshing Freedom*, 24.
48. Copeland, *Enfleshing Freedom*, 24.
49. Copeland, *Enfleshing Freedom*, 52.
50. Cannon refers to this in her work *Black Womanist Ethics*. In her review of this, Karin Sporre uses it interchangeably with "silent grace".

ethicist called to 'debunk, unmask, and disentangle the historically conditioned value judgments and power relations that undergird the particularities of race, sex, and class oppression.'"[51] Her work challenges the theology of anyone dealing with sexism, racism, or classism. Wallace maintains that Cannon demonstrated:

> Black women are the most vulnerable and the most exploited members of the American society. The structure of the capitalist political economy in which Black people are commodities combined with patriarchal contempt for women has caused the Black woman to experience oppression that knows no ethical or physical bounds.[52]

Rather than understanding theology from a Black man's perspective on suffering, or a white woman's perspective on sexism, Cannon argues that we must include the lived experience of Black women. Not only does this acknowledge the insights of Black women, it offers a powerful critique and enrichment of all theology. Rather than limiting the effects womanist theology can have on society to Black women, womanists sought to develop it into a global theology that could help all people. The focus for womanists was toward "organiz[ing] toward the love, justice-making, and transformation of all people."[53] For Cannon, this included focusing on the pedagogical approach to this theology. She desired to teach and empower Black women to work against oppressive systems.[54] In order to understand how Cannon's view of the image of God is developed, I will work through her theology by first understanding the significance of the history of slavery before moving to her development of dignity in the face of oppression.

In light of her practical approach to womanist theology, the starting point of Cannon's thinking in relation to the *imago Dei* is the fact that African Americans experience the world differently because of the chattel slavery and ongoing oppression they have been subjected to. She states:

> The legalization of chattel slavery meant that the overwhelming majority of Blacks lived permanently in subhuman status. No objective circumstance—education, skill, dress, or

---

51. Wallace, "'Black Butterfly' Asking the Question, Womanist Reframing, Conscientization, and Generativity . . . ," 169–79.

52. Cannon, *Black Womanist Ethics*, 4.

53. Kirk-Duggan, "Womanist Theology," 267.

54. Kirk-Duggan, "Womanist Theology," 270.

bearing—could modify this fundamentally racist arrangement. This mode of racial domination meant that as chattel slaves none of my ancestors were human beings legally, culturally, socially, or politically."[55]

As Christian theologians debate the *imago Dei*, they must recognize that the notion that human beings are connected to God through the social roles they assume, their creative actions or their recognition of divine giftings must be challenged. While white theologians discussed these theories as being the "primary location" of the image,[56] Black people were often granted neither the education nor the opportunities to embody God's image in these ways. For centuries, Black people were rendered legally subhuman and strong cultural constraints meant these positive aspects of their *imago Dei* were denied. A strong connection to God was, however, developed through their experience of suffering and oppression. This understanding is crucial for Cannon's work, in which she highlights the importance of understanding how slavery and subsequent oppression have affected Black life, and thus must have a role in the development of a more comprehensive understanding of *imago Dei*. A doctrine of the image of God in humanity must be able to address the specifics of the human, and as Cannon explains, that must confront the "suffering, oppression and exploitation of Black people in society."[57] The oppression placed upon them cannot be held to limit their participation in the *imago Dei*. Rather, womanist theology provides "healing opportunities that expose the muddles and messes of sexism, racism, and classism."[58] Instead of seeing these oppressions as diminishing the humanity of Black women (and others around the world), they can become ways of seeing the world correctly and helping others to also embrace their wholeness. Therefore, in Cannon's work, an understanding of humanity requires confrontation with the oppression that damages the marginalized's understanding of their humanity. But how can oppression be overcome when the evil is so great? Cannon has a hopeful answer to this question,

> "Can God create a rock that God can't pick up?'—is the fundamental query that deals with the traditional theological problem concerning transgressions that proceed directly from human

---

55. Cannon, *Katie's Canon*, 29.
56. Carter, "Humanity," 176.
57. Cannon, *Black Womanist Ethics*, 1.
58. Kirk-Duggan, "Womanist Theology," 270.

sin—structures of domination, subordination and constraints that reinforce and reproduce hierarchies based on race, sex, class, and sexual orientation.[59]

Cannon sees God's work as already addressing this problem through Christ. Like other Black theologians she declares God's work to liberate is focused in Jesus. Jesus's incarnation, life and death, is God's answer to the evil of sin and suffering. Thus, Christ represents the Divine working alongside, and even through, the suffering Black people endure. Cannon's work in womanism allows people to see how theology, particularly Christian theology and biblical studies, has been used to further oppress people, but then it also offers hope in redeeming these practices for liberation rather than oppression.[60]

## Quiet Grace as Resistance

As the above makes clear, for Cannon, there must be an understanding of the *imago Dei* that is not found in asserting an agency that Black women were not allowed to exercise. Instead, it is found in the dignity central to Black theology that comes from the resources not of an individual person but rather from the strength of the community. As Kirk-Duggan explains, Cannon's praxis is informed by her focus on double consciousness. She says, "She embodies and features an epistemological privilege of the oppressed . . ."[61] In doing this, Cannon is able to examine and utilize previous texts, particularly biblical texts and other theologies, to further correct the distortions within these. Kirk-Duggan continues, "The corrective is paradoxical, simultaneously exposing injustice while nurturing and witnessing womanist consciousness."[62] In working through texts and histories like this, Cannon is able to both expose the reality of life's difficulties while inspiring action toward a wholeness that can overcome these problems. Through this, her work examines that of other Black theologians. In the final chapter of *Black Womanist Ethics*, Cannon demonstrates this corrective by exploring an understanding of dignity, drawing particularly on the iconic examples of Thurman and King.

---

59. Cannon, *Katie's Canon*, 101.
60. Cannon, *Katie's Canon*, 101.
61. Kirk-Duggan, "Womanist Theology," 269.
62. Kirk-Duggan, "Womanist Theology," 270.

To begin, Cannon explains that the "cultural and historical support available . . . was the balm of the Black religious heritage."[63] In the work of these two men, she sees a focus on "the ethical themes of *imago dei*, love as grounded in justice, and the irreplaceable nature of community."[64] Developing this theme Cannon lays out the ways community can develop in Black women the inner dignity needed to continue in their struggle. She explains that there are three themes she sees in their developments of theological anthropology: 1) ethical themes of the *imago Dei*, 2) love as grounded in justice, and 3) the irreplaceable nature of community.[65]

Both King and Thurman begin by asserting that all people possess the *imago Dei*, and that it is vital to affirm this in generating liberatory theological visions. For Thurman, understanding the existence of the image in humans allows each individual person to recognize and accept their worth, giving them purpose and power. He believes this affirmation will give meaning to each person's life, allowing them to transform their circumstances, even when facing obstacles and limitations. Much like Tillich, Thurman seems to believe this existential courage will allow the person to see beyond circumstantial injustice and move toward actions that empower. King, similarly, believes that each person's possession of the image grants them inalienable rights which convey to them both freedoms and social responsibility. It also means they are morally unjustified in injuring another person—which would deface the image of God within them.

Secondly, both men see a focus on love as central to the *imago Dei*. For Thurman, this love requires reconciliation and acknowledgment of other's possession of the image. In this, Thurman calls for people to meet each other "where he is"[66] in order to treat the person appropriately. King's conception of love is focused on relationship. Believing that love for God extends into love for neighbor, King called for love for enemies as well as community, and required it to be an "active, dynamic and determined" love.[67]

Finally, Cannon demonstrates how after these two principles, each highlight community as essential. Thurman sees humanity as essentially

---

63. Cannon, *Ethics*, 160.
64. Cannon, *Ethics*, 160.
65. Cannon, *Ethics*, 160.
66. Cannon, *Ethics*, 165.
67. Cannon, *Ethics*, 166.

one, "all life is one, arising out of a common center—God."[68] King, meanwhile, affirms this unity in practical terms. Because of the community rising from our relationships to God and others, we must work practically to end injustice and form a true, realized community in the world.

Having brought into dialogue these important and influential perspectives Cannon then proceeds to apply their conclusions specifically to the situation of Black women. She explains that for Thurman, these principles must bring Black women to "translate the formulation of God's love into the actual phenomena of her human existence."[69] Each woman can see her worth *in* her circumstances and her character. She can transcend her self-doubt through seeing and recognizing the love and faith in her community. From King, Cannon explains that Black women are fully members of the "beloved community," and are thus responsible for the active work toward ending injustice and freeing themselves and others.[70] They are important actors in the work of righting society.

It is through developing these perspectives that Cannon is then able to define her own three characterizations of the image of God in Black women: "invisible dignity, quiet grace, and unshouted courage."[71] These themes underlie the active work Black women can do, regardless of their circumstances, to participate in God's transforming work. As Cannon explains the lack of ability to exert conventional forms of agency means that *imago Dei* theories that require overcoming or active autonomy do not speak to many Black women. Yet Black women who cannot escape oppression are still able to live out the ideals articulated by King and Thurman and can practice them by affirming their own worth and importance in the community. Like King and Thurman, Cannon is particularly invested in emphasizing connection to spiritual roots and emboldening Black women to "seek the realization of their dignity as persons"[72] through this communal inheritance.

In explaining Cannon's definition of dignity, Karin Sporre further examines the "three virtues"[73] mentioned above. These may be the only option for those whose survival depends on finding the resources to endure oppressive circumstances they are unable to change. As Cannon

68. Cannon, *Ethics*, 168.
69. Cannon, *Ethics*, 169.
70. Cannon, *Ethics*, 173.
71. Cannon, *Ethics*, 174.
72. Cannon, *Ethics*, 174.
73. Sporre, *In Search of Human Dignity*, 22.

observes, "one can see that all human beings *ought* to have equal value, but that it does not follow that they actually *have* equal value."[74] Not possessing equal value will affect their actions, and so Cannon says that in the face of oppression, Black women, particularly, exhibit a *quiet grace* that demonstrates their dignity and therefore their *imago Dei*. This quiet grace can be the kind of resistance a person needs in order to connect to their *imago Dei*. For Cannon, even in the direst circumstances, a Black woman's belief that "What is happening to me is not right!"[75] is her resistance. This moral resistance nourishes the life of Black people and means that there can be a way to freedom, for the community if not the individual person. This is not resignation to oppression, but the maintenance of dignity that challenges the oppressive regime established.

For Black women, then, displaying this self-belief with dignity can be salvific to their communities as a whole. They do not need to perform heroic tasks, but instead pass on the belief in dignity. It is this communal belief that restores the experience of the *imago Dei* that the oppressive system denies. Sporre explains that Cannon's work demonstrates this communal value—the community "can form, encompass and promote an alternative value basis."[76] This community is vital. Cannon stresses regularly "how disastrous it can be for an individual who does not live in and through her or his community."[77]

Cannon's community-focused work looks toward the goal of elevating the dignity of Black people. In doing this, she develops an understanding of social justice as a Christian imperative and asks how this vision could be accomplished while oppression exists. This means that reconciliation and redemption are reclaimed as goals for this world rather than simply heavenly promises. She says, "In every sphere where Blacks were circumscribed and their legal rights denied, the Black Church called its members to a commitment of perfecting social change and exacting social righteousness here on earth."[78] Cannon's call for these actions is about praxis, not theory. It is not to hope for a redeemed heaven, but to give courage to women to stand up to injustice in even small ways.

---

74. Sporre, *In Search of Human Dignity*, 24.
75. Sporre, *In Search of Human Dignity*, 24.
76. Sporre, *In Search of Human Dignity*, 25.
77. Sporre, *In Search of Human Dignity*, 25.
78. Sporre, *In Search of Human Dignity*, 19.

Stating that "Christians are morally bound to cooperate with the forces of good and equally bound to refuse cooperation with evil,"[79] Cannon practices what Stephen G. Ray, Jr. describes as sacred rhetoric.[80] In demonstrating this praxis, this functional and active theology, she is linking each person to God through their work in the community and their own dignity. Ray says:

> [T]his enactment of sacred rhetoric in the public discourse of Katie Cannon: 1) restores the divine subjectivity of those made in the image of God but ensnared in the wickedness of slavery, and 2) unmasks the demonic subjection of the Christian faith to the powers of this world mediated through corrupted notions or relationality inscribed through the notion of race.[81]

Through her focus on silent dignity, Cannon is reimagining the *imago Dei* as Saiving had also attempted. Yet Cannon is also shifting the emphasis from equal participation in society, to affirmation of worth in the face of social inequality. When unable to end their oppression, Black women can still acknowledge that they do not deserve the suffering they endure. Instead, they deserve to be acknowledged as full members of the community, in possession of the *imago Dei*.

## Challenges Remain

Reading Cannon in conversation with Barth and Tillich, Cannon's affirmation of the work of Black women is not a full repudiation of their theoretical concepts, but a step forward in a more comprehensive understanding of the image of God in humanity. Barth's Christocentric theology is an obvious influence in Black theology, and practically demonstrated in the ways Cannon depicts the *imago Dei*. Furthermore, like Saiving and Plaskow, Cannon recognizes that the specific ways in which a person claims their *imago Dei* are important. Women must recognize their worth, and for Cannon, Black women must recognize how their contributions can sustain and renew their community. This study of Cannon's work has given me needed challenges—to see "ordinary" lives and work as inherently valuable and necessary in community, and to reject requirements for individuals to overcome systemic injustice

---

79. Cannon, *Ethics*, 22.
80. Ray, "Black Sacred Rhetoric: Katie Cannon and the Power of Memory," 127.
81. Ray, "Black Sacred Rhetoric: Katie Cannon and the Power of Memory," 127.

and oppression in order to embody the divine. Cannon's work to utilize multiple theories is also vital to my own work, as I seek to expand the discussion of the *imago Dei* beyond its current terms.

Cannon's focus upon a multi-oppressed group, articulates an understanding of humanity that locates experience within its social context. While Tillich discussed anxieties in theory, Cannon discusses the reality of people who face physical destruction daily. She recognizes the difficulties of people who must both fight against the evils of oppression while working with or for their oppressors. It is in these real lived experiences that Cannon's understanding of the *imago Dei* is embodied. She says:

> When the soul feels God's presence, individuals are grasped by the divine essence, which heightens awareness of options and possibilities. This built-in sense of the Creator provides oppressed people with ultimate meaning and the ability to transform circumstances.[82]

For Cannon, each person is located within a set of circumstances and community, and thus finds their purpose within that experience. This experiential understanding means that each human's purpose is unique, equal, and accessible. As Daly pointed out, it is important to recognize one's self in connection to God.[83] The work that "ordinary" Black women perform within their communities is not, in fact, ordinary, but it is work in cooperation with the divine. It entails doing the work of Christ in the specific location where one lives. It is a practical recognition and application of the I-Thou relationship and of the courage to be. In her book *Feminist Theory and Christian Theology*, Serene Jones discusses theories surrounding feminist communities. She explains

> [The] utopian, normative dimension of feminist theories of community has its own set of challenges and insights. One challenge is that the everyday experiences of women often resist utopian visions of a better future . . . Irresolvable conflicts leave us unable to imagine the way it should be—for example, communal conflicts in which both sides share the cause of justice and the burden of guilt. We also experience great sufferings that social accounts of oppression cannot exhaustively explain

---

82. Cannon, *Ethics*, 160.

83. As I discussed in chapter 1, she sees God as Be-ing, and thus connected to all of humanity. Daly, *Beyond God the Father*, 29.

> . . . Feminist theories of community need to incorporate such experiences into their utopian vision.[84]

This need to not only acknowledge but include the suffering and oppression women face is built into Cannon's theology, while continuing to look toward the utopia of redemption. These communities allow individuals to see their worth, their dignity, and their connection to each other. The hope is for the heroic arc of the person—that they will overcome the trauma of oppression, even if it is only by internally acknowledging that they deserved better. In Sheldon George's book *Trauma and Race,* he acknowledges that this overcoming is a psychological redemption of identity. Rather than identifying primarily as a racial Other, George wants African Americans to find a *jouissance* that transcends their race.[85] George, like Cannon, wants the Black person to be able to experience a wholeness that sees their personhood as worthy and part of the community.

It is here that I see the needed next step from Cannon's development of the *imago Dei*. Where Cannon emphasizes the communal aspect of Black women's work, and the importance of pointing out their unique ability to bring redemption to a racially torn society, I begin to wonder about the continued focus on dignity that undergirds her work. In each of the theologians I have examined, the focus remains primarily on the person's ability to perceive their place in God's reconnecting work, to recognize the *imago Dei* and then accept the courage it instils in them, or to overcome oppression or destruction. These qualities are obviously ideal. It is understandable to want everyone to recognize their own worth and place in the world, so that they can understand how they might participate in the divine work of redemption. Copeland points this out in her work, explaining that we must remember the slaves and others who were unable to escape their oppression. Some continue to live with their masters, and many continue to be oppressed. Yet, she still points to resistance and the inner overcoming of this bondage in a manner much like Tillich's "courage." She argues that they can

---

84. Jones, *Feminist Theory and Christian Theology*, 131.

85. He describes this *jouissance* in Lacanian terms—"pleasure that would emerge from impossible wholeness" (George, *Trauma and Race*, 4). In achieving this wholeness, African Americans would fix the separation that exists within them of understanding and perhaps resenting their oppression, a "jealouissance" (5). Though George's analysis of this differs greatly from Cannon's, I believe that both are striving toward the same dignity of the person.

overcome by "making means of their suffering" and "defined themselves and dismantled the images that had been used to control them."[86] The desire is always that the person is able to recognize the image in themselves, especially in resistance to those who oppose it.

In her text, *In Search of Human Dignity: Essays in Theology, Ethics and Education*, Karin Sporre examines Cannon's work in dignity and raises questions about the focus on this aspect. She begins by linking oppression and sin, saying

> In a situation where unequal power relations exist, those with power in the relationship also have the power to control the moral situations, which sometimes means the power to identify which situations should be called moral, understand the situations based on their own perception, and also describe the possible alternatives for action.[87]

If those in power are able to define morality as well, finding dignity may be a more complicated issue than discovering or developing love for oneself. The means to survive may, in fact, be deemed "immoral" and even believed to be immoral by the person required to perform them. This disconnect may cause dignity, love for oneself, to be out of reach for a person who is unable to see that the morality of the powerful is disingenuous.

Cannon argues for dignity found within community—particularly the community of Black women. Within this community, a person can recognize and adopt their own dignity. The community embodies the individual and elevates them, regardless of any shift in oppression or circumstances.

Found in community, this dignity is in embracing the value of oneself. Cannon says that when she stopped being a "people pleaser" she was able to see her own worth, which she says was to "experience God's presence within herself."[88] In her Christian theology, this was both an experience of God's presence and an embrace of God in her. Once again, Sporre points out, Cannon has anchored her dignity in something outside of herself.[89] I therefore echo Sporre's question, asking if the experience of being someone is a necessity, of being someone

---

86. Copeland, "Wading through Many Sorrows: Toward a Theology of Suffering in a Womanist Perspective," 149.

87. Sporre, *Human Dignity*, 22.

88. Sporre, *Human Dignity*, 27.

89. Sporre, *Human Dignity*, 28.

in oneself, in spite of, independent of, or rather maybe above the feeling of being less valued that follows the depreciation that comes out of submission in relationship. What of those who lack community, or the outside voice that tells them they are valued? What about those who do not have dignity, or who, because they believe themselves to be acting immorally, feel they have lost their dignity?

Sporre continues her examination of human dignity also asserting that developing this quiet (silent) grace, or dignity, can affect resistance against oppression. Yet, as she's pointed out, developing this dignity may require an outside support. Whether communal or spiritual, there seems a need for relationship in order to restore the ability to embrace of one's own value.

Thus, there is still the question of how to continue to see the image of God in a person who lacks this means to accomplish such work. Having established the need to reject actions as a demonstration of the *imago Dei*, I now must also examine how internal dignity must be understood. If a person cannot or will not see their own humanity, how are we to see it for them? Again, I am confronted with the difficult task of asking whether the image of God is still retained by people who do not overcome, who do not find courage, or who in fact perpetuate their own isolation or destruction. Is there a point in which a person has had stolen, surrendered or irretrievably lost their *imago Dei*?

# PART TWO
## A Turn To Literature

# 3

# Literature as a Challenge to Theology

Forming a Methodology

## Introduction

IN THE PREVIOUS CHAPTER, I began to engage with the challenges of Black and Womanist theology—particularly as these related to the *imago Dei*. I traced the ways in which understandings had been formed out of engagement with dominant theological traditions but also out of the specific contexts and insights of Black people. I also showed how this theology had become a significant resource for empowerment in the face of oppression and also how it reflected the spiritual vitality of Black Christian experience.

My chapter focused particularly upon the work of Katie Geneva Cannon pertaining to the *imago Dei* and specifically her desire to emphasize the importance of community in constituting the image. In pursuing this insight further, it is now important to more fully explore how she sees that community embodied, as well as the methods she utilizes to explore the nature of Black communal life. Particularly significant for my work is the way Cannon employed literature, and specifically Black women's literature in her theological reflection. As Cannon had to primarily draw upon theological sources based upon male experience in her research, she turned to women's literature as a source of the female wisdom required as she sought to develop her community-focused ethics. I will particularly look at her work with the literature of Zora Neale Hurston, as it is central to Cannon's methodology.

While understanding how this engagement with literature informs her stance on the silent grace of the oppressed, and by seeing how she links this to practical outcomes for the Black community, I must also comprehend the manner in which Cannon intertwines her theology with literary analysis. The drawing together of literature and theology is certainly not unique to Cannon, though she is a foundational proponent of it.[1] I will begin this chapter by examining Cannon's particular method of engaging theology and literature. Her approach is invaluable, but it is not unproblematic and so I will consider some of the interdisciplinary conversations between literature and theology that raise challenges to Cannon's method. This will lead me to a review of the way in which other scholars have sought to pursue this interdisciplinary work. My intention here is to build my own understanding of the ways in which literature might make an invaluable contribution to theological reflection and then to lay out my own methodology for the next steps in my research.

## Katie Cannon and Zora Neale Hurston

As Cannon sought a theology that could empower the Black community, she looked to construct this from primary sources that originated within the Black community itself. For Cannon, very significant resources were to be found in the literary work of Black women. These works seemed, to Cannon, to present the best evidence of the real lives of Black women whose experiences were frequently obscured in historical and cultural studies. She turned particularly to the work of the anthropologist, activist, and acute observer of Black life, Zora Neale Hurston. Cannon's work centering the literature of Hurston underpins her theology, and informs her image of the Black community, and particularly Black women. In responding to Hurston's work Cannon explains, "Hurston insisted that Black women seek the realization of their dignity as persons."[2] She sees this realization depicted in Hurston's fictional writing which provides

---

1. In her book *Literature, Theology and Feminism* (2007), Heather Walton demonstrates Cannon as "representative of this significant shift" in developing the combination of literature and theology. (5) In her chapter "Beyond the one and the other," she explains how Cannon saw it necessary to employ literature written by Black women in order to communicate theology pertaining to Black women.

2. Cannon, *Black Womanist Ethics*, 174.

many examples of ordinary Black women actively achieving their personhood and affirming their worth. By looking to these examples, Cannon raises her challenges to existing theories of the *imago Dei* and is also able to answer those challenges with her development of the concept of "silent grace." As stated, in both allowing Hurston's work to challenge and then inform her theology, Cannon also demonstrates an influential model for engagement between literature and theology.

As I discussed in chapter 2, in *Black Womanist Ethics*, Cannon says "The real-lived texture of Black life requires moral agency that may run contrary to the ethical boundaries of mainline Protestantism."[3] While she is searching for an understanding of what allows Black women to achieve the *imago Dei* through silent grace, she allows that, because of the oppression Black women face, they may have to act against the "moral code" of the society in order to become truly moral. To demonstrate what it may look like to achieve Black agency, she looks to Hurston's novels—specifically as they focus on a character's achievement of silent grace. While Hurston's characters may be individually embodying this, Cannon believes the whole Black community can be empowered by their presence and contribution.

## Theology through Reading the Novels of Hurston

In explaining her use of Black women's literature, Cannon begins by stating the foundational goal. Black theology works to understand social justice as a Christian imperative, often specifically linking it to the active work of the Black Church and leaders like Martin Luther King, Jr. This means that reconciliation and redemption are reclaimed as goals for this world rather than only heavenly promises. She says, "In every sphere where Blacks were circumscribed and their legal rights denied, the Black Church called its members to a commitment of perfecting social change and exacting social righteousness here on earth."[4] Seeing humanity as emblematic of Christ in Black theology goes farther than Barth's desire to see Christ as the epitome of the *imago Dei*. Here, there is a deeper focus on the liberative qualities of Christ's life and ministry. As I discussed in chapter 1, Barth's admonition is that "In Christ, the Christian is liberated *to*

---

3. Cannon, *Ethics*, 2.
4. Cannon, *Ethics*, 19.

service of God *and* neighbor"[5] which enacts an I-Thou relationship. This is further developed in Black theology because the social circumstances of the neighbor must be understood for the relationship to be liberating. As I explained, there is the need to look the other in the eye—to recognize their experiences and situation. Hurston's books are used to understand the reality of Black lives, as showing how sight can be achieved. For Cannon, this means Hurston's novels must be read as mirroring reality, demonstrating real experienced oppression.

The novels are not just meant to give insight, however. Because Black theology stressed that "Christians are morally bound to cooperate with the forces of good and equally bound to refuse cooperation with evil,"[6] Cannon also uses literary works to interrogate how Black women do this. The unique activism of Black women, who are both oppressed in their race and their gender, means that they had to find distinctive ways to carry forward this reconciling work. She says, "Hurston insisted that Black women seek the realization of their dignity as persons."[7] She sees this realization depicted in Hurston's work, which provides examples of ordinary Black women actively achieving their personhood and agency. By looking to these examples, Cannon is able to develop a theology of humanity through the insights of the people most often denied their humanity.

## Zora Neale Hurston

As Cannon points out, "Zora Neale Hurston was the most prolific Black woman writer in America from 1920 to 1950."[8] Producing dozens of works, Hurston's description of the Black community showed 'stoutheartedness' and demonstrated "the Black woman as a moral agent."[9] In weaving together stories of community, culture, and realistic actions taken against suffering, Hurston was able to give life to Tillich's idea of "the courage to be." Black women in Hurston's novels did not give in to anxieties, but instead overcame violence and poverty. Cannon recognizes the autobiographical aspects of Hurston's work as well. She argues that Hurston "and

---

5. Barter, "Theology of Liberation," 160.
6. Cannon, *Ethics*, 22.
7. Cannon, *Ethics*, 174.
8. Cannon, *Katie's Canon*, 78.
9. Cannon, *Katie's Canon*, 78–79.

her female characters are Black women who learn to glean directives for living in the here-and-now."[10] Years before King's definition of the *imago Dei*,[11] Hurston recognized that women's achievement of agency requires working within the system they experience. To overcome, to have courage, Hurston and her characters work with what they have, work with whom they can, toward the betterment of themselves and the people they love. She says, "Women who live in the circle of life must discern the genuine choices available or else they will be characterized by one or more of the following disparaging folk metaphors: mule, spit, cut, rut in the road, chewed-up and discarded sugar cane, or wishbone."[12] Cannon believes that in seeing the courage of the characters in Hurston's novels, has the potential to imbue the Black community with the silent grace she discusses in her theology. Acknowledging the dignity of various characters allows Black women to see their own dignity, and the dignity of all Black women, not as striving to resemble white women or achieve white priorities, but instead to recognize their own unique selves.

In order to see how Hurston displays this courage for Cannon, I will briefly explore this with reference to Hurston's most popular novel, *Their Eyes Were Watching God*. In the novel, protagonist Janie journeys through the narrative to discover her "full humanity."[13] In a series of experiences, encounters, and challenges, Janie is able to shed the false identity she was burdened with. Cannon points out that this process is similar to Hurston's overcoming of her father's rhetoric about her. He claimed she "was going to be hung before [she] was grown."[14] Her ambition, passion, and "sassy tongue" would destroy her. Similarly, Janie is taught that she is "not allowed to exist naturally and freely" because of her race and gender.[15] Hurston uses characters like Janie to "demythologize whole bodies of so-called social legitimacy."[16] Janie's Nanny presented her with codes of behavior that had saved her as an enslaved woman, but as Hurston delves into Janie's story we realize that these codes no longer hold for her. Janie is not an enslaved woman. She is not Nanny. She works hard to discover her own agency, as Hurston did, and by doing so leads her community

10. Cannon, *Katie's Canon*, 83.
11. See chapter 2.
12. Cannon, *Katie's Canon*, 83–84.
13. Cannon, *Katie's Canon*, 84.
14. Cannon, *Katie's Canon*, 79.
15. Cannon, *Katie's Canon*, 85.
16. Cannon, *Ethics*, 127.

forward from the "behavioral codes" that were formerly required during slavery. Cannon states, "Moral agency is exemplified each time Janie stands against critical dilution of her personhood."[17] Janie rejects the morality and models of "success" that have been forced upon her community by the systemic racism in the United States. Instead, she seeks to reclaim her dignity by doing what is morally right for her as a Black woman. This distinction is vital in Cannon's silent grace.

For Cannon, Hurston's work in such stories is restorative work. As womanist and novelist Alice Walker demonstrates, Hurston's work embodies "racial health: a sense of Black people as complete, complex, *undiminished* human beings, a sense that is lacking in so much black writing and literature."[18] Walker believes this love of Black people and Black communities stems from an inherent love of herself. Hurston's "confidence in herself"[19] is a unique feature for Walker, and she links it to her choosing to locate herself within a Black community that lived a self-organizing life rather living in a multi-ethnic environment. In this context Black people were not defining themselves continually in terms of their responses to racism but rather "had enormous respect for themselves and for their ability to govern themselves."[20] Walker also sees Hurston's respect for herself as a revolutionary act. She did not desire to be white, nor male, and lived proudly even after she was ostracized by her own community and lived in extreme poverty.[21] Walker wishes Hurston could have found a "family she never had"[22] to support her work and bitterly bemoans her rejection, "*We are a people. A people do not throw their geniuses away.*"[23] Nevertheless, she applauds, as does Cannon her rejection of the oppression of trying to "be white." The theology of Cannon is pointedly aimed at restoring Black women (and by extension, the Black community) in order that they might assume identity on their own terms.

---

17. Cannon, *Canon*, 86.
18. Walker, *In Search of Our Mother's Gardens*, 85.
19. Walker, *In Search of Our Mother's Gardens*, 85.
20. Walker, *In Search of Our Mother's Gardens*, 85.
21. Walker says, "Zora, who worked so hard, was never able to make a living from her work" (90). She discusses Hurston's financial struggle while also discussing her isolation, saying "her last days were spent in a welfare home and her burial paid for by 'subscription'" (87).
22. Walker, *In Search of Our Mother's Gardens*, 92.
23. Walker, *In Search of Our Mother's Gardens*, 92.

Through Hurston's eyes, Black women can claim their lives as their own and begin to make decisions for it. For Janie, the seemingly simple act of falling in love becomes liberation that others theorized about. Janie was able to shed the "false images that said that as a Black and as a woman she is not allowed to exist naturally and freely."[24] At the end of the novel, Janie has rejected "male domination and the empty materialism of white culture."[25] She is then able to find love with her third husband, Tea Cake, who is 18 years younger than she is. It is her developed agency that allows her to reject societal norms and marry a man who frees her soul rather than the "stable" men her grandmother wanted for her. Janie is able to make her own life choices and lives as a full human being. This restoration models what Hurston desired for the Black community, and is the lesson demonstrated through all her books. Black agency can never be achieved by imitating white standards.

As I discussed in chapter 1, Tillich's concept of the "courage to be" is to choose life over annihilation, but he describes this primarily through the language of psychological neurosis. His primary concern is that a person decides to have courage in the face of anxiety. Yet for Janie, this decision to have courage is to decide to be herself despite the social outcome. If Nanny's concern that Janie choose a man who can support her is practically correct, Janie is essentially choosing functional non-survival but survival of her humanity. Tillich does not take into account how choosing to be fully oneself could be detrimental to a person within their social context, but Hurston offers examples of people who are able to do this and yet still survive. Cannon's point in using the example set by these women in her work is that they are demonstrating a specific courage in the face of oppression, rather than a universal form of existential courage.

Because of this difference perspective upon courage, Cannon is reimagining the *imago Dei* in ways similar to Saiving: it is the recognition of one's agency and full humanity. Yet Cannon is also shifting the focus from the ability to participate fully in society, as Saiving outlines it, to agency rooted in an inherent worthiness. Cannon's agency allows women the recognition of their humanity apart from, and despite of, the expectations or requirements an oppressive society may inflict upon them. Furthermore, their silent dignity can spread throughout the community,

---

24. Cannon, *Ethics*, 132.
25. Cannon, *Ethics*, 135.

with the effect of enabling the Black community to experience their *imago Dei* despite the racism that attempts to strip them of it.

## Hurston's Literature in Cannon's Theology

In this analysis, it is understandable that Cannon insists theologians ought to answer directly to the experiences of their community. As she states, "As long as the white-male experience continues to be established as the ethical norm, Black women, Black men and others will suffer unequivocal oppression."[26] Not only must we understand the lived experiences of Black people, but they must be included consistently in theological thinking. It is inappropriate to frame theology, or theological theories, around the experiences of the privileged. By engaging with Black women's literature, Cannon is rejecting the idea that white-male experiences are the norm, and also allowing Black women to see their own lives and experiences central to theological reflection.

Secondly, Cannon is focused on helping Black people to "purge themselves of self-hate, thus asserting their own human validity."[27] In pointing to the silent grace demonstrated or achieved in Hurston's novels, Black women can see it achieved in their own lives. This correlation allows them to begin asserting their own silent grace, their own unshouted courage, and then to pass it along to the community. The communal love she sees in Black liberation theology is passed not through theological texts, but through this wisdom literature.

However, while Cannon's partnership of literature and theology is empowering it does contain a troubling insistence on reading literature as reality. As many scholars have pointed out this is to deny the fictive and creative aspects of literature as art and furthermore supports a dangerous tendency to engage only with literature which confirms a pre-existing view of the world rather than texts that inspire or challenge us to see things differently (as I will discuss further in this chapter, through the work of philosopher Anneleise van Heijst). If theology is to engage with literature on its own terms it is important to acknowledge that this will be a complex and sometimes ambiguous process and that literature might provoke us to encounter things we would rather avoid. Similarly, while Hurston's works are undoubtedly inspiring, it is difficult to see

---

26. Cannon, *Ethics*, 3.
27. Cannon, *Ethics*, 3.

how one character's personal journey, their grasp of the *imago Dei*, is passed through the community to generate wider transformation, as the other characters do not similarly achieve this. Cannon approaches Hurston's works looking specifically for this communal outcome, and therefore Hurston is read as a support to Cannon rather than a creative challenge to her theology. With this unease in mind I turn to see how others have engaged with literature in theological reflection and engage with their methodology before outlining my own.

## Literature and Theology as a Methodology

I have gained much from Cannon's example of interdisciplinary work and see it as a very productive way of developing insights into areas that are frequently marginalized in theological discourse. It is an excellent example of how engagement with literature has opened up many important new trajectories in theological studies. As I shall now go on to explore, attention to literature in the ongoing development of theological work has allowed more inclusive examinations of such important topics as suffering, trauma, intersectional feminism, etc. My focus in this next section of the chapter will be on an example of interdisciplinary reflection upon suffering, as this topic leads directly on from the work the work of Cannon and also relates directly to my own concerns in this work.

As stated, Cannon's inclusion of literature in the development of her theology allows her to open theology to insights not typically included in a predominantly white male-centric study. Similarly motivated, Cynthia R. Wallace's book, *Of Women Borne*, focusses on the ethics of suffering as revealed through close readings of literary texts written by women. Through looking at her work, I can continue to expand my own understanding how literature can challenge established theories of the *imago Dei*, and how I might approach literature to further facilitate my own work on this theme.

Wallace begins by emphasizing the importance of not seeing literature as being simply to be exploited or "used" by theology. It is not a crutch to prop up previously held theological beliefs, or to prove the validity of particular theological stances. She says, "literature's potential to do good in the realm of material justice is strongest when it is attended to as *literature*, when it is read closely, not 'used' for some purpose but given open attention, with a heightened awareness to its singularity."[28] As such, Wallace chooses literature that does not provide answers, but instead provokes questions. She says

> Seeking to do justice to the relationship between word and flesh, I lay out the hypothesis that guides this book—that contemporary literary writings by women challenge and correct the ethical systems of redemptive sacrifice . . .[29]

Wallace demonstrates that by reading specific literary works, the questions and needs of the sufferer, particularly women sufferers, that are not addressed in more traditional, theoretical theology are able to be articulated. In terms of literary texts from minority or nondominant groups, she asks whether they make a particularly important contribution by reminding us of the inadequacy of the dominant symbolic system to address their challenges: "Is the existing language, the existing symbolic, even adequate . . . or is there always something more, some *differend*, that exceeds the given system of signs?"[30]

Wallace's hypothesis is that by engaging with literary texts that portray a "nuanced ethics of suffering," the reader enters into an "ethical relationship with both the text and the material world."[31] This relationship will allow the reader to understand the varied types of suffering and call for action against this. It is not enough, she argues, to "do nothing"[32] after developing the knowledge of suffering. In fact, her definition of liberation theology could be transposed here: " . . . [it] refuses the binaries not just of spiritual/material but also of mind/body: it fundamentally links embodied action with metaphysical contemplation."[33] Wallace's ethic in the face of suffering is developed by both contemplation on the reality of suffering and action to overcome it. She also requires an active change on the part of the reader in a true engagement with the text. As I look back at Cannon's work, the emphasis on developing a supportive community of transformative action is similar. Cannon's desire is that the literature of Hurston will encourage the Black community to support each other, to see their own dignity, and to take any possible actions toward ending

---

28. Wallace, *Of Women Borne*, 34.
29. Wallace, *Of Women Borne*, 10–11.
30. Wallace, *Of Women Borne*, 35.
31. Wallace, *Of Women Borne*, 210.
32. Wallace, *Of Women Borne*, 208.
33. Wallace, *Of Women Borne*, 150.

their oppression. Wallace hopes for the same outcomes in her reader—that they must support those they are now in an ethical community with (for Wallace, this is generally those who are marginalized in their suffering) and do what they can to end that oppression.

Wallace continues to emphasize this requirement throughout her work. While the various narratives she examines bring many questions, she insists we also return to the question of "What is suffering and what do we do about it?" Importantly, Wallace also insists that suffering cannot be ranked, nor can it be dismissed based on worthiness. We cannot decide that a person deserves to suffer, but instead must remain committed to both listen to those suffering, to take action after understanding the suffering, and to allow ourselves to be changed by the experience.

Her chapter on Chimamanda Ngozi Adichie deals with this topic directly. Adichie's book, *Half of a Yellow Sun*, presents a narrative of people living through the Biafran War.[34] Narrated through three perspectives, the novel "undermines the single story, highlighting by its form that stories are always multiple."[35] As it recounts the 1967–70 civil war in Nigeria, it highlights issues of colonialism and poverty, but also political, gendered, and religious hierarchies. Her novel, though, clearly argues against ranking suffering or prioritizing it. She then expands the designation of sufferer, asking "Who is the most guilty?"[36] No longer is it simply a matter of whose suffering is more important, but how can the varieties of suffering, even of those who seem guilty, point us in the direction of transformation. Wallace affirms the play of different narratives to give many perspectives, to open the discussion of suffering beyond narrow boundaries and thus generate a larger recognition of what causes suffering. She ties these to a central call. What will we do now that we see suffering as complex and varied?

Complex understanding of suffering must embrace the ways our suffering affects us physically and emotionally. Our physical selves, wounds to them or oppression power over them, are linked directly to our emotional states. Furthermore, literature provokes us to begin to imagine how the many faceted aspects of suffering can be responded to. As Wallace reflects the "both-and" qualities of literature are particularly significant:

---

34. Wallace, *Of Women Borne*, 197.
35. Wallace, *Of Women Borne*, 197.
36. Wallace, *Of Women Borne*, 202.

> In other words, literature both means something about the world in which we live and also means something about what it is to mean anything at all . . . it seems to me that the texts I have been discussing in these pages have shown the both-and duality of literature as both a space for representing things *as they are* and for hinting at the imaginative potential of how things *could be*.[37]

Representation here is not meant to refer to accurate accounts of specific people, but instead to the ethical dilemmas in which we find ourselves. We are to be challenged by literature to come to new and better actions on behalf of others and ourselves. Cannon asks us to see Hurston's characters as real so that we wrestle with the ways we understand and act on behalf of Black women. Wallace's challenge is rather different. She is reading literature to see complex problems represented and to allow those problems to redefine our understanding of suffering.

It is the need to allow literature to break open our understanding, to give us actionable empathy for others, that also motivates me to turn to literature that asks questions as much as it provides understanding. As Wallace has shown, these works can then move us towards a more open and nuanced theological approach. Again, in a slightly different way to Cannon she is emphasizing that while literature may reveal something of lived experience, we should not require of it heroic character examples or happy endings. As she states, "Suffering must be named, exposed, critiqued, and, at times, chosen, in the name of risky but merciful love . . . "[38] If literary works help us to name suffering they also teach us that we might have to let go of the requirement that it is presented as being overcome within the text. Instead, it is to challenge to the reader to move after putting down the book. As theologian Heather Walton says, " . . . Literature leads us back towards the dark and damp, sacred places where words and forms disintegrate."[39] It is then we turn to reconstruct a theology that must answer these challenges, or, from Walton "Theology seizes language to illuminate and instruct."[40]

As Walton points out, for those who have been marginalized, allowing literature to challenge preconceived notions is an important tool. They look to literature to "challenge, deconstruct and even dismantle the machinery of theological power out of fidelity to a divine encounter

---

37. Wallace, *Of Women Borne*, 215.
38. Wallace, *Of Women Borne*, 124.
39. Walton, *Literature, Theology and Feminism*, 17.
40. Walton, *Literature, Theology and Feminism*, 17.

that literature has pressed upon them."[41] For Cannon, experiencing the divine through the novels of Hurston motivated her to pass those lessons on through her reconstructed theology. Allowing the works of Hurston to give testimony to Black women's experiences enabled her to then construct her theology around "the real nature of the human condition"[42] and foreground Black women's experience. Wallace takes the challenges of inclusivity seriously, but her goal is to allow literature to challenge and complexify theological terms and provoke us to imagine changed worlds. As I seek to expand my own theological thinking on the *imago Dei*, I am also pressed by Wallace's final admonition to her readers, "What will you do, once your hands are again free?"[43]

## Literature that Challenges Us

In light of this challenge, I turn to philosopher Martha Nussbaum, who has written extensively on the engagement between literature and philosophy. While her focus is primarily on philosophical responses to moral issues, her insights into how these can be revisioned through readings of literature are particularly helpful. They have become influential within discussions of the uses of literature within theology.[44] Nussbaum's philosophical work aims to actively change and impact people and achieve transformation. Rather than philosophers avoiding literature because it improperly evokes emotional and empathetic responses, she argues that when we allow the text to speak, it is able to move us into change that includes action. I find it helpful to quote her here at length:

> I have argued that the arts, by nourishing the ability to look on human finitude with delight, assist the personality in its struggle with ambivalence and helplessness. Now, thinking about compassion, we may extend this point . . . We can easily see that such works of art promote compassion in their audience by inviting both empathy and the judgment of similar possibilities. They

---

41. Walton, *Literature, Theology and Feminism*, 3.
42. Walton, *Literature, Theology and Feminism*, 5.
43. Wallace, *Of Women Borne*, 231.

44. Citing work by Nussbaum and others, theologian Jeremy Begbie explains his use of music in theology, "Surely it must be doing more than reflecting our emotional life? Is there not a sense in which music *does something with* our emotions?...This is probably part of what Mendelssohn meant when he said that music is not *less* but *more* precise than words . . . To put this another way, music can play its part in *educating, shaping, and reshaping us* emotionally." Begbie, *Resounding Truth*, 301–2.

also work more directly to construct the constituent judgments of compassion, the judgment of seriousness and the judgment of nondesert. Moreover, they typically have normatively plausible and helpful views of these things: tragedies do not resolve around a shipment of peacock's tongues, but around predicaments that we all ought to see has having "size."[45]

In two of her books, *Love's Knowledge: Essays on Philosophy and Literature* (1990) and *Upheavals of Thought: The Intelligence of Emotions* (2001), Nussbaum argues that literature is an invaluable resource for philosophy. As stated, this method has been adopted by theologians doing similar work. Seeing literature as a helpful supplement to theology helps theologians demonstrate the practical aspects of theology and to connect difficult or seemingly abstract doctrines to emotional aspects of life. However, this method can be seen as undervaluing literature or even behaving as if literature, or other forms of art, were merely there to soften and aestheticize what might be very disturbing theological doctrines. While some of Nussbaum's methods are helpful, it is important to keep this critique in mind. To refrain from simply using literature as a support, it must be emphasized that we must be constantly attuned to the challenges it might force upon us.

To gain greater clarity on the way Nussbaum sees literature and philosophy in productive relationships I turn now to her book *Love's Knowledge*. In the introduction, she cites Henry James's *The Golden Bowl*, which she will further evaluate later. James's work, she claims, demonstrates the fact that some "truths about human life can only be fittingly and accurately stated in the language and forms characteristic of the narrative artist."[46] Philosophical language is obtuse and unable to affect our emotions, and therefore the best way to demonstrate philosophical truths is through the affective language of story. A story told can shift attachments and emotions, causing the philosophy it implicitly embodies to genuinely impact the reader. Similarly to Cannon, Nussbaum sees literature as a means to gain greater understanding of real-world experiences. However, Nussbaum is not as focused upon literature as a depiction of undisclosed aspects of reality, but instead on literature as moral and emotional guide.

Most important, here, is Nussbaum's goal for a better form of moral philosophy. She is not motivated by merely understanding a truth. Instead,

---

45. Nussbaum, *Upheavals of Thought*, 351.
46. Nussbaum, *Love's Knowledge*, 5.

she wants the truth to lead to active change. People should behave differently after learning the truth, which can only be done if they are emotionally affected by the truth encountered. This idea of emotional connection is further developed in her later book: *Upheavals of Thought: The Intelligence of Emotions*. Here she intricately links emotional identification to compassion, which she believes is integral to creating connections between human beings. She begins by laying out her belief that emotion is inevitably linked to connection, examining if "the object of emotion is always valued for some relation it bears to one's own flourishing."[47] She tells us of the death of her mother, the events surrounding it and how she emotionally reacted throughout the time, and connects this to emotional ties we can develop to literary characters. She says:

> The object of the emotion is seen as *important for* some role it plays in the person's own life. I do not go about fearing any and every catastrophe anywhere in the world, nor (so it seems) do I fear any and every catastrophe that I know to be bad in important ways. What inspires fear is the thought of damages impending that cut to the heart of my own cherished relationships and projects. What inspires grief is the death of someone beloved, someone who has been an important part of one's own life.[48]

In Nussbaum's example, this connection is obvious. It is her mother who has died. However, Nussbaum continues her work to demonstrate that we need not have this intimate sense of a connection to a person to attribute value for them in this way. We can develop a connection through imagination, as it is a "a bridge that allows the other to become an object of our compassion."[49] Like Wallace, Nussbaum is envisaging literature as actively changing the reader. However, while Wallace emphasizes how literature embodies complexity and provokes imaginings of change, her emphasis is on the emotional responses of connection and compassion. These are for Nussbaum vital components of working towards a just social order and should be reassessed as such. Nussbaum challenges us to ask:

> [W]hat positive contribution do emotions, as such, make to ethical deliberation, both personal and public? ... Why should a social order cultivate or appeal to emotions, rather than

---

47. Nussbaum, *Upheavals of Thought*, 5.
48. Nussbaum, *Upheavals of Thought*, 30.
49. Nussbaum, *Upheavals of Thought*, 66.

simply creating a system of just rules, and a set of institutions to support it?[50]

## How Not to "Use" Literature

Nussbaum and Wallace have helped strengthen my understanding of how reading literature is not only a means of representing marginalized experience and providing moral examples but also might become a source of imaginative and affective insight. However, I am still wary of the "use" (abuse) of literature in this partnership. Similarly, while Cannon's inspiration from Hurston inspired me, I am still unsure that it challenged and shaped her theology rather than justifying it. As I seek to ensure I allow literature to challenge and inform the theological research that I am pursuing in this book, I now turn to the Dutch theological ethicist, Anneliese van Heijst.

Anneliese van Heijst's book *Longing for the Fall* (1995) specifically argues against reading literature as a clear portrayal of real life which can then be used as a means of evidencing certain predetermined perspectives. Instead, she seeks to use literary forms to highlight the need for certain radical changes in theology and our understanding of theological queries. In explaining the title of her book, she emphasizes that the "fall" she longs for is this letting go of old, harmful dogmas or outmoded stands on religious concerns. She begins by acknowledging the situation of women has been particularly badly served in this way in that their selfhood was continually denied in theological discourses which require the subjugation of selfhood to God. "In short, women are required to lose a self they never actually had. They are becoming a self consisted of self-sacrifice or loss of self. They are still only hesitantly learning to cast off the role of eternal loser."[51] Her goal is to change how women view themselves theologically, in order to prevent them being constituted on the basis of self-sacrifice, and thus become empowered to grasp their own dignity. They must, essentially, lose the sacrificial self. This loss is, as she terms it, allowing oneself to fall. She explains:

> In both the physical and the psychological senses, falling is losing one's grip and being given up to a movement over which one no longer has any control. This can be harmful and threatening,

50. Nussbaum, *Upheavals of Thought*, 298.
51. van Heijst, *Longing for the Fall*, 7.

but it does not, as such, have to be unpleasant, as the cliché, "falling in love" indicates.[52]

Van Heijst proceeds to demonstrate how losing oneself, as she has defined it, allows the reader to gain. It is here that we see clearly how van Heijst's correlation of literature and theology (and philosophy more generally) is employed for challenges and the change literature can bring. Literature should be able to deliver a critique of theology and disturb traditional models and doctrines by forcing the reader to let go of preconceived beliefs. For van Heijst, this requires a reader to be open to the work of the text, letting it speak and shape our imaginings—before bringing our own values or principles to it. Van Heijst's perspective can both helpfully critique Cannon's position and add to the lessons learned from her and the other scholars discussed thus far.

## To Lose Oneself in Text

Following on from her analysis of falling Van Heijst describes interpretation as a loss of self in the text. The reader must note and be willing to set aside the various assumptions and goals they bring to the text and embrace its difference enabling them to "encounter radical alterity."[53] She is aware the reader cannot lose their self completely, but instead she encourages them to become better aware of the many layers that make up each of us. For Cannon, this would mean not overly identifying with the characters in Hurston's novels, but instead to see how they may be even critiquing her own view of Black women. Van Heijst wants us to recognize the layered ways we live—again, Cannon's world and that of Hurston's novels cannot be exactly the same, since their contexts are not the same. Furthermore, we are not simply a gender, or sex, or race, or class, but we are all of these things and many more. Allowing ourselves to "fall" into a text connects us better with each of these intersections—we can see how our own differences with the text highlight things we may not have understood before. For instance, Cannon might see that Janie did not have the educational opportunities she had. How might this have changed the silent dignity she identified? Would it have become even more impactful in this frame? Van Heijst argues that the feminist loss of self, one of three types she identifies, "allows [the reader] to be addressed,

---

52. van Heijst, *Longing for the Fall*, 9.
53. van Heijst, *Longing for the Fall*, 281.

confused, and advised by the alterity of the text, but does bring her/his values and her/his self-respect into the interpretation."[54]

In order to allow the text to fully challenge assumed world views and understandings there are a number of obstacles to be overcome. Van Heijst contends that many theological readings of literature attempt to recreate or shift symbols and images in order to create a cultural system of their liking. In this, they are *using* the novel to create new symbols and myths that support previously held beliefs. Van Heijst's mode of interpretation seeks to avoid this pitfall, though it seems she is pessimistic this ideal can be perfectly achieved as no reader is purely motivated.[55] She insists, though, that the text cannot be approached as a support to an already developed thesis, but instead must be allowed to critique and complicate matters.

In line with this, Van Heijst's second objection is to those who "[read] literary texts, namely, as testimonies to experience and as statements."[56] Literature is fiction, and this fact is important in the framing of literature and theology. Fiction is "constructed representation," and the text has a determinative status in what the reader takes away from it—it must become a moral guide as Nussbaum believes.[57] This critique is also an important warning to anyone seeking to use literature in theological reflection. To confuse the areas of fiction and reality, especially by assuming veracity of literary works, ignores the importance ways in which literature differs from reality. In particular, every aspect of the characters exists to produce the multi-layered meanings of the text, but to view it as realistic allows us to forget these important aspects.

Van Heijst requires that we focus on our reader-centeredness.[58] By being aware of our own bias and desires, we can better surrender to the text as an encounter with that which is different and beyond us. She argues we must lose ourselves in reading literature for theological purposes, rather than centering upon ourselves. Yet, we can only do this by being self-reflexively aware of our own selves and what we are bringing to and requiring from our reading encounter.

It is here I wish to register my own important qualification of the approach van Heijst is advocating. Whilst the emphasis upon literature

---

54. van Heijst, *Longing for the Fall*, 283.
55. See van Heijst's sections on theological reading, *Longing for the Fall*, 237–49.
56. van Heijst, *Longing for the Fall*, 261.
57. van Heijst, *Longing for the Fall*, 261.
58. van Heijst, *Longing for the Fall*, 264.

embodying alterity for us rather than connecting us to reality is a valuable challenge to conventional ways of reading, I would still wish to affirm Cannon's perspective that we can still discover much about lived experience from literature. Furthermore, Cannon's insistence that we value the female author and her insights and wisdom is largely missing from van Heiijst's poststructuralist perspective on literature. In understanding the author's context, we can often discover important ways of understanding the text. In both instances, the reader can allow themselves to become sensitive to the text yet not prevent it from making its own radical challenge. I do not believe that the one approach excludes the other—although they clearly stand in some tension. As van Heijst herself states reading in these ways enables us to "develop a new sensitivity for the contingencies of human existence."[59] In this way, literature retains its power to shift our vision and is not a support or supplement to theology but instead prompts radical shifts in our thinking.

## Rebecca Chopp's Theopoetics

Van Heijst takes us further in our explorations of how literature can reshape theological thinking, yet I remain concerned by her insistence that literature is not, and cannot be read as, a representation of reality. Thus, in this final examination of the engagement between literature and theology I turn to the ground-breaking essay by Rebecca Chopp, "Theology and the Poetics of Testimony." Chopp goes further than van Heijst in exploring the way in which particular forms of communication are best able to testify and provoke change, particularly demonstrating the way an author can use "poetics" as a means to communicate things that are impossible to express in conventional terms, particularly trauma. In Chopp's explorations, however, it is clear that while literature is not merely narrative, it can provide us with a powerful testimony about reality an in particular about the realities of human suffering.

The poetics of testimony inquire into the ability to communicate not just the circumstances or facts of an event. Instead, it explores what it means to testify to their meaning. In her essay, Chopp describes the preface to the Russian poet Anna Akhmatova's collection, "Requiem." In this preface, Akhmatova describes her experience returning, day after day, to stand outside a prison for 17 months, waiting to see her son.

---

59. van Heijst, *Longing for the Fall*, 277.

Rather than explain the weather or other such facts about these vigils, she gives us this image.

> Standing behind me was a woman, with lips blue from cold . . . and asked me in a whisper (everyone whispered there):
>
> 'Can you describe this?'
>
> And I said, 'I can.'[60]

The intimate moment between women gives us not simply a picture, but an emotional connection. This scene allows us to empathize, to experience the line outside the prison rather than simply knowing about it. We can join the women in this moment but more than this it points to the power of the poet to form words about what are unspeakable things. Chopp explains this kind of performative description of the queue as Akhmatova's inviting us not only to fully know the event, but to also make moral judgments about it. This, Chopp states, is the purpose of the poetics of testimony. "The poetics of testimony, expressed in a variety of particular and distinct forms, is fundamentally concerned with human and earthly survival and transformation, and thus renders a moral claim on human existence."[61] By allowing testimony to shape our understandings, she believes this will in turn affect theology.

Such testimony points to a "reality outside the ordinary"[62] and enables us to begin seeing the world in terms of diverse experiences. It allows us to hear from those who are different, and not only hear but begin to understand. It allows us to think in terms of hope and survival for not just ourselves, but for everyone. This is the point of testimonies. Chopp says, "Testimonies are neither subjective nor objective; they are collective and social."[63] Testimony is important to bring awareness, to give voice to a people or situation, and so is not merely giving detail. Instead, testimony highlights that which is important to the speaker. In light of trauma, this testimony can give a voice to the pain suffered, particularly if the listener has not had similar experiences. It is not narrative, but it offers deep insight into other's realities.

This concept of a collective testimony is important in light of standpoint epistemology. Philosopher Sandra Harding explains how feminist

---

60. As quoted in Chopp, "Theology," 57.
61. Chopp, "Theology," 57.
62. Chopp, "Theology," 61.
63. Chopp, "Theology," 62.

standpoint epistemology enables women to "provide points for asking new, critical questions about not only those women's lives but also about men's lives and, most importantly, the causal relations between them."[64] This starting point involves allowing testimonies from diverse voices. As Terrence Des Pres says, "Conscience . . . is a social achievement."[65] As Chopp demonstrates, testimony has the purpose of convincing society (or the listener, at least) of a moral need or fact. It is meant to shape, to change the mindset of those who have not experienced the events of the testimony. The goal of this is to elevate life, and the respect for diverse lives. It is not meant to simply bring facts to light, but instead to actively change those who hear. Much like Nussbaum argued, understanding another's story in this way can move the listener to an emotional response that motivates them to action. For Chopp, testimony of trauma can allow society to understand why change is necessary while connecting people more deeply. It is in this that she develops her method and definition of theopoetics, which is particularly useful in my work. In cooperation with liberation theology, Chopp argues that theopoetics challenges our assumptions by centering the experiences and concerns of the oppressed. In allowing poetry (and, as she explains, other literary writings like novels) to shape the conversation, it is giving both reality and the effects of the experiences—memory, discourse, emotions, actions, etc.—the ability to challenge our previous understandings of a topic. Chopp's explanation of theopoetics is therefore able to guide my theology through both an understanding of reality and the testimony of literature.

Therefore, I again look to those who seek to form a partnership between literature and theology. By actively changing the direction of the conversation, the movement, and the morals, these testimonies are meant to shape theology. When asked what the purpose of telling tragic stories is, I see the answer in Chopp's description of the poetics of testimony. In order to develop a methodology that includes testimony, I must allow testimony to determine the form. As Chopp says, "A testimony requires being heard in its own voice, style, and content, neither as a variation of a common experience nor a representation of that which stands on the margins, opposed by the dominant discourse."[66] Testimony is not the final word, but one that can "describe in real ways

---

64. Harding, "Rethinking Standpoint Epistemology," 55.
65. As quoted in Chopp, "Theology," 63.
66. Chopp, "Theology," 65.

that require people to see these events that reason and theory do not count,"⁶⁷ so that we may better hear and learn.

Chopp ends her ground-breaking essay with three important points that I wish to highlight here. First, she says, "theology has to be responsive to the moral summons of testimony."⁶⁸ Secondly, she believes that theology must be reframed through "poetics."⁶⁹ Her use of this term is to highlight the poetic symbolism, codes, and images that theology already uses and its potential to rework them in order to respond to "the moral summons" of testimony.⁷⁰ She wants to "blur the lines of theory and poetics so as to imagine and create new ways of envisioning human life."⁷¹ As I referenced from Walton, literature leads us to new places, allowing theology a new voice to "illuminate and instruct."⁷²

Finally, she discusses the poetics of testimony in terms of transcendence. Though, as she acknowledges, many feminist theologians are averse to the idea of God as "wholly other," she rejects the notion that transcendence necessitates a distant and uninvolved deity. She argues instead:

> To say it in traditional terms, transcendence expresses the hope that the memories of suffering will be told and not go unredeemed, the hope that personal and social existence can and will be transformed. God as the term of transcendence functions as hope, the promise of liberation, or in terms of David Tracy, the mystical-prophetic God . . . Transcendence is not a conceptual problem but a moral summons to imagine hope.⁷³

And so Chopp ends her essay imploring us to utilize testimony in the purposeful quest for this hope, this reshaping, and this responsive theology. To allow the testimonies of the marginalized to determine the moral direction of our theological endeavors is to imitate the Spirit—to transform ourselves into the likeness of a divine liberator.

---

67. Chopp, "Theology," 64.
68. Chopp, "Theology," 66.
69. Chopp, "Theology," 66.
70. Chopp, "Theology," 66.
71. Chopp, "Theology," 66.
72. Walton, *Literature, Theology and Feminism*, 17.
73. Chopp, "Theology," 67.

## Conclusion

My work in this chapter has been to review the aims and methodologies of others who have sought a dialogue between literature and theology as a means to reshape theological thinking. This will guide my next step in this book, particularly in allowing me to understand how to challenge dominant theories of the *imago Dei*. Cannon's work, both theologically and methodologically, has demonstrated my own need to center the voices of those to whom my work purports to communicate with. In desiring to see how the *imago Dei* can aid the oppressed and marginalized, I must, like Cannon, begin by listening to their stories. I return our thoughts to Lorraine Code's exploration of standpoint epistemology,[74] and the idea that we must be able to listen to and acknowledge another's point of view. Yet, as I saw, Cannon's literature often supports her preestablished theology. As I learned from Wallace, I must prioritize allowing literature to challenge what I believe. Literature allows access to stories and experiences that are not my own, and therefore must be given priority in changing how I understand the world and how I respond to it. This development of viewpoint tied to Nussbaum's valorization of emotion enables the development of compassion. As Nussbaum states, "Compassion takes up the onlooker's point of view, making the best judgment the onlooker can make about what is really happening to the person, even when that may differ from the judgment of the person herself."[75]

Yet, as I saw with van Heijst, I must be cautious not to bring my own desire and motive into the literature—I cannot approach the literature with a set of questions I require it to answer. In order for it to challenge me, I must allow the literature to have its own voice and agenda. I must be wary of the ways in which I may be prone to misuse or misread the literature. Though van Heijst argues against seeing the text as reality, I must also understand the ways in which the narrative can explain reality through fiction. As Chopp's poetics give us the ability to put voice to deep trauma, I must understand that what the fiction teaches is grounded in real suffering. Thus, even as I take account of the fiction of the work, I am enlightened to the real testimonies it embodies.

In forming my method for this research, I approach the following literature section with both questions I have developed from the previous theology section and a reading practice that continues to question

74. See Prologue.
75. Nussbaum, *Upheavals of Thought*, 309.

my desired answers. This partnering of literature and theology should not be unbalanced, and I must remain cautious in my literary analysis. I turn now to my own work, the challenges literature has brought to my *imago Dei* understandings, beginning with the ways in which I will approach my readings.

# 4

# Destruction and Desire

Jean Rhys Novels and a Beginning Theory of the *Imago Dei*

## Introduction

As I DISCUSSED IN previously, literature can raise theological questions and allow us to see others in a new light. Rather than attempting to find proofs of my preestablished theology, the literature I read must challenge and inform me, giving me a better understanding of marginalized people.[1] The principles I developed have shaped my reading of Jean Rhys, as she delivers both a testimonial to marginalization as well as challenges to my approach. As I will demonstrate throughout these two chapters, Rhys's depiction of life focuses on the ways people are excluded in society. She seeks to reveal the degraded and despairing aspects of human life lived as a perpetual struggle. In understanding her own life, as well as the fiction she powerfully creates, I can see vital aspects of humanity, frequently neglected in theological discourse, that help me to understand the image of God more fully.

The fiction of Jean Rhys is distinctly helpful due to the complex characters she creates and themes of marginality we may explore

---

1. In discussing oppression and marginalization, I will be particularly looking at intersectional ways people can be oppressed. Therefore, the focus in these chapters will be based on economic, class, national, and gendered marginalization and the ways being ostracized for these leads to further economic and social oppression.

through them.[2] Her own sense of self, necessary to understand when examining her work, was complex and fluid. She found herself unable to achieve a sense of belonging to communities in the various places where she lived, and her writing expresses a profound sense of outsiderness. In the text *Jean Rhys: Twenty-First Century Approaches* (2015), Erica Johnson and Patricia Moran explain:

> Much has been written about how Rhys's work defies periodization and transcends categories... She is viewed as a modernist, postcolonial, Caribbean, British and Creole writer—yet to parse these identities is to fall short of the complexity of her work and the ways in which it troubles the very categories through which she is read.[3]

Rhys's work is vital to my work for precisely this reason. Her rejection of hierarchy and of simplifying oppression set her well beyond the second wave feminism she did not identify with.[4] Her work, similar to that of intersectional work being done today, is concerned primarily with how oppressions pile on top of each other. As Kimberlé Williams Crenshaw explains in "Demarginalizing the Intersection of Race and Sex: A Black Feminist Critique of Antidiscrimination Doctrine, Feminist Theory and Antiracist Politics," intersectionality is the understanding that separate issues of power often interact in ways that multiply oppression or marginality for people.[5] In Crenshaw's work, this is particularly linked to the oppression Black women suffer due to being both Black and women, and how those two cannot be separated out, but instead understood as interlocking issues. Though Rhys's focus was often primarily on the oppressive power of money, as I said, she is also always simultaneously discussing gender, race, and nationality. Rhys writes a world where these are all weighed against one another, and thus pits people against each other in various and complex ways.[6] Helen Carr states:

> Coming from the fissured and ambivalent world of the colonial margins, with their torn and violent history, to the grim, chill

---

2. As Katie Cannon included stories of Black women to give voice to her theology, Rhys creates the stories of these women to give voice to the oppressed.
3. Johnson and Moran, *Jean Rhys*, 2.
4. Savory, *Jean Rhys*, 11.
5. Crenshaw, "Demarginalizing the Intersection of Race and Sex."
6. In Rhys's work, the challenge of Anneliese van Heijst is vital. Rhys's work must set its own agenda, as it refuses simple readings or approaches that only look for specific outcomes.

edges of metropolitan society, she was able to forge a powerful critique of European values and hierarchies, and to give new insights into the darkness, frailty, pain, desire and hope within the human psyche.[7]

It is her troubling of labels, her complex critique of society, and her consistent challenges to oppression that make her particularly important in this age. Though she has not enjoyed the same popularity of some of her contemporaries, she has proven to be far ahead of her time. It is her ability to present a testimonial, much like Chopp's poetics, as well as establish questions to challenge and makes her the perfect author for this work.

Her complexity, therefore, encompasses a multitude of marginalizations. In her writing, and characters, there is a clear and important rejection of labels that define people either in terms of their allegiances or identity. Rhys continually refuses the categories of social justice activism, though her work is consistently read in those terms. She also rejects labels of nationality, refusing to place herself within a context. Because she was raised in Dominica and later moved to England, she found herself in constant conflict with how she identified. As Rhys scholar Elaine Savory relates, an interview of Rhys shows this:

> To the writer David Plante she was unable or unwilling to answer when asked if she was a West Indian or a French writer and responded quite vehemently when asked about her English literary affiliation: 'No! I'm not! I'm not! I'm not even English'.[8]

Because of this, Rhys has to be read as undertaking an ongoing process of weaving together multiple identities. She is white, Creole, British, West Indian, woman, writer, educated, outsider. Her financial status is a constant shift, from the power and prestige of her family in Dominica, to the poverty she experienced at various times in her life in Europe.

As stated, disconnection from others because of class, race, and/or gender were important experiences in Rhys's childhood. Being white and British in a territory that had resisted colonizing control, along with the isolation she faced in her own family, reinforced in Rhys the sense that she did not belong.[9] Savory points out that it is in these early experiences that

---

7. Carr, *Jean Rhys*, 119.
8. Savory, *Jean Rhys*, 3.
9. "Dominicans of colour resisted colonial injustice when they could . . . Dominica . . . was the only island in the West Indies where white power was successfully

Rhys's complex racial, economic and gender understandings began to take shape. In taking after her (relatively) liberal father,[10] Rhys developed an understanding of racial tensions best described by her belief that people formed understandings of themselves as "not the Other."[11]

This enabled her to conduct a searing examination of how exclusion can shape identity, and this is displayed in the construction of her characters. In the previous chapter I discussed Anneliese van Heijst's rejection of literature as simply a mirror of reality. While I maintained that it is necessary to allow the literature to have its own voice, I argued that it is also vital to understand how the author is constructing that voice. Rhys began with her life experiences, and then shaped them into fiction in order to raise particular challenges. The way she shaped her characters and their environments can be seen as highlighting aspects of the world she knew and the viscous forces of exclusion she encountered.[12] As Helen Carr explains, "Jean Rhys' fiction has been read as the retelling through her heroines of her own melancholy tale . . ."[13] In doing so, she is able to not only able to reflect on aspects of her own life, which she famously did not think it worthwhile to relate in detail,[14] but to point beyond them to the social mechanisms of oppression, marginalization, and rejection.

This is where I must confess my own growth in understanding as I engaged with Rhys's writing. When I began my research, I believed my ideas about the *imago Dei* would be confirmed through engaging critically with an author who writes primarily about suffering. I was looking for an *imago Dei* that was able to comprehend the experience of the innocent victims of injustice who were unable to find the courage to support their becoming or the communal resources that would affirm their identity. In entering into Rhys's work with these pre-set notions, I

---

challenged." Savory, *Jean Rhys*, 4–5.

10. Savory states, "I think Lennox Honeychurch's view of [Williams] as complex is convincing. If he was both liberal (in relative terms) and critical of the mulatto elite, then he was both at one with his wife's family interests and also at times a mildly dissident Celt on the subject of race or religion, just as his daughter was capable of holding both liberal and racist views" (*Jean Rhys*, 6).

11. Savory, *Jean Rhys*, 29.

12. Carr, *Jean Rhys*, 1.

13. Carr, *Jean Rhys*, 5

14. "Jean Rhys began to think of writing an autobiographical book several years before her death on May 14, 1979. The idea did not attract her but because she was sometimes angered and hurt by what other people wrote about her she wanted to get the facts down" (Rhys, *Smile Please*, Introduction).

struggled. My initial readings were, I confess, inadequate. Yet through the process of reading, and re-reading, spending time with her work and with her legacy, my thoughts were broken open.

To begin, I had misconceptions about Rhys herself. Like many, I had made too simplistic an identification between Rhys and her characters who is often portrayed as the victims of circumstances. As Rhys scholar Helen Carr says, "One reason for beginning my account with Jean Rhys in Beckenham 'protesting loudly', as the court reports put it, is to underline the inadequacy of this image of her as a passive, hopeless and helpless victim, from whom her heroines and their bleak lives are cloned."[15] Rhys's work certainly demonstrates a very dismal view of humanity. However, this view is not, as may first appear, a passively bleak view. Rhys certainly did not accept her own life or future as being one of passive reliance on her lovers, though she was certainly dependent at points. Neither was Rhys content to be defined by others, but instead insisted on speaking for herself in ways that continually seemed contradictory; expressing how those who long for inclusion also pass judgement on the society that excludes them. Thus, her positions on many social issues are deeply ambivalent and many readings of her work debate whether she was a feminist or not, a racist or not, a prostitute or not as these defined positions are not established in her writing.

In fact, I experienced my own struggles with her work for a time for these reasons. Furthermore, reading her novels in succession, I despaired of her characters. They seemed, at times, completely helpless and victimized, and at other times to be complicit in their own destruction. I wanted to save them and berate them simultaneously. I wanted to dispute their sense that they were inherently doomed and tell them they simply did not have enough faith in their own talents. Though I was motivated to act,[16] I had not discovered the appropriate type of action needed.

This was a naïve reading of Rhys, and of her characters and I assume she would have been displeased with many of my original interpretations of her work. However, the process of understanding Rhys is challenging because her work is deeply complex and varied. Her characters are not singularly anything, nor are they interchangeable. To truly understand what Rhys is doing, it takes time to see how she allows the forces that

15. Carr, *Jean Rhys*, 5.

16. Martha Nussbaum's desire to see literature challenge us to action is present here, but it is vital (in both Nussbaum's view and my own) to know what that action should be.

alienate her characters to intersect, how she develops narrators who work through their own complex views, and how, in the end, she allows herself to protest loudly for those at the margins. As Helen Carr explains:

> ... her chief loyalty is not to her sex, but to the group with which she identifies, in her case the disempowered and dispossessed, which are neither so homogeneous nor so easily identified as a group held together by race, nationality or even class.[17]

Rhys is not so much interested in specifically pointing out the oppression faced by particular groups, but rather, to draw her reader into the mind of the characters and allowing us to see the connections between the differing experiences of the disempowered. By multiplying her focus, she is not campaigning for one particular group, but instead seeking to side with the marginalized in every situation.

Her novels are thus not simply narratives based on personal experience. Instead they serve as important commentaries on how the struggle to develop identity is often linked to systemic mistreatment of people—they are challenges, much like Cynthia Wallace examines for her work. In this respect, her fiction helps me to conceive a model of the *imago Dei* that is not reliant on problematic concepts of ability, goodness, assimilation or even communal belonging. In the following two chapters, I will first examine Rhys's own life to highlight key themes that were then elaborated upon and creatively mediated in her fiction. I will then move to explore her interwar novels to see how those themes are embodied and may be drawn upon in order to form a more complex and inclusive discussion of the *imago Dei*.

## Jean Rhys: An Isolated Life

Ella Gwendoline Rees Williams was born in Dominica in 1890,[18] the third child of Reese and Minna Williams. However, only one of her two siblings had survived. An older sister had been born, Brenda Gwenith Maxwell Rees Williams, who died at nine months old. In her biography on Rhys, Carol Angier explains that according to custom, her mother, Minna, was encouraged to have another child immediately. This was thought to help with the pain of loss. As Angier states:

17. Carr, *Jean Rhys*, 23.
18. Rhys lists her birth year as 1894 in *Who's Who*, however according to *Smile Please* her passport recorded 1890 (Rhys, *Smile Please*, 11).

Often, perhaps mostly, this works, and pulls the mother back into life. But sometimes it doesn't. Then there is a phenomenon which doctors also recognise: what can happen to a child with a mourning mother. It can be left with a lifelong sense of loss and emptiness, of being wanted by no one and belonging nowhere; of being nothing, not really existing at all.[19]

Rhys and her mother struggled to connect, due to the grief Minna was still suffering. Rhys recalls in her autobiography, *Smile Please*, that she is sure there must have been "an interval before she seemed to find me a nuisance and I grew to dread her."[20] However, upon the birth of her younger sister, Rhys felt she was cast aside. She experienced her mother as abusive; humiliating her and causing her to focus on her flaws from a young age.[21] She felt an outsider in her own family, noting that when looking at a picture of her family, "My brothers and sisters all had brown eyes and hair, why was I singled out to be the only fair one . . . ?"[22]

This early division between Rhys and her mother was further complicated by the social status and attention her mother brought to the family. In her book, *Jean Rhys*, Elaine Savory states that Minna's family was respected on the island, and Rhys was often referred to as "a Lockhart."[23] Her inherited social status, dependent on a relationship to her mother, only highlighted for Rhys how unlike her mother and sister she was becoming. The lack of a loving relationship with her mother opened a gap between Rhys and others; she felt herself "disconnected" from earliest childhood and this becomes a major theme in her work. This sense of disconnection influenced her relationships throughout her life, even with those she most cared for.

The primary example of this is Rhys's relationship with her father. In contrast to her mother, Rhys idealized him yet, as she admitted, "I probably romanticised my father, perhaps because I saw very little of him."[24]

19. Angier, *Jean Rhys Life and Work*, 11.
20. Rhys, *Smile Please*, 42.
21. Angier explains that it is unknown how exactly Minna behaved toward Rhys. "We cannot know, of course how often this happened or how bad it was. Perhaps Jean exaggerated . . . But that her mother did punish her, at least sometimes physically, is almost certainly true" (*Jean Rhys*, 24). It seems Rhys also focused on her mother's attempts to change her, as Angier explains, "Her mother watched her, disapproved of her, tried to change her" (*Jean Rhys*, 18).
22. Rhys, *Smile Please*, 20.
23. Savory, *Jean Rhys*, 9.
24. Rhys, *Smile Please*, 71.

Despite this, Williams's influence can be seen in many aspects of Rhys's persona. Having moved to Dominica as a doctor, Rees Williams built a prominent reputation on the island. He was wealthy; in fact Savory lists him as one of the wealthiest people in Dominica.[25] He was also influential in the island's politics, and his social views seem to have influenced Rhys's own. Not terribly consistent, both expressed opinions that can be seen as "racist and anti-racist, both hostile and sentimental, both patronizing and egalitarian."[26] Her father's paternalist form of liberalism meant he was "kinder" towards black people than some white occupants of Dominica, but it did not motivate him to side with the colonized Dominicans in their fight against the British empire.[27]

Rhys's childhood may have been spent idolizing her father from a distance, but he left the parenting work to Rhys's mother. She explains, "My father never seemed to notice us at all, far too engaged in either abuse or praise of various English politicians, while my mother watched us the whole time."[28] Believing that he lived an exciting life and was kindly disposed towards her, she ascribes the positive aspects of her childhood to his influence. "It was he who stopped the hated plate of porridge my mother suddenly expected me to eat every morning, and arranged that I should have an egg beaten up in hot milk with nutmeg instead."[29]

Rees Williams died when Rhys was 18. His death was "remote" in that Rhys had already gone from the island and was distanced from her family by that time. Yet she remained deeply attached to him, and upon hearing, late in her life, that the Celtic cross that marked his grave had been knocked down, she wrote, "I hated whoever had done this and thought, 'I can hate too.'"[30] Despite these strong feelings her emotional attachment to her father was always distanced, and so his

---

25. Savory cites Sue Thomas, who argues that in 1910 Dr Williams was listed as one of the seven richest men in the community, demonstrating that he could not have been in bad financial standing in the 1890s and early 1900s (*Jean Rhys*, 7–8).

26. Savory, *Jean Rhys*, 34.

27. Savory lists the many ways Williams reputation was contradictory in this area. He was known as respected among the poor in Dominica (*Jean Rhys*, 9), and offensive to the "anti-colonial middle class" (9). However, he was also part of the Crown Colony Government, which opposed Dominica's autonomy in favor of continued rule from Britain (7). Savory states, "For those however who had a critical and resisting eye on colonialism and racism, Dr Williams might easily have been just another opportunistic white migrant from Britain" (9).

28. Rhys, *Smile Please*, 72.

29. Rhys, *Smile Please*, 72.

30. Rhys, *Smile Please*, 73.

absence during traumatic times of her life is poignant. Again, threaded throughout her life is this constant feeling of disconnection with those she longs to be in relationship with.

Just as her home life left Rhys feeling isolated, her social life was also unfortunately characterized by separation. Meta, her "nurse and the terror of my life,"[31] repeatedly and purposefully terrified Rhys. Meta taught Rhys things to be afraid of, including zombies and cockroaches. These interactions with Meta caused fear and distrust, as "[Meta] both made the young girl afraid and reminded her of her exclusion from the African world of the spirit."[32] She played tricks on Rhys, laughed at her distress, and physically abused her.[33] Rhys explains, "Meta had shown me a world of fear and distrust, and I am still in that world."[34]

Rhys was also divided from her classmates. While she does not speak directly about her white peers, she recounts being rejected by the Black girls she wanted to befriend. As Savory explains, "For Rhys racial difference factored into painful childhood relationships at times."[35] *Smile Please* recounts several examples of Rhys's interactions with Black children, which developed in her a sense that they were happier than she.[36] She poignantly recalls trying to initiate a conversation with a Black girl at school, but the girl gave her an irritated look which Rhys interpreted as hatred.[37]

Rhys painfully felt the separations between herself and those she wished to form relationships with. Although from a wealthy background she displayed a willful misunderstanding of the conventions of race relations and class hierarchy. However, once again this should not be seen as a simple rejection of privilege. While Rhys spent most of her adult life protesting against the power of money to determine status,

31. Rhys, *Smile Please*, 29.

32. Rhys, *Smile Please*, 32.

33. "She was forbidden to slap me and she never did but she got her own back by taking me by the shoulders and shaking me violently" (Rhys, *Smile Please*, 31).

34. Rhys, *Smile Please*, 32.

35. Savory, *Jean Rhys*, 32.

36. This includes her memories of the Riot, Josephine the family cook, and interactions with Black children. She says after one example, "They hate us. We are hated" (Rhys, *Smile Please*, 49). Yet, she also discusses the reasons she is jealous of Black people. She believes they are "free" because she doesn't see many Black marriages, believes they were happier because of their colorful clothing, and says, "They were more alive, more a part of the place than we were" (Rhys, *Smile Please*, 50–51).

37. Savory, *Jean Rhys*, 33 and Rhys, *Smile Please*, 49.

she also loved things money provided—fashion, luxury, etc. Savory tells us Rhys had "strong sympathies for the underprivileged. But she had strong contradictions there as well."[38] Rhys believed that things were not fair for both the workers and "the other side."[39]

Rhys is aware of these contradictions, and inserts the same complex outlook in her protagonists, giving us characters who are both able to experience "otherness" and also marginalize others as they continue to strive for stability. In her examination of Rhys's work, Helen Carr believes that it is through this overlap of victim/victimizer that Rhys is able to reshape our understanding of social relationships. She says:

> For Rhys to make sense of existences like hers meant understanding the historical and social forces which had made them what they are . . . It is impossible to separate her readings of the psyches of those whose lives are misshapen and coerced by the hierarchical machinery of organized society from her analysis of the working of that machinery itself . . . She constantly, in Bhabha's words, 'relat[es] the traumatic ambivalences of a personal, psychic history to the wider disjunctions of political existence.'[40]

It is this unusual ability to highlight the complex overlapping of various marginalizations that is particularly important in my work as I seek to discern the image of God in those who can neither be classed as virtuous, courageous or innocent victims of hostile circumstances.

The consequences of her disconnection from others then leads me to another important theme that can be seen in Rhys's life and work. As she felt constantly othered, we begin to see her acceptance of this status. Not only does Rhys accept a feeling of distance, but she begins to accept abuse, both emotional and physical, as she devalues her personhood. This abuse shapes how she continues to form, or attempt to form, relationships.

An important example of her acceptance of abuse comes from another significant event during Rhys's Dominican life. When Rhys was fourteen, Mr. Howard, a friend of Dr. Williams, and his wife visited Dominica on their way to England. During a walk, as Rhys tried to behave "in the most grown-up way she could," Mr. Howard put his hand on

---

38. Savory, *Jean Rhys*, 23.
39. Savory, *Jean Rhys*, 23.
40. Carr, *Jean Rhys*, 114–15.

her breast.[41] Rhys records a similar assault in her short story, "Goodbye Marcus, Goodbye Rose," giving us perhaps a glimpse of her feelings about this assault. His hand having moved down to her waist, he was interrupted by a couple on a walk, yet Rhys was constrained to continue walking with him for months. Though, as Angier says, "He never touched her again,"[42] Mr. Howard gained an abusive control over the young woman. He constantly repeated themes of owning her, her necessary submission to him, and the ubiquitous violence of gendered relationships. Angier explains, "That was love, he told her, that was making love: not kindness, but violence and cruelty."[43] This abusive relationship ended when Howard and his wife left for England, and Rhys claims to have "forgot it."[44] It is clear, however, that the effects of Mr. Howard's 'instruction' lasted through Rhys's entire life. Her understanding of her place among people is characterized by separation, by violence, and by oppression. Mr. Howard's assault and subsequent treatment of her, consolidated her sense of isolation. Her adult relationships with men were complicated, and it seems she came to identify love with being owned by someone. In *Smile Please*, as she discusses her relationships, she says:

> It seems to me now that the whole business of money and sex is mixed up with something very primitive and deep. When you take money from someone you love it becomes not money but a symbol. The bond is now there. The bond has been established. I am sure the woman's deep-down feeling is 'I belong to this man, I want to belong to him completely.'[45]

Howard impressed upon Rhys that love was ownership, and once again she developed an acute understanding of a divide between people. As she endures abuse, she also begins to act in ways defined by that abuse. Rhys both longs for relationships and also consistently acts against herself in that pursuit. This pattern is rehearsed throughout her adult life.

At the age of 17, Rhys and her Aunt Clarice boarded a ship to England, leaving Dominica behind. She was travelling in order to attend school in England, as was normal for many white Dominicans.[46] She

41. Angier, *Jean Rhys*, 27.
42. Angier, *Jean Rhys*, 27.
43. Angier, *Jean Rhys*, 28.
44. Angier, *Jean Rhys*, 27.
45. Rhys, *Smile Please*, 121.
46. Angier, *Jean Rhys*, 33.

recalls her father telling her to write if she is "very unhappy," but not too soon or he'd be disappointed in her.[47] Going to her cabin, she saw that a brooch, which she had previously loved, had been crushed. She says, "I took it off and put it away without any particular feeling. Already all my childhood, the West Indies, my father and mother had been left behind: I was forgetting them. They were the past."[48] As she attempts to disassociate from her former life, though, she finds her life in England to be equally filled with isolation and rejection. She may have believed she was able to put her past behind, but the themes of her past—difference and isolation from those around her, recognition of social hierarchies, sexual trauma, and financial concern—continue during her adult life. Rhys had been enrolled in acting school, but on the insistence of her parents had to leave after the second term.[49] After hearing of her father's death, Rhys decided to pursue a stage career and worked for a time as a chorus girl. She was routinely rejected for more prestigious acting roles. Rhys often cited her father's financial difficulties as the sole reason she could not continue at drama school, yet her difficulties in getting cast also point to a problem with her West Indian accent.[50] Savory explains, "If anything would have impressed upon Rhys her colonial and marginal status it would have been this painful failure to achieve her dream of acting because of her accent."[51] This failure, coupled with her father's death and even further isolation from her family, also contributed to Rhys's financial struggles. She often found herself living in extreme poverty, unable to sustain herself through her stage work.

At the age of 20, Rhys began her first "love affair."[52] Lasting eighteen months, this initiated a series of relationships with men on whom Rhys became financially dependent. Rhys describes this in *Smile Please*, stating that her lover began sending her money through a law firm. When she received the first cheque, with a note that she would be getting a

---

47. Angier, *Jean Rhys*, 93.
48. Angier, *Jean Rhys*, 93–94.
49. Her mother wrote to her that they could not continue to pay for the Academy, but as Angier points out, it was likely coupled with reports that her accent could not be altered. Her father, prior to his death, probably believed it would be too expensive to continue her schooling for as long as was needed to "fix" her speech (*Jean Rhys*, 49).
50. Savory, *Jean Rhys*, 8.
51. Savory, *Jean Rhys*, 11.
52. Rhys, *Smile Please*, 11.

monthly allowance, she says, "It is at once humiliating and exciting."[53] She saw the cheque as both a "bond" and as distance, because it came from a lawyer.[54] Once again, Rhys experiences love as being owned by another person—as she had been taught by Mr. Howard during his abuse—this time through money. She accepted that first cheque, tried to find a job, but because of her fear of rejection and isolation, continued to take money until she got used to it. "You think: I'll never do that; and you find yourself doing it."[55] This move into a form of sex work places Rhys into another marginalized community and highlights the way in which these many forms of oppression combine and intersect.

During these years of sex work, Rhys continued to make some attempts at developing an acting career. In 1917, as she was taking dancing lessons, she lived in a cheap boarding house called Torrington Square. It was here that she met her first husband, Jean Lenglet. He fascinated her, and within weeks of meeting they were engaged. Her family disapproved, and Angier records that her sister asked her to end the engagement.[56] Rhys married Lenglet a year later, and she moved to Holland to be with him in 1919. She was thrilled to leave England and believed this would be the start of a better life. Lenglet, though, had many secrets—including the loss of his Dutch citizenship for eight or nine years and a previous wife he had not divorced.[57] Their marriage was defined by financial struggle, Lenglet's troubling and disreputable associations and actions, and Rhys's naivety about him. The couple soon moved to Paris, where Lenglet succeeded in making some money; almost certainly through illegal means. It was during this time that Rhys had her first child, William Owen. But her baby became sick, and because of their poverty, they left him at the Hospice des Enfants Assistés. Anxious and distressed Rhys became insistent that they christen the baby, even though she and Lenglet were atheists. Lenglet did not want to do this, and to distract her he bought champagne

---

53. Rhys, *Smile Please*, 121.
54. Rhys, *Smile Please*, 121.
55. Rhys, *Smile Please*, 122.
56. Angier, *Jean Rhys*, 99.
57. "[Lenglet] was not divorced from Marie Pollart when he married Jean; in fact he was not divorced from her until 1925. According to Dutch law, this did not make Jean's marriage invalid, *so long as no one challenged it*. No one ever did, so it never ceased to be perfectly legal." This, and his one month service for the French army that cost him his Dutch citizenship, are only two examples of the difficulties Lenglet brought to Rhys's life, as Angier details in her biography (Angier, *Jean Rhys*, 104–5).

and they drank through the night. The next day, Rhys learned that her baby had died while they were drinking.[58]

Rhys kept numerous journals during these times, writing about these events and shaping them into stories. After travelling in Europe, with an extended stay in Vienna, the couple returned to Paris bringing with them their two-year-old daughter Maryvonne. It was then, in 1924, that she met the publisher Ford Maddox Ford. Rhys had been writing more seriously, and Ford took an interest in her work. This interest turned into an affair, but also the beginning of Rhys's professional writing career. The relationship, which became notorious in the literary world, inspired her first novel, *Quartet* (1928).

Rhys and Lenglet divorced in 1932, and she married Leslie Tilden Smith the same year. Tilden Smith died tragically in 1945, six years after the publication of Rhys's final "interwar novel" and the last writing she would do for many years. Her adult life, the events surrounding her time as a chorus girl, her marriages, her poverty and sex work, all became the resources she used to craft her novels and stories. In these, power is held on the basis of gender, money, race and nationality, and she examines this oppressive interlocking system through her fiction. During this period of her writing career she did not achieve the kind of fame and financial rewards that would arrive very late in her life and she struggled to feel welcome within the literary world. Even as she moved to Paris, living among other expatriates, bohemians and writers, she saw herself the "outsider of outsiders,"[59] unable to feel acceptance even in the company of exiles. As she says in *Smile Please*, "I would never really belong anywhere, and I knew it, and all my life would be the same, trying to belong, and failing."[60]

As I reflect upon Rhys's life, the two prominent themes of disconnection and abuse (both done to her and by her, to herself and to others) are the tragic poles around which her work and life unfold. Although, there is much of Rhys's life left to be discussed, I break here to begin looking at how these two themes impacted on the first novels I will examine, *Voyage in the Dark* (1934) and *Quartet* (1928) and the challenges she delivers through them. By examining these novels in the light of these two themes, I believe they will raise important questions for my re-visioning of the *imago Dei*. I will review the books not chronologically, but in order of the author's life stages to which they correspond.

58. Angier, *Jean Rhys*, 112–13.
59. Savory, *Jean Rhys*, xiv.
60. Rhys, *Smile Please*, 124.

## *Voyage in the Dark*

### Anna Morgan, Woman Divided

*Voyage in the Dark* tells the story of Anna Morgan, who was born in the West Indies and moved to England with her stepmother after her father's death. As with most of Rhys's characters, she pursues a life in which her sexuality is commoditized. Like Rhys, Anna's move took place in her late teens. As she pursued a life as a chorus girl, her accent often kept her from finding success, friendship and real community. We see Anna isolated because of her cultural difference, and she struggles to find a sense of home in England. Eventually, she begins to live off the money given to her by her first lover, the older Walter Jeffries. Anna is Rhys's youngest protagonist in her interwar novels, and her story highlights the transition most of the women characters make into forms of sex work to survive. This novel captures the first theme explored—that of disconnection and non-belonging. Through Anna's life, Rhys demonstrates the various ways Anna has lost connection to others and to herself, which I will work through in the following section.

Like Rhys, Anna is unable to connect to people in either of her homes. She remembers the West Indies in attempts to warm herself in a land she finds cold and unwelcoming, but simultaneously reflects that she did not "fit in" in Dominica either. She says, like Rhys, "Sometimes it was as if I were back there and as if England were a dream. At other times England was the real thing and out there was the dream, but I could never fit them together."[61] Her time in England is also marked by loss of connection to her family. Having travelled there with her stepmother, Hester, after her father's death she does not maintain regular contact with her, and in the middle of the novel, this is lost completely. Her stepmother had tried to have Anna's uncle take her back to the West Indies, and he has written a rejection. Hester reads, "If you feel that you don't wish her to live with you in England, of course her aunt and I will have her here with us. But in that case I insist—we both insist—that she should have her proper share of the money you got from the sale of her father's estate."[62] Hester insists it is impossible to give her money, as "It's an outrageous thing to accuse me of cheating you out of your father's money. I got five hundred pounds

---

61. Rhys, *Voyage In the Dark*, 8.
62. Rhys, *Voyage In the Dark*, 61.

108 PART TWO: A TURN TO LITERATURE

for Morgan's Rest, that was all."⁶³ Hester's rejection, paired with the clear rejection from her uncle as well, begins a fight between the two women, which ends their relationship.

## Disconnection and Isolation

Rhys uses several factors to highlight Anna's disconnection to' both England and the Caribbean. In the Caribbean, her family was apparently prestigious. She had servants and felt close to her father. In England, she is now noticeably poor, leaving her unable to assume her former class position. With her father's death, she has lost connection to her family, and her stepmother is clearly not fond of her. Anna believes this is because Hester thinks her mother was black, and therefore Anna is not "white."⁶⁴ Though Anna considers herself white and West Indian, she realizes these descriptors also put her outside the groups she envies. Elaine Savory explains that Anna's world is that of dualities, demonstrating "many subordinate oppositions."⁶⁵ The differences of the two communities are in opposition to each other, and so for Anna, she is at war with herself as well. In a letter, Rhys says of Anna, "The difficult thing is the only worthwhile thing. The girl is *divided*. two people *really*. or at any rate a one foot in the sea & on land girl." (emphasis original)⁶⁶ It is important to keep in mind that for Rhys, Anna represents this divided self, and the consequences that come from it. Even in her division, she belongs to neither community, and internalizes this as a rejection of who she is essentially.

Anna's desire to be black is further examined by Savory. As she explains, Anna understands blackness to be tied to not only happiness, but to sexual agency and the ability to engage autonomously with others. She says, "Anna makes sure Walter knows how much she has wanted to be black. Later in the novel, a man speaks to her in the street and she feels violent towards him but sees a policeman looking at her, and the violence turns towards him, verbally. She makes him 'a damned baboon—a

---

63. Rhys, *Voyage In the Dark*, 61.

64. "'I always pitied you. I always thought that considering everything you were much to be pitied.' I said, 'How do you mean, "considering everything"?' 'You know exactly what I mean, so don't pretend.' 'You're trying to make out that my mother was coloured,' I said. 'You always did try to make that out. And she wasn't'" (Rhys, *Voyage In the Dark*, 65).

65. Savory, *Jean Rhys*, 91.

66. Savory, *Jean Rhys*, 85.

fair baboon too, worse than a dark one every time."[67] This reversal of the racist use of monkey highlights her problematic understandings of Black people's power. For instance, in her attempt to cope with her first sexual experience with Walter, she imagines herself a young slave woman whose name she once saw on a family estate list: "Maillotte Boyd."[68] She is, in this, naming herself as a slave. Her inner connection to the slave list, particularly through naming Boyd at this point, highlights her problematic understanding of racial power relations. Savory explains that while Anna feels identifying with Black Caribbeans motivates her to stand up for herself, it is not in healthy ways. She sees her ability to act against Walter, particularly when she stubs a cigarette on her hand, as akin to the Dominicans rise against white colonization. This fetishization of Blackness is particularly rooted in the violent struggle of peoples against each other. We also hear her say, recalling the slave relation she has assumed, "I like it like this."[69] However, her belief that she is assuming the role of a "passionate black slave woman"[70] does not empower her as she believes it will. Rhys, as I noted previously, also had similar fantasies. Violence and love are linked for Anna, and Savory cautions that this slave motif is used to justify sexual predation for Anna.[71] Men and women, in her understanding, act against each other just as, for her, black and white people do not exist peacefully. Instead they are essentially at odds and one can only assert themself at the expense of the other.

This desire to be black is mirrored in an oppositional desire to be in a higher social class in England. Again, Anna recognizes that the social class she now belongs to is powerless, looked down upon, and she therefore desires inclusion in the class with power. In her work on Rhys, Sue Thomas discusses the symbols that represent the clash between the classes. As Anna feels confined, and suffocated, by the grey and cold of England, she also feels this in how wealthier people are constraining her. Thomas says "Walls figure in Anna's sense of the English sneering at women of her class and in her desperate situation: 'their damned voices, like high, smooth, unclimbable walls all round you, closing in on you.'"[72]

---

67. Savory, *Jean Rhys*, 95.
68. Savory, *Jean Rhys*, 95.
69. Rhys, *Voyage in the Dark*, 56.
70. Savory, *Jean Rhys*, 96.
71. Savory, *Jean Rhys*, 96.
72. Thomas, "Jean Rhys and Katherine Mansfield Writing the 'Sixth Act.'"

Again, Anna sees the hierarchy as a dominating power, crushing the lower class and keeping them from freedom.

The differences in her worlds are mirrored in Anna's divided self. The Caribbean is warm and colorful. England is cold and grey—"[it is] cold and . . . the towns we went to always looked so exactly alike."[73] Whereas in the Caribbean she suffered from fever, wore white in mourning, and wished she could be Black. In England, Anna wears black in an attempt to signify sexual agency, is always cold and clammy, and wishes she was wealthy. Anna is never satisfied in herself. Yet she always believes that if only she could change an important aspect of herself, she might be happy. In the Caribbean, she believes she would be happy if she was Black. In England, she believes better clothes would change her life— "I'll do anything for good clothes. Anything—anything for clothes."[74] These contradictions are not merely part of Anna's instability, but instead another demonstration of her lack of connection to herself and a lack of recognition of others. As she cannot find community, she also cannot find herself because her focus always seems to remain on the divisions that separate people. Anna is not trying to bridge gaps in the opposing cultures, but instead plays directly into their contesting moves for power. She is unsuccessful, however, and remains a constant outsider.

This brings me to the second theme I wish to highlight here: the complex consequences of not belonging. Anna, having lost connection to both her home(s) and herself, begins to both accept abuse and to abuse others. She is made fun of for her accent, her nationality, and her virginity— "the girls call her the Hottentot. Isn't it a shame?"[75] It is the perceived acceptance she receives from Walter Jeffries, the older man whom she first entered into a relationship with, that truly seduces her. She confesses several times that she does not particularly like Walter— "Oh God, he's the sneering sort"[76]—but despairs he might also reject her. When he does finally break with her, she attempts to make a living through various forms of sex work, beginning with receiving allowances from other lovers

---

73. Rhys, *Voyage*, 8.

74. Rhys, *Voyage*, 25.

75. As Savory points out, during her time as a chorus girl, she was dubbed "the Hottentot." Upon explaining this to Walter, encourages her to "'call them something worse back,' thus reinforcing the name as a negative" (*Jean Rhys*, 94).

76. Rhys, *Voyage*, 22.

and then moving into more explicit forms of prostitution.⁷⁷ Eventually she becomes pregnant by one of the men she sleeps with.

Rhys does allude to various traumas, including rape and abuse, which have obviously contributed to Anna's isolation and disconnection. However, Anna is not innocent herself and inflicts wounds upon those around her, with increasing violence as the novel progresses. In one instance, as she is with Carl, a lover she has had multiple encounters with, they are listening to music in her flat. She tells us:

> We started to dance and while we were dancing the dog in the picture over the bed stared down at us smugly . . .
>
> I said, 'I can't stand that damned dog any longer.'
>
> I stopped dancing and took off my shoe and threw it at the picture. The glass smashed.⁷⁸

At the end of the novel Anna has undergone an abortion, which went badly wrong. She is very sick—"I was dying"⁷⁹—and her friend Laurie tries to care for her. The novel ends with Anna thinking, "I lay . . . and thought about starting all over again. And about being new and fresh. And about mornings, and misty days, when anything might happen. And about starting all over again, all over again . . ."⁸⁰ However, these lines do not convey a sense of hope but rather that Anna is utterly caught up in repetitive cycles of destruction she can no longer escape from.

Even though Rhys does not give us a clear answer to whether the novel ends with Anna's death, I believe the ambiguity is part of Rhys's evocation of Anna's death as a person. She has lost all connection to the world, and her increasing drift between spheres indicates that she has become a "ghost" long before her death. This "death" highlights a challenge Rhys's writing makes to dominant understandings of the *imago Dei*.⁸¹ In understanding this death outcome, I look more in depth at Anna's relationship with Ethel.

---

77. We see evidence of this, though it is never overtly addressed. Anna begins to have male visitors more frequently while she lives with Ethel, but it is pointed out in Ethel's letter toward the end of the novel. "It is one thing for a girl to have a friend or two but it quite another for it to be anybody who she picks up in the street and without with your leave or by your leave and never a word to me" (Rhys, *Voyage*, 166).

78. Rhys, *Voyage*, 161.

79. Rhys, *Voyage*, 178.

80. Rhys, *Voyage*, 188.

81. Rhys's work can be understood as giving voice to the "dead" in this sense, while simultaneously directly challenging how life is understood, particularly in light of my

## A Type of Death

Anna's disconnection, and the consequences of her abuse and subsequent reaction to that abuse, has evolved into Anna's complete disconnection from herself. She has, in essence, died to herself. Her dreams of happiness are implicated in this death—she believes she would be happier if she was someone other than herself, just as she wishes she could be Black. This rejection of her own self, consolidated by the rejection she receives from those around her, is then enacted in her rejection of others. Towards the end of the novel, she is renting a room from Ethel Matthews, who we see is also quite isolated. Her relationship with Ethel is a clear demonstration that Rhys does not allow her protagonists to be merely victims. Rhys paints a clear picture that Anna has become a destructive person, and this division, this disconnection from self, is a "death" of Anna.

While Ethel desires connection and friendship, Anna cannot recognize any healthy forms of relationship offered to her. She seeks superficial admiration from men, even those she doesn't like, and continues to seek to modify herself in order to get this false acceptance.

During Anna's time with Ethel, they fight over a situation with a client. As Ethel complains about Anna's inability to perform manicures as she ought, the conversation turns to Anna's exclusion of Ethel in social settings. Ethel cries:

> But it's always the same thing. You didn't even ask me . . . And oh God, what a life I've had. Trying to keep up and everybody else trying to push you down and everybody lying and pretending and you knowing it. And then they down you for doing the same things as they do.[82]

In fact, this same speech could have been made by Anna. She has been trying and wishing to be included, but always senses that she does not belong. Yet when encountered by another human who is similarly isolated, she is unmoved. In fact, she pays them no more attention than an irritating insect, "A fly was buzzing round me. I couldn't think of anything, except that it was December and too late for flies, or too soon, or something, and where did it come from?"[83] She does not recognize

---

work in this book.

82. Rhys, *Voyage*, 146.
83. Rhys, *Voyage*, 146.

the humanity of Ethel, demonstrating that for Rhys, Anna's humanity is now also unrecognizable.

We see then that Anna's isolation does not motivate her to be kind or inclusive of those she recognizes are also isolated, but instead leads her to despise them. She hates Ethel and she hates herself. In an imagined conversation with her then-lover, Carl, she imagines how he would describe her. She thinks he would say, "'I picked up a girl in London and her ... Last night I slept with a girl who ...' That was me. / Not a 'girl' perhaps. Some other word, perhaps. Never mind."[84]

## Increased Disconnection

*Voyage in the Dark* was disturbing for Rhys's early readers, because of the explicit sexual and racial material it contained. She was made to change the ending by her publishers and substitute a more ambiguous outcome to the abortion. Rhys stayed with this altered ending even in its later reprinting.[85] Primarily, Anna's story is about abandonment, loss of connection, and an increasing inability to recognize herself as part of the world. Her narrative most clearly highlights the ways wounded identity becomes destructive, producing the type of "death" Rhys focuses on in her work. Wounded identity is a key theme in what we now call postcolonial literature. As critics have reviewed the novel the themes of economic, gendered, and racial violence have been discussed, and their combination noted as constituting one of the first examples of novels directly dealing in postcolonial themes. Ania Spyra states that, as an early and pioneering work in "new world literature," comparison is a constant theme.[86] She continues, "Reading *Voyage* as an example of comparison literature suggests that its critique of uniqueness is not so much a recent phenomenon . . . but has roots in the transnational or (post)-colonial

---

84. Rhys, *Voyage*, 157.

85. Adlai Murdoch discusses this in her chapter, "The Discourses of Rhys: Resistance, Ambivalence and Creole Indeterminacy." She explains the novel "appeared with an ending in fact suggested—if not mandated—by the publisher, and different from the one originally proposed by Rhys. This fact was unequivocally demonstrated when the original ending was found and published some six years after Rhys's death by Nancy Hemond Brown in 1985, lengthening Part Four of the novel by over two and a half thousand words. Indeed, as Mary Hanna points out, 'Rhys's original ending in which Anna dies, was rejected by three British publishers—Cape, Hamish Hamilton, and Constable." (Johnson and Moran, *Jean Rhys*, 148).

86. Spyra, "Alternatives and Alterities," 71.

situation of its author."[87] The comparisons in *Voyage* demonstrate the problematic competitiveness between cultures placed in binary and hierarchical opposition to each other—challenging agendas that could be placed upon the work, in the same way van Heijst rejects preconceived answers to text. Spyra continues:

> Because of the imbalance of power, uniqueness—difference, opacity—becomes the domain of the disempowered. If there are no grounds for comparison, or when one side of the compared binary is considered the standard, comparison has to stall because the party which is not the standard is always already in the lost position. If England is the standard of beauty, then the Caribbean cannot compare and cannot be beautiful according to the same standard.[88]

In its exploration of such problematic relationships, *Voyage in the Dark* demonstrates hierarchy in relationships. Anna has experienced "love" through oppression. Power imbalance, oppressive hierarchies, and loss have defined how she understands connection to others. Therefore, seen through Anna's experiences, a relationship with a God who is powerfully "over us" could not be comforting or indeed loving. Looking back to previous *imago Dei* theories, I must question how they are to be received by the oppressed when they are still modelling these features of oppression.

As Anna continues in her disconnection and participates in destructive comparisons, she increasingly "dies." This disconnection is, as Murdoch explains, "reciprocal . . . she is as alienated and culturally different and distant from her metropolitan counterparts as they are from her."[89] The novel's end, either in the intended original or the published compromise, is not really about whether Anna survives her abortion. To Rhys, Anna has died inwardly already. She could not even be connected to her own pregnancy, as is evidenced by her sustained inability to admit her condition to herself or others. Her last disconnection is the final chapter in a life of an outsider in all circumstances and contexts. As Anna demonstrates this disconnection, I move now to Marya. In her story, a profound sense of disconnection is directly tied to her disconnection to God.

---

87. Spyra, "Alternatives and Alterities," 72.
88. Spyra, "Alternatives and Alterities," 82.
89. Murdoch, "Discourses of Rhys."

## Quartet

### Marya, Woman in Competition

As stated, *Quartet*, published in 1929, is Rhys's first novel—although it reflects a later period in her life. It draws creative inspiration from the complex relations between the real quartet of people Rhys was involved with at that time, including her writing mentor turned lover Ford Maddox Ford and Stella Bowen, a painter and Ford's wife. While with her first husband, Jean Lenglet—and likely during his prison sentence[90]—she became involved with Ford. Their affair was documented by all four in published works. Because Rhys, Ford, and Lenglet were novelists (and "sometimes plain liars"[91]), their accounts cannot be taken as purely factual.[92] Savory explains:

> *Quartet*, which was Rhys's highly fictional version of the affair and its consequences, caused a great literary scandal, especially in England, as Ford was so famous and many felt Rhys had behaved badly in exploiting the privacy of Bowen and Ford after being helped by them.[93]

As with *Voyage in the Dark*, although the novel is a literary work references to Rhys's life can be useful in highlighting the social concerns Rhys is exploring through fiction. *Quartet* similarly demonstrates a keen sense of competitive relationship, destruction of self, and the imbalance between social classes.

Stephan and Marya Zelli, married and poor, move around Europe as Stephan attempts to make money through various illicit schemes. His crimes come to light, and he is arrested, leaving Marya to support herself, a task she is woefully unprepared for. In this realization, her fear grew: "It was a vague and shadowy fear of something cruel and stupid that had caught her and would never let her go."[94] Having recently met a wealthy couple, Lois and HJ Heidler, she goes to them for help. "Now, look here, we want you to move into the spare room at the studio," says Lois.[95] This

---

90. Angier, *Jean Rhys*, 140.

91. Angier, *Jean Rhys*, 140.

92. Even though Bowen's account is thought to be more accurate, it is not highly detailed (Angier, *Jean Rhys*, 139–40).

93. Savory, *Jean Rhys*, 40.

94. Rhys, *Quartet*, 33.

95. Rhys, *Quartet*, 48.

kind gesture is not without an underlying motive, though, as Heidler then forces Marya into an affair, that Lois is aware of. The affair is constantly shown in violent, divisive, and abusive ways.

Most obviously, this is manifested through the destructive relationship with HJ. Marya, initially afraid of and intimidated by HJ, is repeatedly abused, raped, and manipulated by him. When Marya falls in love with him, it is obvious that it is not healthy love, mutually beneficial or supportive, but instead the kind of abject love of an abused creature for its master.

Marya and Lois, meanwhile, do not fair better in terms of supportive relationship with each other. There are brief moments during the affair in which a connection is almost made between the two women. Marya admires Lois. Yet jealousy between them causes fights, and Lois makes clear that HJ holds the power in their marriage— "I'm talking about the man, the male, the important person, the only person who matters."[96] Marya believes Lois hates her, and she comes to hate Lois as well. The women's fighting causes Marya to move out, though she is still entangled in the affair.

After a year, Stephan is released from prison. HJ wants assurances that Marya will not return to her husband, "your going back to live with him would make an impossible situation."[97] However, the arrangement with HJ is also becoming problematic. In the face of his increasing disinterest Marya tries to protest she loves HJ; "quivering and abject in his arms, like some unfortunate dog abasing itself before its master."[98] But he has clearly tired of her. In her desperation at this situation, she tells Stephan of the affair and declares she is leaving him. He rages, saying he will kill Heidler. In their ensuing fight, "He caught her by the shoulders and swung her sideways with all his force."[99] The novel ends with Stephan heading to a hotel with another woman.

## Unseen Identity

Rhys emphasizes Marya's disconnection throughout this novel by the literary device of highlighting sight, eyes, and looks. While in *Voyage*,

---

96. Rhys, *Quartet*, 81.
97. Rhys, *Quartet*, 132.
98. Rhys, *Quartet*, 131.
99. Rhys, *Quartet*, 185.

Anna's disconnection was largely framed through Anna's desire to be someone else, here we see Marya wishing to be known (seen) by someone. Beginning with the first dinner Marya has with the Heidlers, we see Lois's tendency to look past Marya.[100] Marya regularly has unsatisfactory eye contact with Heidler, as he seems to either turn away from her or seek to possess her through looking.[101] Meanwhile, we become aware that Marya believes the ability to look at people, or to watch people, comes with elevated status. In a description of Lois, she emphasizes her ability to look at people. We are told:

> Lois was extremely intelligent. She held her head up. She looked at people with clear, honest eyes. She expressed well-read opinions about every subject under the sun in a healthy voice and was so perfectly sure of all she said that it would have been a waste of time to contradict her.[102]

Lois's ability to look at people demonstrates her significance and status, though Rhys also demonstrates what harm it might do to have such people look at you. Marya is clearly hurt not only by not being looked at, but also by being watched. This difference in wording is important, as it emphasizes that the watcher is elevated above the watched; to really look at each other would be to recognize the humanness in the other.

As stated, Marya is watched by Heidler in her sleep,[103] once again highlighting the many ways we are told that Heidler's relationship with Marya is oppressive and abusive. His presence is regularly referred to as heavy, crushing, and domineering.[104] However, even as his presence is oppressive, it is the ways he watches her that seems to have the most effect.

---

100. "She looked past Marya at a girl dressed in red, followed by two young men, who passed the table with coldly averted head" (Rhys, *Quartet*, 39).

101. "His eyes met hers for a second, then he looked quickly away" (Rhys, *Quartet*, 48). "He would thank her without looking at her and disappear behind the newspaper" (59). "He spoke slowly without looking at her" (71). "When she saw his hostile eyes she stopped laughing and her lips trembled" (121).

102. Rhys, *Quartet*, 60.

103. "Your door is open because I come up every night and open it. Then I look at you and go away again" (Rhys, *Quartet*, 72). "His cool eyes that confused and hurt her" (118). "She undressed, and all the time she was undressing it was as if Heidler were sitting there watching her with his cool eyes that confused and hurt her" (145).

104. ". . . and his huge hand lay possessively, heavy as lead, on her knee" (Rhys, *Quartet*, 13). "He was a rock of a man with his big shoulders and his quiet voice" (43). "He was too formidable standing over her" (83). "He was large, invulnerable, perfectly respectable." (148).

We learn, too, that Marya believes this "watching" is common for men. "And they look at you with hard, greedy eyes. I hate them with their greedy eyes," she thinks.[105] She regards Heidler's eyes as "cool," but begins to accept how they see her and thus define her. In the midst of the abusive relationship, Heidler's opinion becomes fact for her. Again, we are told:

> What mattered was that, despising, almost disliking love, he was forcing her to be nothing but the little woman who lived in the Hotel du Bosphore for the express purpose of being made love to. A *petite femme*. It was, of course, part of his mania for classification. But he did it with such conviction that she, miserable weakling that she was, found herself trying to live up to his idea of her. / She lived up to it. And she had her reward. / . . . He had everything on his side—right down to the expression on the waiter's face when he brought up her breakfast.[106]

As Heidler physically "bore her down"[107] he also breaks down her own view of herself. She has become, in her mind, what he believes her to be—useless except to be used. She is not to be considered anymore. What matters is merely what she can do for him.

And so, we come to a significant passage in which Marya's image of God, and of Heidler are revealed to the reader. Marya dreams about Heidler praying; his supposed "divine" connection having affected her own ability to pray herself. Rhys explains how in her dream, "Marya turned to watch Heidler go down on one knee and cross himself as he passed the altar. He glanced quickly sideways at her as he did it, and she thought: 'I'll never be able to pray again now that I've seen him do that. Never! However sad I am.' And she felt very desolate."[108] Then she imagines he tells her about his relation to God. "God's a pal of mine," she hears him say. God has the same "cold eyes" and is in Heidler's image. She is not even worthy of an introduction to this divine figure because "Lois is a good woman and you are a bad one." Transformed into who he believed her to be Marya must acknowledge, "Nobody owes a fair deal to a prostitute."[109] In her dream Marya is not loved by God/Heidler, nor should she be, and this extinguishes the last of her hope. In trying to wake from this terrible nightmare, she finds herself sick from

105. Rhys, *Quartet*, 72.
106. Rhys, *Quartet*, 118–19.
107. Rhys, *Quartet*, 119.
108. 95 Rhys, *Quartet*, 161.
109. Rhys, *Quartet*, 161.

drink and unable to force her eyes open. "She shut them and again the bed plunged downwards with her—sickeningly—into blackness."[110] She then imagines herself trying to climb out, "so weighted down that it was impossible to hoist herself to the next rung . . . She was going to fall. She was falling. The breath left her body."[111]

Stephan's unsuccessful reunion with Marya is again focused largely on how others see her. In her rambling, she repeatedly references Lois's opinion of her, that she "is too virtuous."[112] Stephan, upset, asks for details, but Marya "stared unseeingly with the eyes of a fanatic" and begs him to "be good to her."[113] She says:

> I wanted to beg you to be good to me, to be kind to me. Because I'm so unhappy that I think I'm going to die of it. My heart is broken. Something in me is broken. I feel . . . I don't know . . . Help me![114]

Stephan, still enraged, determines to kill Heidler, though Marya begs him not to. As they fight, she looks at him.

> She saw the expression in his eyes and was afraid. / 'No,' she said piteously, backing away from him. 'I didn't mean . . . ' / He caught her by the shoulders and swung her sideways with all his force. As she fell, she struck her forehead against the edge of the table, crumpled up and lay still.[115]

So yet again Marya is conquered by the way a man looks at her. She is crushed once more, left without even a thought—destroyed.

## Invisibility

To understand how Rhys displays Marya's death, I look to an earlier scene in which we see Marya's desire to be recognized, not simply watched or looked at. When Heidler tells her that he is done with her, she looks across the café at a man. "It seemed enormously important that she should remember the name of the little man who, staring at

---

110. Rhys, *Quartet*, 162.
111. Rhys, *Quartet*, 162
112. Rhys, *Quartet*, 179–81.
113. Rhys, *Quartet*, 181–82.
114. Rhys, *Quartet*, 182.
115. Rhys, *Quartet*, 185.

her, was obviously also thinking: 'Who is she, where have I met her?'"[116] In the midst of her breakup with Heidler, Marya desires to be not just watched but known, recognized. This last insight Rhys gives us again distinguishes between the act of watching and seeing. It is not that Marya is afraid of being seen, it is instead that she longs to be known and recognized in that sight. She finally remembers the little man's name, but it comes along with a strong feeling of nostalgia about days past when she still hoped in life. The connection she develops to this man is strained between the shame she feels at his seeing her now, being dumped, and the memory of who she then was. As this connection to her former self is now also ruined, Heidler sees the change in her eyes.[117]

Marya's oppression is clearly tied to several aspects of her being in *Quartet*. Rhys points out her gender, constantly showing us that Marya believes it is always the man "who matters."[118] Marya identifies men as her primary abusers, and while we do not get information about her trauma before the novel begins, it is obvious she has suffered abuse.[119] Marya's social and economic status is also clearly part of this marginalization, as Lois points out.[120] Marya is unable to climb the social ladder, and so acceptance by the Heidlers in this way is another type of oppressive control. Marya admires Lois for being knowledgeable, hinting that she is insecure about her own intelligence. Finally, Marya's move into becoming "*petite femme*" or prostitution, seals her fate as an unvalued member of society. As I will explain, though, it is not Marya's "image" (or personhood) that dies in this novel, even though it is badly wounded.

## Destruction

Though received as a fictionalized account of Rhys's own relationships, *Quartet* succeeds in portraying her four characters as variably

---

116. Rhys, *Quartet*, 148.

117. "She turned and looked at him, and when he saw her eyes he put his hand up to his tie, fidgeted with it and said: 'Oh God! Oh God!'" Rhys, *Quartet*, 149–50.

118. Rhys, *Quartet*, 81.

119. "It was a vague and shadowy fear of something cruel and stupid that had caught her and would never let her go. She had always known that it was there—hidden under the more or less pleasant surface of things. Always. Ever since she was a child" (Rhys, *Quartet*, 33).

120. "I suppose you're the sort of person one does feel responsible for . . ." (Rhys, *Quartet*, 52). Lois explains here that Marya has little economic ability to go against the Heidlers's plan for her.

problematic. Rhys is certainly not painting herself as innocent victim. As Savory states, it is an indication of her great talent she was able to "keep herself from being either simple heroine or simple villain."[121] The novel is a prime example of Rhys's expertise in writing, as none of the narrations are trustworthy, and the "reader learns quickly to measure a word or a phrase in a context carefully."[122] *Quartet* firmly establishes Rhys's goal to keep us from assuming simplicity in the ways society oppresses and moves people into self-destructiveness. In this, the novel is particularly important in reframing the questions we normally ask in determining who is, and is not, "good." As I discussed earlier, Rhys is challenging how we understand power. In *Voyage*, she identified how other's power over us can destroy us. Here, Rhys also wants us to reframe what we understand as our own power. For Rhys, power cannot be good if it crushes others. Heidler's power over both his wife and Marya is a demonstration of his oppressive nature. Likewise, Lois's power over Marya positions her as guiltily complicit in abuse, even as she remains powerless with HJ. For Rhys destructive power and the hierarchies it creates cannot be good, and therefore, she challenges us to acknowledge the problems that ensue when we represent God through the terms of hierarchical power relationship. In her discussion of *Quartet*, Helen Nebeker argues that women, in Rhys's fiction, live in "a distorted world where man's only view of woman is sexual and woman's only hope, submission."[123] Nebeker's argument that women become sex workers not because of "uncontrollable desires"[124] but as a mode of survival is again evidence in the destructive competitiveness between oppressor and oppressed. The encounter between women and men is one of economic struggle. She says that in the struggle between Stephan and Marya, we see that Stephan's violent response is tied to Marya's economic dependence on him. To quote:

> In this final revelation of man's despair, of woman as man's economic, if not moral and spiritual, albatross, Rhys transcends her time, suggesting that much of man's real dislike of woman—perhaps even his sexual exploitation of her—is rooted in his unconscious sense of perpetual economic obligation. Since the obligation exists, perhaps he exploits it to the fullest. Conversely, as woman rails against man's sexual exploitation, berating him

121. Savory, *Jean Rhys*, 48.
122. Savory, *Jean Rhys*, 53.
123. Nebeker, *Jean Rhys*, 7.
124. Nebeker, *Jean Rhys*, 7.

for assuaging his guilt with money, she nevertheless feeds and lives upon him like some parasitic vine.[125]

As Rhys powerfully displays, the ways in which the powerful maintain their power leads the oppressed themselves to operate in light of this, often in ways that involve them also in compromise and guilt. Just as in this unequal fight for power we cannot allow the powerful to image God, nor can we always simply declare the oppressed innocent. As Rhys makes clear the abused and traumatized can also damage others. Nebeker's interpretation of *Quartet* certainly has problematic aspects to it. Nonetheless, it is helpful to my discussion here. While Marya and Stephan's conflict is a far deeper one than simply frustration about economic inequality, that destructive competition is still present. Marya and Stephan, Marya and Lois, Marya and HJ, Lois and HJ, and Stephan and HJ all seek to secure their own status through the destruction of the others.

Marya's relationships with the three other characters are all, in various ways, demonstrations of different ways in which hierarchical society can be crushing and destructive. Her relationship with her husband, Stephan, highlights a number of national and racial prejudices, as his Polish name and nationality affect Marya's ability to move within society in Paris. What's more, Stephan is an example of an oppressed person making decisions society deems unacceptable (though in this instance, they are truly destructive and violent) and then re-enacting oppressive relations in his responses to other people (particularly Marya). Her relationship with Lois, first viewed by Marya as one of help and compassion, highlights internalized misogyny and the destructive competition between women that results from this. Lois, the wife, is clearly in a position of power over Marya, and even in fleeting moments of weakness, Marya is constantly torn down by her contact with Lois. This relationship, in its overlapping oppressions, give insight to how class and status can overpower gendered compassion, in keeping with Rhys's suspicion of a one-dimensional feminism.

Marya's part in this competitive relationship, unlike Anna's in *Voyage*, is focused on desire for recognition of her true self. As Anna pursued change in herself through constant appropriation of other people and cultures, Marya desires someone to know her as she is. This focus on connection as recognition is demonstrated through Rhys's use of sight and understanding. Therefore, this novel demonstrates Rhys's challenge

---

125. Nebeker, *Woman in Passage*, 13.

to perceptions concerning who is worthy of recognition. Recognition, highlighted earlier in my work through Stephenson's four points of the *imago Dei*, is a key aspect to being able to participate in the world as God does. This type of recognition includes recognition of the self and of others, leading to a mutually beneficial and loving relationship. As I discussed through the theology of Karl Barth, Katie Cannon, and the philosophy of Martha Nussbaum, developing recognition of others is essential to understanding the *imago Dei*. However, now in light of Rhys's novels, I am able to see that recognition's importance particularly for those who do not recognize themselves.

Therefore, *Quartet* links Rhys works most directly to the discussion of the *imago Dei*, both in the novel itself and in the understanding of the image as sight. As Stephenson says, to image God we must begin by looking one another in the eye, and then participating in that knowledge of the other. Marya desires recognition, even as she does not believe herself worthy. The other characters, who do not give her this recognition, are in her belief more worthy. It is here that I see the *imago Dei* more truly reflected in Marya than the others.

As *Voyage* demonstrates our participation in the image of God requires us to be vulnerable and also acknowledge our own woundedness, *Quartet* shows us that this participation must not be superficial. Marya, in her desire to be seen and known by the others, does not, herself, see and know them. Resentment between the four is, as Nebeker helps to demonstrate, due to the destructive relationships through which they are positioned. However, the destruction they enact is not equal. HJ's ability to crush the women (and Stephan's power as well) is far greater due to his privileged role. Marya, suffering from gendered, economic, and class disadvantage is the most injured.

## Challenges Raised

These two novels present the many of the challenges I see Rhys raising to contemporary theories of *imago Dei*. In *Voyage*, Rhys emphasizes the brokenness and isolation of Anna, leading me to question how our understanding of the image could be localized in attitudes of dignity or courage. Is Anna not able to represent the image because she did not see herself as worthy or capable? Similarly, Rhys does not show us that Anna, or others, are able to lift themselves out of their isolation through their own efforts. In *Quartet*, Rhys challenges the notion that Heidler images "his pal" God. I also understand her to be questioning the characteristics we valorize in the divine, specifically that of power over others such as Heidler boasts of. I also am led to look at Marya's longing to be recognized for herself, even as she believes she can never image God.[126] Her sense of agency and selfhood is often compromised, and she certainly damages others in the process of trying to be accepted into the world. I therefore must continue to question how community, or participation in relationships, has been required in alternative *imago Dei* theories as I look further at Rhys's remaining interwar novels.

---

126. Her dream of Heidler's speech indicates that she sees him as imaging God. She hears him say, "I'm in His image or He's in mine" (Rhys, *Quartet*, 161).

# 5

# Wounds and Connection

Reflection on Isolation and Relationships in Rhys

## Introduction

IN MY DISCUSSION OF her previous two novels, I outlined how Rhys demonstrates competitive and destructive dualisms in social and personal lives, which produces a form of "death" in her characters. For Rhys, this kind of death, as I have stated, is a loss of both connection to the self and to the world/others.[1] By linking these states of separation to the destruction of the human person, Rhys challenges us to look specifically at the way in which power over others can be exercised as a destroying force. Loss of connection, and the abusive patterns it perpetuates, require me in this work, to re-examine the disconnection presupposed between humanity and God in some traditional theological schema, including that of the *imago Dei*, and acknowledge the possibly abusive patterns of relations that could come from that. In reading Rhys, I am also motivated to discover the presence of God-not in "power-over," but in participation with. This is a theme I will continue to explore in the following chapters as well.

By emphasizing the problems hierarchical divisions cause, Rhys is also able to move beyond needing to make clear separations between the oppressed and oppressors. As I demonstrated previously, her characters are both victims and victimizers. In this chapter, I will examine two more

---

1. See chapter 4, above, under the subheading A Type of Death (page 112).

of Rhys's interwar novels, *After Leaving Mr Mackenzie* (1931) and *Good Morning, Midnight* (1939), in order to further complicate how "victimhood" can be defined. Rather than allowing us to analyze oppression as if all who are oppressed are victims, or all who have privilege are victimizers, Rhys gives us characters who cross between these categories because of the layered way marginalization truly works. These novels also expressly highlight the major role economic status plays in oppression, increasing the ways people are marginalized. When her characters attempt to transform themselves, as many *imago Dei* theories would require, money becomes key to their success or failure.

As well as continuing to challenge understandings of moral goodness or moral agency as means of participation in the *imago Dei* these later two novels challenge us to recognize the *imago Dei* in their leading characters not in spite of the women's difficulties or shortcomings, but because of them. As I will demonstrate, particularly in relation to the final novel, *Good Morning, Midnight*, Rhys locates the humanity of her characters at the very point where we are most aware of their inability to transform themselves. In their worst moments, either because of oppression or their own actions, these women are still worthy of dignity. Her goal is not to offer models of women who achieve changes in their lives or circumstances, but instead to change how we respond to them.

## *After Leaving Mr. Mackenzie*

### Julia, the Lost Sister

*After Leaving Mr. Mackenzie* (*ALMM*) is a narrative of two sisters, Julia and Norah.[2] Told primarily from Julia's point of view, the story explores Julia's return to London after years of living abroad in continental Europe. Julia, a woman older than the characters Rhys has given us so far, is beginning to have concerns about her life and her future that we have not encountered in Anna or Marya. She has become dependent on her lovers for money but is starting to doubt her ability to attract them in future.

---

2. Again, it is important to see how Rhys's work gives voices to various oppression, once again bringing Katie Cannon's literary method to this work. In understanding the stories as "voices" for the concerns Rhys raises, not only does it allow the reader to experience life as another, it also continues to reject any attempt at bringing in one's own agenda to the story. Therefore, the novels are particularly suited to embody both the principles of Cannon, Anneleise van Heijst, and Cynthia Wallace.

To begin, Julia's story is framed by rejection. The novel opens with her dismissal by her patron Mackenzie. Julia receives this in something of a daze—"she felt bewildered, as a prisoner might feel who has resigned herself to solitary confinement for an indefinite period in a not uncomfortable cell and who is told one morning, 'Now, then, you're going to be let off today. Here's a little money for you. Clear out.'"[3] She argues with Mackenzie in a restaurant, attracting the attention of another man, George Horsfield. While Mackenzie is only slightly fazed by this encounter, Horsfield is drawn to Julia. Thinking she "looked pretty lonely,"[4] he sits with her and they spend the night drinking and talking. Later, in his room, she explains her situation, and he gives her some money. Horsfield, feeling "powerful and dominant"[5] then encourages her return home to her family.

Julia's decision to return to London is provoked by the encounter with Horsfield, but it is also clearly taken out of desperation. Even while making the decision we see that she "felt so tired. How to do all that must be done while she was feeling so tired?"[6] Comforting herself with the idea of buying new clothes, she sets out to prepare for her trip but, in her anxiety, she spends almost all the money on these purchases. Upon arriving in London, she is immediately in need of money again. Her economic insecurity puts her in a position of reliance upon her family members, her sister Norah and Uncle Griffiths, who both immediately turn down her requests for help. These early rejections allow us to see the kind of fractured relationship Julia has with the world, but also with herself. She says to Uncle Griffiths, "Yes . . . it was idiotic of me to come. It was childish, really. It's childish to imagine that anybody cares what happens to anybody else."[7] She has become so accustomed to her way of living, she is no longer able to believe anything different may be possible for herself.

Julia's return to London has introduced us to her sister, Norah, who becomes an important figure in the novel. The narrative form of *ALLM* allows us to see glimpses of Norah's life, separate from Julia's. We learn that having spent much of her adulthood caring for their ailing mother, Norah has a similar sense of loneliness and abandonment to her sister. She confesses that she feels annihilated by her family and the world, and that

3. Rhys, *After Leaving Mr. Mackenzie*, 19.
4. Rhys, *After Leaving Mr. Mackenzie*, 39.
5. Rhys, *After Leaving Mr. Mackenzie*, 47.
6. Rhys, *After Leaving Mr. Mackenzie*, 57.
7. Rhys, *After Leaving Mr. Mackenzie*, 84.

she no longer feels alive— "My life's like death. It's like being buried alive. It isn't fair, it isn't fair."[8] Norah's energies have been exclusively focused on caring for her non-responsive mother, and there seems a divide in Norah between who she wishes to be and who she is. The inability to live an autonomous life is compounded by her the need to conceal her relationship with Miss Wyatt; a theme which Rhys uses to subtly introduce queer relationships. Yet even with this hidden intimacy, Norah feels wasted. She complains, "They just stood around watching her youth die, and her beauty die, and her soft heart grow hard and bitter."[9]

Julia succeeds in acquiring a little money from a past lover she contacts and begins to think in terms of her future again. Yet, in this awkward encounter, Julia feels again betrayed. "She had hoped that he would say something or look something that would make her feel less lonely."[10] She receives financial support, but she leaves lacking the thing she really desires. In her depressed state, she gets word that her mother is dying and goes to the home to see her one last time. As she's visiting, her mother dies, and the sisters' only connection to each other is gone. They fight, each accusing the other of not caring enough, and Miss Wyatt tells Julia to leave. Julia leaves, saying, "I shall never bother any of you any more after this. Really."[11] She reunites with Horsfield, and their affair continues for a short time.

However, the death of her mother and the loss of her family, have left Julia in a very low state. She thinks about aging, that "suddenly something happens and you stop being yourself; you become what others force you to be. You lose your wisdom and your soul."[12] One night, as Horsfield is following her up the stairs to her room, she gets confused in the darkness. His touch alarms her, and she yells out, "Oh God, who touched me?"[13] This breakdown causes the end of their relationship, and ten days after her arrival in London, she goes back to Paris. Having arrived in Paris, she once again encounters Mr Mackenzie. "Lend me a hundred francs, will you?"[14] she asks, and he obliges. The novel ends as

8. Rhys, *After Leaving Mr. Mackenzie*, 103.
9. Rhys, *After Leaving Mr. Mackenzie*, 104.
10. Rhys, *After Leaving Mr. Mackenzie*, 116.
11. Rhys, *After Leaving Mr. Mackenzie*, 138.
12. Rhys, *After Leaving Mr. Mackenzie*, 158.
13. Rhys, *After Leaving Mr. Mackenzie*, 163.
14. Rhys, *After Leaving Mr. Mackenzie*, 191.

they part ways, leaving us with the belief that Julia will continue as she has done or further decline.

## Disconnected Sisters

Rhys uses the character of two very different sisters to deepen the challenge made in *Quartet*—and to ask, "why do we only question the moral and spiritual status of those who do not follow social norms?" She questions further whether those who do abide by conventional moral codes are really more able to live fulfilled lives or are they not also enslaved by economic and social constraints they cannot change or avoid. While Julia's story is similar to that of many of Rhys's other characters, Norah's is one of outwardly following societal expectations and family obligation. The differences in the sisters' paths, however, does not change the ultimate outcome for either of them. Both Norah and Julia are disconnected, and their wounds ignored and left unhealed.

As I discussed previously, competitive relationships can be destructive, and are often unequally so. *Voyage in the Dark* gives us insight into how the competitive relationships cause wounds, but with *ALMM* we are able to see the wounds as they fester. Julia's and Norah's wounds are old. Their interaction as played out in the novel prove that unhealed wounds reopen, causing even deeper damage. Norah sees Julia's new clothes and imagines her living a glamorous life in Europe. She believes that Julia has forsaken her family responsibilities and escaped the restrictions of society. In her jealous response, "she felt a fierce desire to hurt her or see her hurt and humiliated."[15] This is not due to hatred for Julia, but instead hatred for her own life and a misguided comparison between this and her sister's fortunes. Julia, in turn, is jealous that Norah had the love of their mother[16] and a seemingly stable life and believes her family has rejected her. Neither sister really knows the other, but they both believe themselves to be the despised one.

---

15. Rhys, *After Leaving Mr. Mackenzie*, 102.

16. "Her mother had been the warm centre of the world . . . And then her mother—entirely wrapped up in the new baby—had said things like 'Don't be a cry-baby. You're too old to go on like that. You're a great big girl of six.' And from being the warm centre of the world her mother had gradually become a dark, austere, rather plump woman, who, because she was worried, slapped you for no reason that you knew" (Rhys, *After Leaving Mr. Mackenzie*, 106–7).

Thus, the sisters' situations and relationship highlight the theme I have been pursuing in my research into Rhys's novels. Rhys uses the differences and animosity in the sisters to emphasize the difficulties of the oppressed in forming communal and supportive bonds. Rhys characters are not "less valuable" or "less human" because they have become sex workers or have not lived up to society's expectations. They also have not been mere victims, or people without agency, in their situations. Instead, what I—and I believe, Rhys—observe is that various forms of lack of connection to the world are destructive and one of their most destructive elements is to separate us from those who are similarly marginalized.

## Survival and Dependence

Julia's story through the novel reveals the different ways that she attempts to sustain herself but simultaneously demonstrates their ineffectiveness. Despite the continuing rejections she faces Julia makes great efforts to maintain appearances. She fears "looking like that woman on the floor above" who has given up.[17] That woman, realizing she has nothing left to offer, has stopped trying. Yet this leaves her "a shadow, kept alive by a flame of hatred for somebody who had long ago forgotten about her."[18] Nevertheless, Julia keeps "trying" even as she fails.

Mr. Mackenzie, her previous benefactor, is given some narrative room, allowing us to know his perception of Julia. We learn that he never intended to keep his promises to her,[19] and that he knew she had been "principally living on the money given to her by various men."[20] He is concerned about how others will perceive him in relation to Julia, and even as she tells him how he has hurt her, he only cares whether anyone else is listening. To Mr. Mackenzie, Julia is of no value in her personhood. This break in relationship is an example of what Moran believes adds to the chronic shame of Rhys's protagonists. She says:

> Our sense of self, both particular and universal, is deeply embedded in our struggles with the alienating affect. Answers to the questions, 'Who am I?' and 'Where do I belong?' are forged in the crucible of shame.' These questions are central to

17. Rhys, *After Leaving Mr. Mackenzie*, 14.
18. Rhys, *After Leaving Mr. Mackenzie*, 15.
19. Rhys, *After Leaving Mr. Mackenzie*, 25.
20. Rhys, *After Leaving Mr. Mackenzie*, 26.

the Rhys protagonist, who struggles with feeling unloved and unwanted at the personal level, and marginalised and despised at the social and cultural level.[21]

As I stated previously, after her break with Mr. Mackenzie Julia meets George Horsfield who was witness to Julia's painful conversation with Mackenzie. Horsfield, though currently sexually interested in Julia, proves no better than Mackenzie. He regularly feels "detached" from her.[22] He begins to give her money, but not because of concern for her, but rather because it makes him feel "powerful."[23] In fact he feels more attracted to her when she is more obviously upset,[24] and even as their relationship ends, he believes she'll be desperate enough to contact him again.[25]

Two other men from Julia's past are introduced in the novel. Her Uncle Griffiths and Neil James, a former lover. The attitudes of both toward Julia mirror what we see from Mackenzie and Horsfield. They find her desperate, pathetic, and only worth helping because of the power it gives them over her. Julia is, to all of them, less than human. She tells us, as she's beginning to ask for money from Neil James, "Because he has money he's a kind of God. Because I have none I'm a kind of worm. A worm because I've failed and I have no money. A worm because I'm not even sure if I hate you."[26] Julia is not unaware of how these men view her, but in fact, agrees with their judgments. She has no compensatory support from a female realm that values and sustains her. As Elaine Savory also comments on Julia's separation from the others in the novel, saying, "Since she is alienated from her physical mother and far from her mother's culture, Julia . . . is double-divorced from a space where she might be known."[27] Her relationships in all areas have been destroyed, leaving Julia unknown and unable to participate meaningfully with anyone.

21. Savory, *Jean Rhys*.
22. Rhys, *After Leaving Mr. Mackenzie*, 39.
23. Rhys, *After Leaving Mr. Mackenzie*, 47.
24. "He noticed that Julia appeared frightened, as if she had been crying. Yet he thought, too, that her face was thinner and somehow more youthful than when he had last seen her" (Rhys, *After Leaving Mr. Mackenzie*, 145).
25. "And then he wondered how he should send money to her if she did not write. 'But, of course, she will write,' he told himself" (Rhys, *After Leaving Mr. Mackenzie*, 175).
26. Rhys, *After Leaving Mr. Mackenzie*, 112–13.
27. Savory, *Jean Rhys*, 63.

The final severing of ties to the world in the breakdown of family relationships has broken Julia completely. Savory states, "Her paralysis and silence act as a physical embodiment of this social and emotional isolation."[28] Even as she thinks she may be able to win another man, she feels she is unable to interact with them. "Something in her was cringing and broken, but she would not acknowledge it."[29] She wishes she could talk to someone, tell them about herself, but time and again is unable to do so.[30] She is unable, even, to care for the plight of things she used to be moved by. Rhys says, "Now she felt indifferent and cold, like a stone."[31] Julia has lost her ability to participate in the world at all.

Meanwhile, Norah has tried to live according to social expectations by caring for her mother and has sacrificed her own life to the domestic demands made on women. Like her dress, Norah has "lost [her] freshness."[32] She is also economically disenfranchised through the social role she has assumed. Norah's place in society is indelibly marked upon her. "Middle class, no money" was seen in every aspect of her.[33] As Rhys relates, this means she was "brought up to certain tastes, then left without the money to gratify them; trained to certain opinions which forbid her even the relief of rebellion against her lot; yet holding desperately to both her tastes and her opinions."[34] Norah cannot achieve a fulfilled life without risking herself by overthrowing these impossible restrictions. She is not willing to take this risk, though, and so even her one friendship[35] with Miss Wyatt is not able to be revealed in truth. Norah, in an attempt to maintain the little financial stability she does have, must sacrifice her own self and her loves for that money. Her sacrifice is very like Julia's, though on the surface might seem to have made "better" life choices she is no less oppressed economically and no more able than her sister to assert her own agency or achieve meaningful connections with others.

28. Savory, *Jean Rhys*, 75.
29. Rhys, *After Leaving Mr. Mackenzie*, 182.
30. Rhys, *After Leaving Mr. Mackenzie*, 184, 186.
31. Rhys, *After Leaving Mr. Mackenzie*, 188.
32. Rhys, *After Leaving Mr. Mackenzie*, 71.
33. Rhys, *After Leaving Mr. Mackenzie*, 73.
34. Rhys, *After Leaving Mr. Mackenzie*, 74.
35. Though it is clearly more than a friendship, and thus Rhys has also introduced the marginalization faced by lesbians in this society.

## A Theory of Life

In opening her discussion of *ALMM,* Elaine Savory discusses at length the previous scholarship on Rhys. Included in this is the idea of the "Rhys woman," and the idea that the protagonists from the four interwar novels can be seen as one woman at different stages, probably representing Rhys herself.[36] She sees this as particularly erasing the Caribbean and racial aspects of Rhys, and concludes that:

> The Rhys woman is a subversive not just in intention and reaction to social conditions but in her very existence as a puzzling, riddling, self-questioning loose cannon who continually destabilises conventional values for women, sexuality and male behaviour towards women and easy definitions of national, class and ethnic identity.[37]

This complicating of issues, particularly evident in *ALMM*, problematizes the idea of the unitary Rhys woman. Moreover, I believe that the juxtaposition of Julia and Norah demonstrate that Rhys is creating a tapestry of ways people are marginalized and oppressed. That the women characters have commonalities, and the fact that they can be read in life stages (as I have done) does not mean they should be autobiographically localized as one woman. It can mean, though, that Rhys is prefiguring the possibility of solidarity between the oppressed. She may be read as implying that those who are damaged and marginalized might connect in their woundedness.

If this possibility is present it must also be clearly stated that this coming together does not happen in this novel. *After Leaving Mr. Mackenzie,* like *Voyage,* shows us two women who have stopped participating in the world. For Rhys, and in my analysis here, these women have died by the end of the novel, not physically, but rather have become "ghosts."[38] They are both unable to risk relationships, even with each other, and they both grow more dead as the narrative progresses. As we see Julia at the end of the novel, she is even unable to perform the basic actions needed to secure more money for herself. She leaves Mr. Mackenzie with only

---

36. Savory, *Jean Rhys,* 57–60.
37. Savory, *Jean Rhys,* 83.
38. "To be a ghost means to be insubstantial in certain important ways to those still living and unable, usually, to communicate with them . . ." (Savory, *Jean Rhys,* 74). This is particularly well-done in Rhys's short story "I Used to Live Here Once," where the character is invisible to those around her.

a small amount and seems simply too weary to try and gain more from him. Instead of acting as Marya does, desiring to be recognized, which indicates a desire for the I-Thou, Julia acts as Anna does—disconnected to the point of willing death. Neither she nor Norah will allow themselves to be affected by the world anymore, and therefore are not truly "alive" in the sense Rhys is symbolizing. The importance in recognizing the similar fates of the women is seen in that Rhys frames both outcomes clearly, while demonstrating how differently the sisters have lived. Norah has seemingly done everything right. If we were to take Heidler's understanding of the "good woman" Norah should be considered exemplary. She may not have much money, but she is not a prostitute. She has lived, outwardly, according to conventional standards. Yet she is still described as dead. Julia, on the other hand, has been continuously damaged by others. She has suffered obvious trauma and marginalization. Without economic independence, she has taken to living the only way she can by surviving on sex work. However, Rhys does not absolve her of responsibility. Rhys shows us how Julia still hurts both her sister and her mother. The sisters' futures are that of the ghosts that haunt all of Rhys's novels. Their constant wounding of each other inflicts further damage and they find no support through connecting to their common oppression. There is no recognition, no "looking the other in the eye."

## Connection and the Image

As stated, Rhys clearly highlights the break in these sisters' relationship, and I see this as her way of signaling their need for reconnection. Norah and Julia's relationship is one of competitive disconnection. Norah desires to be seen as reputable and holds this over Julia. Julia, thinking herself the outcast of the family, looks for this affirmation in men. Julia believes Norah, along with the rest of their family, must hate her and see her as less than human. Savory says that we begin to see Julia as a *zombi*, a "Caribbean form of the living dead."[39] Neither sister, though, changes. Even a recognition of the need to change, particularly shown in Norah's reflection upon how her choices have left her isolated,[40] does

---

39. Savory, *Jean Rhys*, 83.

40. "Everybody had said: 'You're wonderful, Norah.' But they did not help. They just stood around watching her youth die, and her beauty die, and her soft heart grow hard and bitter" (Rhys, *After Leaving Mr Mackenzie*, 104). Though Norah gets approval from society, they do not participate in her life meaningfully.

not move them to make new decisions. Along with Rhys, the sisters continually desire that someone else will impart dignity upon them, creating change for them. However, as no one does or can and their lack of money symbolizes their captivity. the sisters return to the destruction they faced in the beginning of the novel.

Julia and Norah are characters who are deeply wounded by their pasts. In Patricia Moran's analysis of Rhys, she states, " Rhys's courageous exposure of the mechanisms by which chronic shaming underwrites the social transactions that have multiplied and relentlessly disenfranchised her protagonists is one of her most brilliant and important contributions to modernist and postcolonial discourses."[41] For Julia and Norah, these wounds from trauma and oppression, leading to the chronic shame both sisters carry, continue to keep them from the ability to move within a society built on economic status. This story demonstrates clearly the inability to reject oppression, even inwardly as Cannon offers, without significant outside support. Having noted this, I now move to Rhys's final interwar novel, in which this requirement for mutuality, recognition and human contact is most clearly depicted.

## *Good Morning, Midnight*

### Disconnected Memories

*Good Morning, Midnight* (*GMM*) is the last of Rhys's four interwar novels. It focuses on Sasha, the oldest of Rhys's characters, who lives in Paris. While the plot is much simpler than the other novels, we frequently switch back and forth from current time to the memories Sasha has of her past life.[42] Like *Voyage in the Dark*, *GMM* is told in the first person, from Sasha's point of view. Through this, we are able to see Paris from Sasha's perspective, and to discover how she understands both the world and herself. It is important to note that because the novel has a fairly simple plot, we are drawn to focus on Sasha's complex state of mind and see how her despair has disconnected her from the world.

41. "The Feelings are Always Mine," in Johnson and Moran, *Jean Rhys*, 191.

42. This novel also is particularly helpful in seeing examples of the kind of testimony Rebecca Chopp describes in her poetics. While it is not the only novel with these testimonial sections, I will be highlighting many of them in order to demonstrate Rhys's depiction of Sasha's inner voice as well as how Rhys expertly identifies the Nussbaum ideal of emotional response (and thus the appropriate actions) we should be having from these testimonies.

As the novel begins, Sasha is leaving London to return to Paris, thinking about her original trip to Paris with her then-husband, Enno. Arriving in Paris, she rents a room, "More dark rooms, more red curtains . . . ,"[43] which is next door to a man who, throughout the novel, wears a dressing-gown. Sasha seeks to order her days based on interacting only with people she believes will like her. "The thing is to a have a programme," she tells us, "not to leave anything to chance—no gaps. No trailing around aimlessly . . . "[44] But the routine she sets out to follow is one which brings up many memories from her past. She remembers jobs she's had, including one in a shop. A fluent French-speaker, Sasha was the receptionist. However, she was nervous around the owner and is unable to communicate with him. Due to his inability to speak French, she is unable to complete a task he has given her, and she loses her job. Yet, Sasha knows the incident was not her fault. She recognizes she has been wrongfully treated, but she cannot speak up for herself. This memory leads her to recall other jobs in which she appears to have failed; unable to evoke confidence in herself, she has been let go.

## Memories of Loss

These haunting memories disrupt Sasha's planned routine. Dwelling on a series of disastrous encounters she thinks of lashing out at the people she believes have wronged her, and the day she has planned begins to unravel as past memories thwart all her attempts at new beginnings.

This disastrous day has also brought back extremely painful memories of her pregnancy and the death of her baby in Paris. She had struggled to care for her child, having no money and being unable to feed her baby. Having taken him to the hospital and having been bandaged herself by a midwife to remove the marks of her pregnancy, she is informed that he has died. She remembers gazing at him with the trees of her motherhood already removed from her body.

> And there he is, lying with a ticket tied round his wrist because he died in a hospital. And there I am looking down at him, without one line, without one wrinkle, without one crease . . .[45]

---

43. Rhys, *Good Morning, Midnight*, 12.
44. Rhys, *Good Morning, Midnight*, 15.
45. Rhys, *Good Morning, Midnight*, 61.

Sasha may have no physical marks of her baby, but this memory tells us she carries these wounds of his loss. On her next day in Paris, in an effort to change her fortunes, she has her hair dyed "a nice blond cendré."[46] She plans to buy a new hat as well, and as she continues her day, things begin to look up.

Her memories become happier, but less frequent. She is more grounded in the present with her new confidence. It is in this mood that she encounters an interesting group of Russian emigrees. She also meets a new man, René, who clearly is hoping to get money from her—we learn that he is a gigolo as the story continues. She finds this reversal of roles to be empowering, and they spend the day together. However, again, in the next morning, her spirits are low. Her plans to meet with her new Russian friends are the only thing that gets her out of bed, but during their outing she is drawn back to her memories. She thinks of times she had no food, her thoughts of suicide and she struggles to remember what reality is. "Pull yourself together, dearie. This is late October 1937, and that old coat had its last outing a long time ago."[47] In each of these instances, Sasha tries to enact a change that will fix her life, or at least give her more confidence. She is seeking outside affirmation of her personhood, but primarily does this through superficial means. Sasha's understanding of change never goes deeper than immediate physical or material change, and Rhys uses this to demonstrate the futility of these attempts.

## Sinking and Drowning

Rhys uses constant unsuccessful efforts at transformations Rhys uses it to show Sasha's inability to change is another way of being "dead." In *GMM*, Sasha often likens her state as something like dying or death. In order to comprehend this, I quote at length.

> On the contrary, it's when I am quite sane like this, when I have had a couple of extra drinks and am quite sane, that I realize how lucky I am. Saved, rescued, fished-up, half-drowned, out of the deep, dark river, dry clothes, hair shampooed and set. Nobody would know I had ever been in it. Except, of course, that there always remains something. Yes, there always remains something . . . Never mind, here I am, sane and dry, with my

---

46. Rhys, *Good Morning, Midnight*, 61.
47. Rhys, *Good Morning, Midnight*, 91.

> place to hide in. What more do I want? . . . I'm a bit of an automaton, but sane, surely—dry, cold and sane. Now I have forgotten about dark streets, dark rivers, the pain the struggle and the drowning . . . Mind you, I'm not talking about the struggle when you are strong and a good swimmer and there are willing and eager friends on the bank waiting to pull you out at the first sign of distress. I mean the real thing. You jump in with no willing and eager friends around, and when you sink you sink to the accompaniment of loud laughter.[48]

Sasha articulates a key theme in Rhys's novels here. The importance of various forms of privilege, or connections to the world, which I have been highlighting in the works, are presented as being "strong and a good swimmer and there are willing and eager friends." Sasha realizes that she lacks these things. Rhys is using this analogy to highlight the systemic difficulties her characters face in their economic and social positionings, their gender and nationality, and to press upon us that "the loud laughter" means Sasha (and others) are not merely drowning because no one notices. In fact, their struggle is the entertainment society provides for the successful. When the multiple oppressed begin to drown, they not only cannot find someone to help them, they are surrounded by people actively hurting them. As Moran explains:

> The Rhysian protagonist is painfully aware of contemptuous gazes, ranging from the sneers on the faces of landladies, waiters, servants and taxi drivers to the open contempt written on the faces of family members. The protagonists' obsessive concern with clothing registers a common strategy of fending off contempt, as if clothing functioned as a form of camouflage: Julia speaks of her fur coat as a 'protective colouring' and Sasha similarly images clothing as 'protective armour'.[49]

As I have been arguing, Sasha, like Anna Morgan, believes she can improve her life by superficially changing who she is. As she remembers her past, she tells us "It was then that I started calling myself Sasha. I thought it might change my luck if I changed my name."[50] She lives behind a mask: "Besides, it isn't my face, this tortured and tormented

---

48. Rhys, *Good Morning, Midnight*, 10. This is also my first example of both the testimony Sasha offers, and the actions Rhys expects of her readers. It is here that we hear the demand to aid those who are drowning.
49. Moran, "'The Feelings are Always Mine,'" 101.
50. Rhys, *Good Morning, Midnight*, 12.

mask. I can take it off whenever I like and hang it up on a nail."[51] She believes if she can only change her appearance, and thus how people look at her, her whole life will change for the better.[52] As Carr explains, this desire to change is rooted in her own self-hatred:

> Like the Creole, she has internalized the condemnation and scorn of those around her. Rhys's psychic patterning of those excluded and humiliated is something far more complex than the pathos of oppression. Hatred breeds hatred, brutality breeds brutality.[53]

Her self-hatred turns to hatred for others, and so Sasha struggles to survive in this death-like state.

In the face of so much rejection Sasha attempts to catalogue places and people where she might find acceptance. Much like Marya's experiences of "knowing/recognition" in *Quartet*, Sasha analyses the ways people look at her, interact with her, and respond to her. Through this practice she makes adjustments in her life and only goes to places where she is liked, or at least where people feel neutral about her. She says:

> My life, which seems so simple and monotonous, is really a complicated affair of cafés where they like me and cafés where they don't, streets that are friendly, streets that aren't, rooms where I might be happy, rooms where I shall never be, looking-glasses I look nice in, looking-glasses I don't, dresses that will be lucky, dresses that won't, and so on.[54]

There are many examples of this process in the novel, but one in particular is paradigmatic: Sasha's trip to a café, Théodore's. She decides to eat there, though she isn't sure yet whether it is "friendly" or not. She wonders if the patron will recognize her and debates the consequences of this. As she thinks, she says, "Today I must be very careful, today I have left my armour at home."[55] She observes the people around her,

51. Rhys, *Good Morning, Midnight*, 43.

52. "If I had been wearing [the dress] I should never have stammered or been stupid" (Rhys, *Good Morning, Midnight*, 28). "Who says you can't escape your fate? I'll escape from mine, into room number 219" (37). "Watching her [try on hats], am I watching myself as I shall become?" (68) "I feel saner and happier after this [hat shopping]" (70). "Tomorrow I'll be pretty again, tomorrow I'll be happy again, tomorrow, tomorrow . . ." (57). "You're judging by my coat" (75).

53. Carr, *Jean Rhys*, 71.

54. Rhys, *Good Morning, Midnight*, 46.

55. Rhys, *Good Morning, Midnight*, 49.

also very aware that they might be observing her. She soothes herself with saying they are too interested in themselves to notice her, but her panic grows. "I told you not to come in here, I told you not to."[56] Then, as she's finishing her meal, two girls enter. Théodore talks to them, and Sasha tells us that the girls turn to look at her.

> "'Oh, my God!' the tall one says.
>
> Théodore goes on talking. Then he too turns and looks at me. 'Ah, those were the days,' he says.
>
> 'Et qu'est-ce qu'elle fout ici, maintenant?' the tall girl says, loudly."[57]

Sasha believes the whole café is looking at her now; her worst fear realized. She tries to look at the tall girl, who then averts her eyes. Sasha's panic grows, bringing her near to tears.

It is at that point Sasha distracts herself by focusing on changing her hair color. The ideal, she tells us, is blond cendré. It's a difficult color, though. She explains, "First it must be bleached, that is to say, its own colour must be taken out of it—and then it must be dyed, that is to say, another colour must be imposed on it."[58]

Are those in the café really behaving as Sasha perceives them? Even she is not sure, as she leaves and questions the meaning of Théodore's smile. However, the event allows us to see how her two protective devices work to keep her functional. She needs to believe that people like her, or at least are neutral to her, and that she belongs where she is. Feeling like an imposter in Théodore's, she immediately dreams of changing who she is.[59]

---

56. Rhys, *Good Morning, Midnight*, 50.

57. Rhys, *Good Morning, Midnight*, 50.

58. Rhys, *Good Morning, Midnight*, 52. This scene is also particularly poignant, as Sasha wishes she could also remove her own self and have another identity imposed upon her.

59. This desire to change her looks is not merely vanity, though. It also has economic implications. In Andrea Zemgulys's work on economic issues in *GMM*, she points out that Sasha, and the other women in the novels, are trading on their looks. She says, "women, specifically poor women, manage the market as a system of exchange that structures the world and values them for their exchangeabilty as things." Sasha's work, and the casual sex work of Rhys's other protagonists, does require them to focus on their looks. However, it is the understanding of themselves as things to be traded and finding security in disconnecting from themselves in this way, that both helps the women survive and continues in their woundings.

## Beyond Death in Life

Throughout the novel, Sasha reflects on death and life, and her beliefs about them. She references murder, suicide, and the afterlife frequently.[60] Yet, her references are clearly not only to a physical death. Sasha does consider suicide in a desperate state in Paris and, as Savory says, this represented not as tragic but "something to consider as a next step, a proper move."[61] Physical death assumes this "thinkable" status for Sasha because, as she tells us throughout the novel, she considers herself already dead. Her "real end" came long ago. But it was not a quick death. It was a series of events in a process of being disconnected.

> 'What happened to you, what happened?' He says. 'Something bad must have happened to make you like this.'
>
> 'One thing? It wasn't one thing. It took years. It was a slow process.'[62]

Her sense that she has died, that her existence is disconnected from her body and from other people, is what directs Sasha's actions for the majority of the book. She acknowledges that, even if she isn't fully aware of the meaning. Attempting to look like someone she is not, or to avoid places she might be recognized, are the continuation of not being "marked" by her life. The elusive "tomorrow" cannot come, because tomorrow is the hope that she will, in fact, become someone wholly different.

---

60. Describing a dream: "But blood is streaming from a wound in his forehead. 'Murder,' he shouts, 'murder, murder'" (Rhys, *Good Morning, Midnight*, 13). "Paris is looking very nice tonight . . . You are looking very nice tonight, my beautiful, my darling, and oh what a bitch you can be! But you didn't kill me after all, did you?" (16). "But no, you must have the slow death, the bloodless killing that leaves no stain on your conscience . . ." (23). "He has recognized me . . . Very unlikely. Besides, what if he has, what's it matters? They can't kill you, can they? Oh, can't they, though, can't they?" (49). "One day, quite suddenly, when you're not expecting it, I'll take a hammer from the folds of my dark cloak and crack your little skull like an eggshell" (52). "'Why didn't you drown yourself', the old devil said, 'in the Seine?'" (41). "It was then that I had the bright idea of drinking myself to death" (43). "As soon as you have reached this heaven of indifference, you are pulled out of it. From your heaven you have to go back to hell. When you are dead to the world, the world often rescues you, if only to make a figure of fun out of you" (91). "Well that was the end of me, the real end . . . The lid of the coffin shut down with a bang. Now I no longer wish to be loved, beautiful, happy or successful. I want one thing and one thing only—to be left alone" (42–43). "But when I think 'tomorrow' there is a gap in my head, a blank—as if I were falling through emptiness. Tomorrow never comes" (159).
61. Savory, *Jean Rhys*, 127.
62. Rhys, *Good Morning, Midnight*, 175.

It is here that the end of the book, and its deep ambiguity, are important. Sasha brings René, the gigolo, to her room, but as they argue, she asks him to go. Instead, he rapes her. The scene, in its difficult detail, must be quoted here.

> 'You think you're very strong, don't you?' he says.
>
> 'Yes, I'm very strong.'
>
> I'm strong as the dead, my dear, and that's how strong I am.
>
> 'If you're so strong, why do you keep your eyes shut?'
>
> Because dead people must have their eyes shut.
>
> I lie very still, I don't move. Not open my eyes . . .
>
> 'Je te ferai mal,' he says. 'It's your fault.'
>
> When I open my eyes I feel the tears trickling down from the outside corners.
>
> 'That's better, that's better. Now say "I tell you to go and you'll go".'
>
> I can't speak.
>
> 'That's better, that's better.'
>
> I feel his hard knee between my knees. My mouth hurts, my breasts hurt, because it hurts, when you have been dead, to come alive.[63]

Sasha tells us she is coming alive, but we must understand what she means by this. After the gigolo leaves, having also taken her money, she cries. She says, "Who is this crying? The same one who laughed on the landing, kissed him and was happy. This is me, this is myself, who is crying. The other—how do I know who the other is? She isn't me."[64] Sasha has finally recognized herself. This is the first instance of meaningful change for one of Rhys's characters. Though seemingly a small step, Sasha not only has recovered a sense of survival, she has also reconnected to herself. The Other, who begins to tell her to do things, is the protective voice in her head that has kept her from connecting all these years. The Other is the one that tells Sasha to believe her neighbor has heard everything and so she must be quiet. The Other is the one who believes the gigolo has taken all her money, though in

---

63. Rhys, *Good Morning, Midnight*, 181–82. Here I am reminded specifically of Chopp's testimonial poetics from Anna Akhmatova, as described on page 79.

64. Rhys, *Good Morning, Midnight*, 184.

fact he has left her a little. "I appreciate this, sweet gigolo, from the depths of my heart. I'm not used to these courtesies."[65] After this horrible experience, we would assume Sasha would retreat farther into her disconnection. Yet, here we see a glimmer of hope. Sasha's situation is not much changed, but she sees a very small kindness and connects to it. She meaningfully changes herself. In this moment of hopefulness, Sasha unlocks the door, wishing René would come back.

He does not come back, but Sasha is visited by her dressing-gowned neighbor, the *commis*, who she has interacted with throughout the novel. Their interactions have not been monumental events. She avoids him, and he seems to want to talk to her, but they never have a real conversation. He is always wearing either a blue or white dressing gown. She is afraid of him, but primarily because she seems to think he understands her. When the *commis* enters, we are left with this final scene.

> He doesn't say anything. Thank God, he doesn't say anything. I look straight into his eyes and despise another poor devil of a human being for the last time. For the last time . . .
>
> Then I put my arms round him and pull him down on to the bed, saying: 'Yes—yes—yes . . .'[66]

Savory discusses this last line and its reference to James Joyce's *Ulysses*, in which Molly Bloom repeats "yes" as she expresses and embraces life and love.[67] In her opinion this saying, "yes—yes—yes" demonstrates that Sasha "gives herself up most chillingly to a death-in-life, to a *zombi* state."[68] This idea of a "death-in-life" is certainly something I see regularly in Rhys's novels, but I interpret the passage quite differently. As I demonstrated with Rhys's other novels, the character's death-in-life comes with both giving up on themselves and on others. Here, Sasha surprisingly appears to possess renewed hope. She sees her death as having happened long ago. This, then, must be different to death, while in Joyce's novel, the "yes" spoken is tied to Molly's affirmation of life and love,[69] Rhys shows us that Sasha's affirmation is of herself. This scene demonstrates her restored acceptance of herself and, perhaps, through the *commis*, also the others that she has previously despised. Therefore,

65. Rhys, *Good Morning, Midnight*, 186.
66. Rhys, *Good Morning, Midnight*, 190.
67. Joyce, *Ulysses*, 1078.
68. Savory, *Jean Rhys*, 131.
69. Ellmann, "James Joyce," 338.

I agree with Tamar Heller's assessment of the conclusion to *GMM*, this ending is hopeful; a "potent antidote to despair."[70]

## Connection and the Image

Savory describes *GMM* as Rhys's "masterpiece, mordantly funny and at times highly satirical . . . but it has generally been far less noticed and definitely far less loved"[71] than *Wide Sargasso Sea*, her final novel. As she remembers her life, we can clearly see how Sasha has been wounded. As she goes about her days, we see Sasha's attempts at protect and disguise those wounds. It is the ending of the novel, though, that sees Sasha begin to heal and allow her wounds to transform and redeem her. While the novel has another controversial conclusion it is, as I have argued, one that, finally, offers a small glimmer of hope. Sasha's life is no better than that of Rhys's other protagonists, but there are glimpses of a different attitude, and the way Rhys portrays this hope is important for my research.

Sasha's life has numerous named traumas, but more importantly, it begins with a woman who has stopped attempting to participate in the world and is rather shielding herself from it. While these actions are methods of protection, they are also demonstrations of Sasha's paralyzed state. They also show how Sasha moves in the world after her "death." By not leaving her in this state, Rhys uses this novel to gesture towards the difficult movement back into life. Sasha's wounds are not fully healed, but finally not ignored when she is "reborn." They are acknowledged and given air. She allows herself to be recognized as wounded, and in turn recognizes another human in their woundedness. It is this moment that does not negate but rather completes the many challenging insights concerning the *imago Dei* that I have begun to discern in Rhys's novels.

As I have stated some critics read the ending of *GMM* pessimistically, insisting that Sasha is dead and hopeless in her surrender to the *commis*.[72] Others discern a more optimistic conclusion, insisting that Sasha is at last able to love. In her article, Heller even goes as far as naming Sasha's final act as a direct imitation of Christ. She says, "Imitating Christ's assent to a sacrificial death, decreation purges the will of its

---

70. Heller, "Affliction in Jean Rhys and Simone Weil," 176.
71. Savory, *Cambridge Introduction*, 66.
72. Savory, for example, says, "This is a deeply disturbing conclusion, but very powerful: a surrender to the end of love, a female wasteland." (*Cambridge Introduction*, 79)

inherent lust for power by replacing it with purely disinterested love."[73] As I examine the novel, I agree with those who read it with hope. The *commis* may conceivably have killed Sasha or, more plausibly, simply made love to her. Whatever the case it is Sasha's attitude that is significant. Her declaration that she will not hate, paired with her earlier admission that she is being reborn, describe a person who has, as Heller says, experienced a second creation. This, as I will argue, is the movement into a love of self and others that causes me to reflect further on God's vulnerable participation within the world.

Sasha's "rebirth," rather than death, is the final key to my reading. She has been traumatized as much, or more, than Rhys's other women. As Helen Carr discusses, Sasha's forms of protection regularly fail her: "She shows a fragmented, volatile, destructive psyche born of a torn, destructive, violent history."[74] However, in the end, Sasha realizes that she wants to be alive. This simple desire, awoken in her when she allows herself to be wounded by the rape rather than to ignore it numbly, makes her want to be connected to people—even the ones who have hurt her. This may not be the way we want her to "come alive." We might even recoil from this response to a violent assault upon her. Yet I cannot refuse the point Rhys wants to convey. Our standards for success and failure are badly biased toward those who make money, gain power, and can control their own lives completely. Rhys here shows us how she envisions a truly alive human—a woman willing to continue to participate in the world even in the face of trauma and oppression. It is this theme of participation rather than power that is now come to full fruition in her fiction.

## To Find Identity

Rhys challenges my understanding of identity in pointing out the many ways identity is formed in relation to processes through which the self is placed in opposition to others. These oppositions mimic and sustain relations of hierarchy and power. If we continue to uphold these in our theological reflection, we will always remove the *imago Dei* from those who have no power and who fall short of our ideals of fulfilled personhood. Rhys challenges me to shift my understanding of the divine image away from the perfections of power that I (and society) too often

---

73. Heller, "Affliction in Jean Rhys and Simone Weil," 174.
74. Carr, *Jean Rhys*, 73.

equate with God likeness. Like Heidler, by perpetuating them we implicitly image God as a powerful oppressor. By challenging the belief that the *imago Dei* is located in power, Rhys pushes me to reorient my understanding of the image to consider how Godself participates in our weakness and woundedness.

This is why the theories of the *imago Dei* I explored at the beginning of the book struggle to answer the challenge Rhys has pressed upon me. Barth's and Tillich's theories relied heavily on a sense of ability in oneself, which Rhys's women cannot achieve. Cannon's belief that one must understand they do not deserve to be oppressed relies on a self-acceptance that Rhys did not achieve in her life, nor did she allow her characters to enjoy. Rhys, in her isolation and continued marginalization, often blamed herself for her misfortunes or concluded that she was inherently less deserving of love than other people. She recounts in *Smile Please* that her mother believed "black babies were prettier than white ones,"[75] and, as we have seen, she spent much of her life wishing she were Black. She recounts in her autobiography as well: "I am a stranger and I always will be, and after all I didn't really care."[76] This kind of self-blame that Rhys demonstrates challenges the theories of the *imago Dei* Cannon and the other feminist theologians I noted have developed, and so I must allow Rhys's challenges to shape my understanding as well.

Her novels have much to offer beyond her own self-reflection. In dealing with her divided self, she acknowledges the widespread problem of hierarchical oppression and the destructive consequences of identities developed in opposition to each other and to the powerful others. Further, Rhys explores multiple themes of oppression, particularly how women "struggle to survive in the modern world, against the sadistic power of men, poverty, and society."[77] The women, in various ways, are "outsiders among outsiders."[78] Rhys carefully constructs her stories to demonstrate how each of the women are wounded, but also how they wound others. Rhys moves from disconnection to destruction.

Yet she is not so much interested in specifically pointing out the oppression faced by particular groups, but rather, by drawing her reader into the mind of the characters, allows us to see the similarities in the experiences of the disempowered. She is wary of identifying which

75. Rhys, *Smile Please*, 42.
76. Rhys, *Smile Please*, 124.
77. Flynn, "Alternatives and Alterities," 43.
78. Flynn, "Alternatives and Alterities," 2.

groups are most marginalized and she could also be disturbingly racist and classist herself. By multiplying her focus, she is not campaigning for one particular group, but instead attempts to side with those who are misrecognized, abused and excluded in every situation.

## Conclusion

I have read the work of Rhys as a literary challenge to theological thinking as outlined in chapter 3. It sheds light on the occluded experiences of marginalized women, it reveals the complexity of suffering and helps me to begin to imagine ways it can be overcome. It evokes an emotional response in me and enables me to grasp that divine compassion must also be evoked by the suffering it describes. Finally, it challenges me to confront disturbing perspectives that destabilize my own preconceptions and it points to the death in life that is the continuing outcome of oppression and trauma.

In relation to the specific concerns of this research, my readings of Rhys's interwar novels lead me to argue that the *imago Dei* must be able to comprehend the following challenges if it is to speak meaningfully to oppressed and wounded people and point towards transformations in the way we encounter God and others. To begin, it must not be a misdirected attempt at achieving perfection. To simply desire the perceived perfections of God to be imposed upon humanity both excludes a vast amount of humanity, but also presents problematic understandings of God's transcendence as I shall go on to explore further in the next chapter.

Secondly, as it would be impossible for everyone to achieve these characteristics, a requirement of achievement (even when labelled as "courage" or "overcoming") must be rejected. It is a continuation of the very system that places people in positions of oppression and marginalization to attempt to become the oppressor. Even in situations such as Cannon imagined, in which a community is seen as lifting each other into silent dignity, those without community are left behind. Rhys's depiction of interlayered oppressions confronts the notion that everyone has a community—her characters are socially ostracized in so many categories that there is no one left to pull them out of their isolation. Economic paralysis, patriarchal power, hatred of self, and the many other ways they are pushed to the margins ensure that they are unable to receive communal affirmations of their God likeness. In fact, as Rhys has shown, the women believe that they do not deserve such affirmation. The women do not feel a connection to God and lack the power to transform this situation.

In order to build a theory of the *imago Dei* that can effectively include those who resemble the women in Rhys's novels, I must focus instead on the very fact of their woundedness. When we recognize the trauma they have suffered as essential to who they now are we must also seek to understand how this trauma connects them to God. Instead of attempting to erase or ignore their wounds, I must look to them *specifically* to see how God is present within them.

This leads me directly to the vulnerability God demonstrated in the incarnation. If Christ is in fact the true image of God, this event should be primary to understanding how the image is displayed, for it is the way God revealed Godself. By connecting to humanity, God took on the wounds (quite literally) and vulnerabilities of being human—and specifically a human who was in various ways marginalized. Christ took on an intersectional oppressed life, suffering in economic, social, and national ways, even unto death. It is in this self-emptying that God demonstrates love toward us—connecting with humanity not in power, but in wounds.[79] We must then recognize the woundedness of God, and of ourselves, in order to see that it is not our work or ability or even our beliefs that makes us worthy. It is God's recognition of our trauma, and the glimmer of hope God gives by being present within and through trauma. In reading the novels this way, I am challenged to recognize Rhys's women characters as imaging God just as they are. God is not imaged as oppressive and powerful, like Heidler, but instead weak and vulnerable, like Marya. God is imaged in Sasha, who in her woundedness finally affirms her connection.

---

79. The New Testament gives connections between death and the image of God, in fact. Beyond Christ's death, we also see references to the death of the old self. Romans 6 describes the death of the old self, in particular verse 4—"We were therefore buried with him through baptism into death in order that, just as Christ was raised from the dead through the glory of the Father, we too may live a new life" (NIV).

# PART THREE

# Reconstructing a Theory of the *Imago Dei*

# 6

# Reframing Definitions

Trauma and Immanence

## Introduction

As I concluded in the previous chapter, Rhys's work requires me to understand the *imago Dei* in light of the weak, the disconnected and those unable to escape continuing cycles of trauma in their lives. Through understanding Rhys's concerns of marginalization, I also demonstrated that Rhys calls for connection. In their wounds, the characters are united, though most of them do not recognize this. It is the connection of wounds that I now seek to examine.

Encountering Rhys's deeply wounded characters, I can no longer seek a theology of divine likeness that erases or ignores wounds. Instead I must attempt to understand how the *imago Dei* itself incorporates woundedness. People are not only in God's image if they are healed of their wounds. Indeed, their wounds may become an integral part of who they are. Therefore, in beginning to trace a "wounded" image of God, I must consider wounds in relation to Gods own self and ask whether this woundedness is key to the *imago Dei*.

These challenges cause me to look back at the works I began this book by examining. Having surveyed understandings of the *imago Dei* presented in the work of significant theologians from Karl Barth to Katie Cannon, I was dissatisfied primarily because I considered they were in danger of overlooking or eradicating the brokenness which characterizes many people's lives and identities. Even in theories that sought to address the situations and concerns of oppressed groups, representations of the *imago Dei* still seem to implicitly communicate that persons should overcome their suffering—if only inwardly.

Yet, as I have begun to discern through my readings of Rhys's novels, this understanding of the *imago Dei* is inadequate. Furthermore, I am challenged to complicate the idea of innocent victims, wounded by the acts of others, and insist that theological representations of humanity must engage with the morally ambiguous victims as well as complex and ambivalent forces of oppression. Rhys's work requires me to acknowledge that a sense of not belonging, or a lack of community, paired with abuse can lead to a person's actions being destructive to both themselves and others. I think particularly of Anna in *Voyage in the Dark*. Her increasing disconnection led to her own destruction, but she also inflicted great damage upon other people. Many of Rhys's characters similarly appear disassociated from the world and themselves. They are incapable of discovering the silent dignity Cannon celebrates. They also cause hurt by acting out of the trauma they have suffered. Yet, Rhys challenges me to discover the image of God in these figures as well.

In essence, my reading has led me to reflect that theories of the *imago Dei* are consistently seeking to replicate the qualities traditionally attributed to God in human form. We desire that the divine attributes of power and freedom be extended to humanity. Yet if the image is identified primarily within these attributes that represent authority, attributes that are not available to everyone, the image must become the preserve of privileged people. Rhys challenges me to look instead at weakness of those who lack agency and contemplate, through them, the possibility of weakness in God. Through this chapter, I will discuss how brokenness and wounds are not only a significant aspect of our lives but are embraced within God's self also. I will draw upon the work of theologians who are addressing this theme and particularly those who focus on theological responses to suffering or trauma such as Shelley Rambo and Mayra Rivera.

## Brokenness Defined

It is from this challenge that I look specifically to theologies engaging with brokenness in various forms. I use this word in response to the thinking of the Caribbean philosopher Édouard Glissant. His important work, *Poetics of Relation* (1990), defines relation in an entangled manner. We are not merely related to each other superficially, but essentially, though these relations have been broken. He states, "Today the individual, without having to go anywhere, can be directly touched by things elsewhere."[1] This connection, the ability to directly impact others, is what he says allows us to "'know' that the Other is within us and affects how we evolve..."[2] However, acknowledging this and establishing these relations must be a conscious effort. Glissant emphasizes that the world is moving toward relationality, but that this is not yet achieved or always realized. Glissant is inspired by Caribbean thought, which he believes "may be held up as one of the places in the world where Relation presents itself most visibly."[3] Moreover, Caribbean poetics function as a significant resource for Glissant, particularly the work of Derek Walcott, who describes the Caribbean as a "gathering of broken pieces."[4] Imaging the Caribbean as a site of broken pieces coming together to affect each other and be in relation, does not mean that the broken parts disappear. The brokenness, in fact, is important to the relation. Therefore, in discussing brokenness, I highlight both the various ways people are broken and the poetic understanding Glissant has conveyed that a vision of relation does not deny the breaks that have taken place. As Rhys's work demonstrates, these cracks remain and affect how we engage with the world. I think particularly of Sasha, and her many strategies to survive without enduring more hurt. Ultimately, she was unable to protect herself by this withdrawal from life and in recognition of this she began to heal, "to come alive."[5] Her brokenness in fact becomes the way she connects with the *commis*. Therefore, it is vital that I continue to see how these fractures can be both enduring and redeemed.

## Rambo: Looking at Scars

In responding to this understanding of brokenness, and thinking back to Rhys, I want to be sure my analysis acknowledges trauma without

---

1. Glissant, *Poetics of Relation*, 27.
2. Glissant, *Poetics of Relation*, 27
3. Glissant, *Poetics of Relation*, 33.
4. Walcott, "Antilles, Fragments of Epic Memory: The 1992 Nobel Lecture."
5. Rhys, *Good Morning, Midnight*, 182, and see chapter 5.

seeking its erasure. Therefore, I must look at theologians who study trauma without superficially healing it. Too often people are advised to see difficulties or oppression as a means of coming to value alternative aspects of life they might be grateful for or hopeful about. This prevents us giving serious thought to how the event(s) may change people, perhaps for the worse. There are lasting consequences of trauma, and they must be properly understood.

The enduring consequences of brokenness are a major concern in the challenging writing of Shelly Rambo, who focuses much of her work on suffering. Her commitment to both constructive and systematic theology is particularly helpful for me, as this leads her to engage with the traditional doctrine of the *imago Dei* in contemporary and practical ways. Her work explores how Christian theology might be formed both out of and in relation to trauma. In particular, her second book, *Resurrecting Wounds: Living in the Aftermath of Trauma* (2017), explores the ways we might understand and seek healing while not erasing the significance of the scars that trauma leaves. The book is presented in four parts, each exploring a different way Christian theology has dealt with trauma, and she threads these understandings together to generate a theology of suffering that allows wounds to retain enduring significance. Her work, employing both the insights of theopoetics and yet rooted in context and practice, gives an understanding of resurrection that centers upon Christ's death and the wounds that endure in resurrection—rather than on the glorified post-resurrection body so often represented in Christian theology.

It is the focus on scars and the remaining consequences of trauma that are particularly helpful for my work. Like Glissant, Rambo insists that the wounds of events remain. They do not disappear. In relation to this conviction she evaluates John Calvin's commentary on the disciple Thomas and his direct encounter with the wounds of Christ. Rambo is concerned about the theologian's desire to move beyond, and then erase, the trauma this scene embodies. As she explains, Calvin's commentaries were initially sermons. His emphasis is primarily upon convincing his listeners of the effectiveness of receiving truth through hearing without the need for physical proofs. She says, "He wants to turn attention away from the sensuality of touch and instead emphasize that the process of faith is nurtured by way of hearing the word and responding to it."[6] Thus, as he analyses Thomas's words after the death of Jesus, Calvin sees his need to

---

6. Rambo, *Resurrecting Wounds*, 20–21.

see and touch Christ's wounds before believing as "displaying both obstinacy and stupidity."[7] Calvin acknowledges God accommodates Thomas, as God accommodates all human limitations, but this is as a concession to human failure. In her critique of Calvin, Rambo says that his erasure of wounds demonstrates a mistrust of doubt: doubt is lazy, sinful, and unfaithful. Thomas is displayed as an example of human inadequacy.

Instead, Rambo believes Thomas's encounter with Christ's wounds emphasizes God's good cooperation with humanity. She regards the displaying of wounds as not only a response to Thomas's lack of faith, but also a sign of God's redemptive identification with human suffering. She explains, "The marks of the wounds are God's accommodation to human weakness, and they are important insofar as they ensure our salvation."[8] Calvin only sees this accommodation as the result of sin. For him, we are so damaged that God has to allow us to see these wounds to help us believe; it would be better if we could believe without God's assistance.

Rambo questions Calvin's perspective on this matter and offers a much more positive interpretation of woundedness that directly connects with the *imago Dei*, "Why, then, would wounds not be the ultimate sign of limitation and humanity—marks of the human—that would affirm that the full range of humanity is, in the end, united with God?"[9] This statement is essential. Rather than seeing the weakness of humanity as something shameful, Rambo sees God uniting with it and bringing it into relationship with Godself. Her understanding of wounds reminds me again of Glissant's approach to brokenness. The cracks are not only evidence of trauma, but of relationship. Christ's wounds mark his body eternally, demonstrating God's suffering. God has embraced humanity, and the embrace includes and empowers the marked bodies of real human lives. Yet also, God is affected by God's participation with humanity—not just affected but wounded. Therefore, not only are we transformed by encounter with God, but God is transformed as well.

In Rambo's estimation, the love of God not only allows us to touch Christ's wounds, but invites such encounters. Christ's physical body is essential to the reconciling work, and therefore, the wounds are important to the resurrection. As Jessica Coblentz states in her review of Rambo's text, "Healing is not a clean break. Christ's marked body discloses the enduring presence of suffering's wounds within resurrected life. In fact,

7. Rambo, *Resurrecting Wounds*, 22.
8. Rambo, *Resurrecting Wounds*, 29.
9. Rambo, *Resurrecting Wounds*, 33.

wounds serve as ongoing sites of resurrection, though not in the instrumental fashion of redemptive suffering."[10]

Rambo's critique of Calvin emphasizes his failure to "give meaning to an important juncture in which things are shifting."[11] She continues to explain this, saying, "The danger in erasing these wounds is that the erasure occludes a testimony to what is most difficult about traumatic histories, whether personal or collective: that the wounds remain."[12] This notion is essential to consider. As I have emphasized, in revisioning the *imago Dei* our previous definitions of "weakness" or "flaw" must be revisited, and Rambo's work allows us to do so through a direct look at wounds. What we might have wished could be erased, instead, allows us to achieve a deeper comprehension of God's presence in the world.

In understanding the healing or resurrection that accompanies these wounds, Rambo allows us to fully grasp that wounding (or trauma) does not distance us from God. My first significant insight into the *imago Dei* gained from Rambo's work, then, is this understanding that wounds not only remain but must be acknowledged and understood. Allowing wounds to tell their story, and to recognizing the importance of that story, is central to understanding of the healing that accompanies those wounds. It must be particular and personal. Again, I look back to the challenges literature brings to theology. Rhys's penetrating depictions of the complexity of the wounds her characters suffer allow me to truly see them in their woundedness. In observing the wound, Rambo explains, we can then allow the wound to be acknowledged while also working toward true healing rather than erasure.

Secondly, I wish to highlight the claim that God is transformed in relation to human wounding and woundedness. In insisting that God embraces our wounds, Rambo also discusses the suffering God experiences in incarnation, drawing us from the experience of Thomas further toward the drama of God's relation with the world. In this, her perspective accords with that of panentheist theologians, like Mayra Rivera (whose work I consider further below) that the reconciliation between God and the world is a recreation. This recreation, she says, "is a reorientation *to* the world."[13] Like Rivera, Rambo insists that God is concerned with and affected by our lived experiences, and that because of God's interaction

---

10. Coblentz, Review of "Resurrecting Wounds," 497.
11. Rambo, *Resurrecting Wounds*, 42.
12. Rambo, *Resurrecting Wounds*, 42.
13. Rambo, *Resurrecting Wounds*, 41.

with the world, the world can be transformed to the likeness of God. Again, drawing insights from Glissant, the fractures in relations paradoxically serve to connect God and the world more fully. Rambo believes the transformation from wounds is something that involves both us and God. To demonstrate this, I return to Rambo's discussion of the story of Thomas, and the physicality of Jesus's wounds. She says:

> [W]hen Jesus appears to the disciples, he presents them with wounds . . . The memory comes forward in order to surface wounds, but it also brings the possibility that wounds, once surfaced, may yield something new . . . Suddenly, what they think they see is altered by the presencing of wounds . . . Through dismantling sight, Jesus opens the disciples to a kind of witness that involves affective work, signaled through his invocation of breath and touch. He turns them to the wounds and to the surface of skin. He invites them closer to touch.[14]

Jesus exposes the wounds and allows the physicality of breath and touch to begin the healing. Rambo reminds us that Jesus also promises the paraclete in this moment, bringing the Spirit who will "guide them into truth."[15] Therefore, the wounds themselves become the way of healing. They are now "a productive site in which difficult memories are held (and not erased); they can also be the site of potential transformation . . . "[16]

Looking at Thomas's story, Rambo reminds us that God took on these wounds. As she says, "Christianity is distinctive in its claim that God suffers."[17] God embraced the world in a way that interlaces divinity with humanity so that the suffering of the world also marks God. In being marked in this way, God can then enact healing: the resurrection Christ brings through his wounds. In a similar redemptive process, allowing the memories of woundings to affect us can be part of the process of healing. She says, "The wounds can be a productive site in which difficult memories are held (and not erased); they can also be the site of potential transformation, in which the crossing of memories might bring about healing."[18] This move generates an understanding of atonement that declares God does not require suffering to achieve redemption, but instead sees God as affected by us, freely choosing to take on suffering in order to empower us and

14. Rambo, *Resurrecting Wounds*, 87.
15. Rambo, *Resurrecting Wounds*, 89.
16. Rambo, *Resurrecting Wounds*, 92.
17. Rambo, *Resurrecting Wounds*, 88.
18. Rambo, *Resurrecting Wounds*, 91–92.

even in order to enable us to attend to our own wounds. In light of this, the atonement is God achieving reconciliation with the world through the incarnation of Christ, in suffering and woundedness.

Continuing her focus on how woundedness might enable the development of a liberative theology, Rambo then turns to highlight the suffering of God in light of Black theology, particularly through the work of James Cone. As I discussed earlier in this book, Cone points to a Black Jesus to demonstrate the oppressive and traumatic experiences Jesus endured and how these are mirrored in the experience of Black people. Understanding this, Rambo uses this section of her book to further explore how suffering and redemption are intertwined. She, however, explains that we must first surface the wounds—we must gaze upon the cross, even as we find it horrific. Horror is mixed with redemption, but Rambo points out that we cannot ignore the horror and only look for the redemption. Citing theologian Willie Jennings, she says that white theology has too long focused solely on redemption as a means of avoiding complicity in suffering and injustice. She says this willed blindness is false, and states:

> Christian theology is produced by erasing wounds. It sanitizes and purifies. Theology birthed from this wound is dependent on ongoing practices of erasing these origins. It insists on pure beginnings that hover above the soil. And if and when theology hovers above the soil, it denies harm done to bodies on the ground.[19]

We cannot ignore the suffering being done. Further, we must also see the complex roles we play in prolonging the suffering. As Rhys demonstrates, we are often also complicit in suffering, even if we are victims. We must confront the wounds in order to understand them, and in looking particularly at racism, Rambo notes that we must see how different responses are required when acknowledging wounds.

Here Rambo cites author Wendell Berry, who "narrates racism within the United States by employing the image of a hidden wound."[20] Berry believes that racism is a "collective wound" within the United States, but this does not mean it is equally shared or that we can respond in the same ways. Instead, we must understand our particular roles in the

---

19. Rambo, *Resurrecting Wounds*, 77.
20. Rambo, *Resurrecting Wounds*, 71.

wounding, acknowledge how the wound is caused, and then accept our roles and responsibilities in relation to healing.

At this point Rambo directly discusses Christianity's role in the wound of racism. While it claims to be a healing faith, "'White man's Christianity' renders the Christian story in a particular way, offering a justification of white superiority."[21] Therefore, the "sacred bandages" of Christianity are trying to conceal the wounds rather than heal them.[22] Here, she returns to James Cone's theology of the cross, saying that it "offers both judgment and healing," again stressing the varied ways suffering laces through humanity.[23] While we must all look to the cross, as we must acknowledge wounds, our responses must be different. White America must "turn to the cross to see the suffering that they have enacted there."[24] Therefore, it is my responsibility to acknowledge what I, and my inherited legacy, have done to wound others. I cannot forget how I am implicated in racism and must work to repent of this. Looking at the cross must change me radically so that I actively work toward a healed world. Rambo also addresses the intersectional oppression of Black women, employing Melissa Harris-Perry's image of a crooked room. The crooked room, she explains, is the predicament of Black women in the United States. Their attempt to stand straight is hindered by this room, and they can become so used to the crooked room that they believe the room to be "oriented correctly."[25] Harris-Perry believes the problem is in recognition—Black women are not recognized meaningfully and then "wounds cannot surface, truths cannot be told."[26] As I discussed previously, Cannon believes that the silent grace of Black women is to believe they do not deserve the treatment they receive. Even if they cannot overcome their situation, they can believe themselves worthy of better. What I questioned then, and Rambo highlights here, is the possibility that some will not achieve this silent grace. Misrecognition may define the ways the oppressed sees themselves as well as others, and like Rhys's women, they may not resist their oppression but accept and perhaps perpetuate it.

Furthermore, a theory of the redemption of suffering can lead to a valorization of suffering, which Rambo warns us against. She explains

21. Rambo, *Resurrecting Wounds*, 74.
22. Rambo, *Resurrecting Wounds*, 74.
23. Rambo, *Resurrecting Wounds*, 75.
24. Rambo, *Resurrecting Wounds*, 75.
25. Rambo, *Resurrecting Wounds*, 85.
26. Rambo, *Resurrecting Wounds*, 86.

that when we look at a redemption that requires sacrifice, we begin to see Christ as a "soldier-saviour."[27] This common theme in certain atonement theories has led to a problematic connection between Christianity and the "American war story,"[28] which she then examines in the final section of her book on veterans' healing. She reminds us of Thomas's story, affirming again that redemption is embodied here as "a vision of communal care" rather than a sacrificial suffering.[29] Jesus's suffering came as a consequence of his life, and God's embrace of the full range of humanity. Rather than a victory narrative, we need the sense of physical presence and the breath of the Spirit released into the room. Theology, Rambo says, "can reposition suffering so that it may be engaged rather than idealized."[30] Therefore, Rambo cautions us that the atonement is not merely to be seen through the cross. Jesus's suffering there is not where redemption happens. Instead, she says, the redemption is the recreation of that suffering. Through the work of Delores Williams, she explains that the cross demonstrates the destruction of the life Jesus offers us. The cross is the wounding. Yet, in the resurrection, Jesus offers recreation to that life. This, Williams argues, is a revaluation— "the return of Jesus, the defiled one, reassigns value to those denied value."[31] The wounds are not covered or erased, but examined in order to present value to those "the world deems of little value."[32]

In concluding her work, Rambo reemphasizes three points she believes brings theology into conversation with wounding. First, she says that "wounds cannot be easily seen or accessed."[33] We must be willing to truly look, to touch, to listen. It takes invitation, as Jesus invited Thomas to touch his wounds. Secondly, she "emphasize[s] that a spirit is breathed into this place."[34] Jesus breathed new life into the room, and recreation transformed the disciples. Finally, a "new community is formed and given shape."[35] New valuations are able to move us forward, transforming the world. I look back to my analysis in chapter 1 of Lisa

27. Rambo, *Resurrecting Wounds*, 113.
28. Rambo, *Resurrecting Wounds*, 113.
29. Rambo, *Resurrecting Wounds*, 113.
30. Rambo, *Resurrecting Wounds*, 141.
31. Rambo, *Resurrecting Wounds*, 102.
32. Rambo, *Resurrecting Wounds*, 107.
33. Rambo, *Resurrecting Wounds*, 147.
34. Rambo, *Resurrecting Wounds*, 147.
35. Rambo, *Resurrecting Wounds*, 147.

Stephenson's understanding of the *imago Dei*.[36] We "[look] the other in the eye" in order to assist the other, to be assisted by the other, and to recognize the impossibility of being "an 'I' without a 'Thou.'"[37] It is in this way, as in Glissant's understanding of relation, that we affect each other in our brokenness. I think specifically here of Rhys's portrayal of Sasha's "coming alive." It was in a moment of violence and hurt that her desire to be connected to others returned. Brokenness is not to be ignored or avoided, but instead may become the means that allows us to be in true relation with each other.

## Brokenness and God

Having developed an understanding of how woundedness can become integral to relationship, I now seek to further explore how we might explore God's interaction with, or redemption of, human brokenness in the light of this. Here I keep in mind the challenges drawn from Katie Cannon and womanist theology to avoid requiring overcoming in those who suffer, whilst practicing silent grace. I also keep in mind my challenge from Rhys that even such silent grace may not be attainable for many. As Glissant teaches, I must focus on the brokenness, looking for God's work within these cracks. In doing this, I turn to systematic theologian Serene Jones and her work on trauma and grace. Jones places trauma within the context of *imago Dei* by declaring that human beings embody God's will despite the marks of sin and separation they bear. As she explains:

> I would recall the doctrines of justification and sanctification and the truth they insist upon: that in the very moment we are marked as sinful by the world, God marks us as loved, as recipients of divine forgiveness. Marked in this way, we are freed to act not as perfect creatures, but as fallen people who are nonetheless called to persistently seek ways to embody God's will for the flourishing of all creation.[38]

Jones argues that in trauma we can look to God's presence for grace that transforms. Jones sees a transformation of trauma not as overcoming or

---

36. See chapter 1, page 17.

37. Stephenson, "Directed, Ordered and Related: The Male and Female Interpersonal Relation in Karl Barth's *Church Dogmatics*," 439.

38. Jones, *Trauma and Grace*, 37.

erasing of woundedness, but instead requiring "new imaginings"[39] that themselves emerge out of the context of trauma itself.

*Trauma and Grace* (2009) explores the way in which the Christian Church can declare God already present in traumatic events and the way Christians can both lament and hope in the wake of trauma. Two particular sections in her book explain this juxtaposition and serve as useful comparisons to Rambo's dialogue with Calvin. Jones also turns to his work and employs his *Commentary on the Psalms* as containing a methodical three step process to living with and restoring trauma.

This is seemingly quite a different view of Calvin than Rambo offers in her critique of his commentary. Yet, in following more closely the three steps Jones describes, I maintain we might develop a rather a more positive appreciation of Calvin's position than Rambo offers. To begin, Jones identifies the three steps in psalmody: "psalms of deliverance, psalms of lamentation, and psalms of thanksgiving."[40] The first, psalms of deliverance, represent an articulation of the reality of wounding people suffer. Here, Calvin sees the psalmist asking God for help in specific circumstances, crying aloud against the trauma of evil. Like Thomas asking to touch the wounds, this is the request for God's intervention. Yet, instead of seeing Calvin dismiss this request as demonstrating the sinfulness of humanity, Jones focuses on Calvin's belief in God's intervention. Jones does not deny that Calvin sees weakness or sin in humanity, but instead understands Calvin to care more about God's response. She says, "With this stabilization comes the possibility of imagining that one is, in the most ultimate sense, safe. It becomes possible to imagine that the deepest truth about oneself is that God loves you."[41]

The second step, the psalms of lament, are understood as Calvin's reminder that the pain people experience should be released, as "groans of the violated,"[42] so that they can begin to mourn. Once this is done, the third stage follows in "psalms of thanksgiving," which are able to occur because the wounds are healed. Rambo believed this requirement for healed wounds was an erasure, but Jones does not agree. She states, "What is crucial, therefore, is not to have the pain disappear or the forces

---

39. Jones, *Trauma and Grace*, 21.
40. Jones, *Trauma and Grace*, 55.
41. Jones, *Trauma and Grace*, 56.
42. Jones, *Trauma and Grace*, 59.

of violence cease to bear down upon us, but to reduce the hold ... [it] has upon ... the one who suffers."[43] Jones explains:

> What is also remarkable is how Calvin accomplished this reintegration into the mundane: not by pretending that the traumas never happened or will somehow magically disappear because they have been remembered and mourned, but rather by allowing the reality of violence testified to in the first two types of psalms to continue to echo through the praising prayers of this third type of psalm.[44]

While I think Jones's commentary on this process is a persuasive reading of Calvin's work, I must agree with Rambo that it can be difficult to avoid attempts to erase or forget the wounds when the emphasis still falls so strongly on healing. Instead, a balance between the two views is necessary, particularly as I look to understand how trauma changes both God and humanity, while not allowing woundedness to destroy us. Jones's way of articulating how brokenness must be allowed to remain, as Glissant encourages, is a vital step in her being able to affirm praise and rejoicing later.

Continuing to look at trauma, Jones then moves from the psalms to examine the Gospel of Mark, in its original inconclusive state.[45] By leaving the women in a state of shock, refusing the tidy ending of the other gospels, she believes this ending gives space to the trauma of the Cross. It allows those suffering to see that this trauma isn't merely "gotten over," but that it lingers in post resurrection experience. Yet, in this, God is still present. There is a hope of transformation in the resurrection of Christ. She says, "Expecting the world to be broken and expecting grace to come—it is the air and gravity of sin-grace imagination. That's what makes Christians such inveterate hopers. In our minds,

---

43. Jones, *Trauma and Grace*, 63.
44. Jones, *Trauma and Grace*, 63.
45. She says in her introduction: "I further suggest that we resist giving Mark a cohesive ending but instead use his non-ending to remind us that, in a world filled with vast and unresolved traumas, Jesus comes to us anyway, in the midst of our faltering speech, our shattered memories, and our frayed sense of agency. This is truly what grace is, in its most radical form: not the reassuring ending of an orderly story, but the incredible insistence on love amid fragmented, unraveled human lives" (xiii). The final verse, then, is Mark 16:8 (ESV), "[The women] went out and fled from the tomb, for terror and astonishment had seized them; and they said nothing to anyone, for they were afraid."

something is always about to happen. And then it does."[46] The broken remains and the rejoicing will come but allowing both to fully exist is integral to the Christian faith. This is, for Jones, a living out of Calvin's three steps. It is acknowledging the trauma, crying to God, and then hoping for redemption.

Jones's theology of trauma brings me back to the glimmer of hope I see in *Good Morning, Midnight*. While the trauma of that fateful end is not resolved, and we are left with only variously problematic interpretations of what has happened. The hope that I see in that novel is like the hope Jones sees in the ending of the Gospel of Mark. It is the unexplained belief that God will transform the brokenness. Again, I quote her:

> The cross trains us in these dispositions of body and imagination. It narrates for us, again and again, two paradoxical stories about who we are: God's inevitably broken children, and God's constantly renewed beloved; these two stories run down parallel tracks of flesh and soul. They are not, however, driven toward evolving resolution. We are not becoming better or worse: we just are these two things, in the juxtaposed tension of our everyday life.[47]

As Rhys does not allow us to see her female characters "become better," Jones does not require improvement. This tension allows for those broken pieces to come together to form the Relation Glissant talks about. As he explains, this relation is "not merely an encounter . . . but a new and original dimension allowing each person to be there and elsewhere, rooted and open, lost in the mountains and free beneath the sea, in harmony and in errantry."[48] Therefore this tension brings us into a new state of being where a form of reconciliation without the eradication of wounded identities can take place.

## The Immanence of God

The theological interrogation of brokenness I have undertaken with reference to the work of Rambo and Jones now prompts me to inquire further into the ways in which God meets us in and engages with our trauma. Traditionally Christians have stressed God's immanence as a

---

46. Jones, *Trauma and Grace*, 154.
47. Jones, *Trauma and Grace*, 165.
48. Glissant, *Poetics*, 34.

way of comprehending how God fully enters into the "travails" of creation at every level, while maintaining this in tension with the belief that God is also transcendent. However, reflections on the immanent presence of God can be overshadowed by a felt need to stress and defend transcendence. As Barth declared, God is an ineffable Other,[49] and some have seen this radical otherness in conflict with God's immanent presence in creation. As I continue to develop my research on the *imago Dei*, I must now engage with contemporary theological struggles to reimagine immanence and transcendence. As I strive to comprehend God's image in wounded humanity, I must locate this in a wider understanding of the relation God has with the world. To form this, I begin with a critical examination of Catherine Keller's panentheist understanding of God as immanent within the processes of becoming that pattern the universe and the life of all creatures.

### Keller's Immanence and My Questions

To begin, Barth's insistence on God's separateness is disputed in Keller's works on the doctrine of God. Practicing a hermeneutics of suspicion, she sees a patriarchal hierarchy operative in his theology particularly in his conception of otherness. Her work regularly focuses on how gendered power is encoded within hierarchical social models and theologies. She is particularly concerned that these types of understandings of God directly impact upon social relationships in the world. It is within this context that her disagreement with Barth is played out. Reacting against "the individualism of the Enlightenment," she says, "his reinscription of the *imago dei* as relational rather than an ontological endowment"[50] demonstrates his understanding that human beings do not represent God's image in their essential being. This allows Barth to maintain that God must be conceived as wholly other, and for Keller, this means that God retains "absolute" difference.[51] Barth's insistence on the difference and the total sovereignty of God sustains the patriarchal and domineering social order Keller seeks to overcome. She says, "Barth seems to have transferred to the Lord's account our most modern claims

---

49. "Whichever way I look, God is hidden for me and I am blind to Him" (Barth, *Church Dogmatics* I/2, 29).
50. Keller, *Face of the Deep*, 48.
51. Keller, *Face of the Deep*, 87.

to certainty and property."⁵² For Barth, this is done in order to differentiate creature and Creator. However, in this, she argues that he has made a Creator who deals in domination; the form of domination that has "driven women to the shelters."⁵³ Furthermore, Keller argues this kind of omnipotence and separation from creation is part of Barth's understanding of a hierarchical cosmic order. This order is such an important part of Barth's theological worldview that it "takes precedence over any other understanding of relationship."⁵⁴

Although opposing violence against women, Barth equally opposes women asserting their autonomy in opposition to the divinely ordered system in which they might find their fulfilment.⁵⁵ Keller argues that this vision supports a patriarchal system by implying women's submission to male headship is integral to their response to God.⁵⁶ As demonstrated previously, critics of Barth argue that this perspective leaves women forever vulnerable to male oppression. Keller objects to Barth's doctrine of God on these grounds and further questions whether understandings of divinity that maintain a hierarchical order and separateness between creator and creation can ever lead to anything other than domination. For her, any discussion of God as entirely outside of us requires God to be oppressively above us. Therefore, she sees Barth's understanding of God's freedom and power as oppressive, linking it with a warrior ethos that develops a need to possess because of the anxiety of nonbeing.⁵⁷ Instead, Keller represents the world and God as connected essentially. She likens it to connections within the body, saying that differences between the hand, wrist, and arm do not allow us to separate them without damaging them.⁵⁸ These are ideas she elaborates further in her book *On the Mystery* (2008) in which she explains:

> Because we are radically interdependent, we are unbearably vulnerable to each other. We are each other's power. But power does not mean dominance. Power is manifest concretely in the flow of influence, the flow of me into your experience, of you

---

52. Keller, *Face of the Deep*, 90.
53. Keller, *Face of the Deep*, 90.
54. Keller, *Face of the Deep*, 95.
55. Keller, *Face of the Deep*, 96.
56. Keller, *Face of the Deep*, 96.
57. Keller, *Face of the Deep*, 23.
58. Keller, *Face of the Deep*, 192.

into mine, by which we consciously and unconsciously affect each other.[59]

In this frame God's power, or influence, is expressed in participation rather than control. Keller's book *From a Broken Web* (1988) explores the intertwined relationship she sees between God and creation. In discussing relationship with God, she argues that traditional models that see God as self-sufficient are "a bizarre double standard."[60] This view of God "is the absolute instance of the traditional sin" of being "curved in upon himself."[61] God, she argues, must be interdependent with creation or else incapable of truly loving the world.[62] Likewise, she believes that we must be interdependent—or immanent- to each other in order to truly image God.[63]

In discussing imaging God, again, we must continue to remember the relation model as outlined by Glissant. As Keller states, the divine/human relation leads to the "crown of thorns, not domination".[64] Relation means seeing the wounds of the other, and as I demonstrated through Jones and Rambo, allowing those wounds to remain as we see in the example of Jesus. Keller here offers an important insight into the *imago Dei* through developing this perspective. She sees God's participation in the world as risk—that is God risks being weakened by us. Likewise, then, the *imago Dei* requires risk in human beings also. Here, she explains:

> . . . in the name of our humanity in the image of God, we are empowered not to lord it over others, nor to settle into a serene and dispassionate piety, but to risk an adventure? To go off on an uncertain journey? To take untoward chances?[65]

We must be willing to risk in love, to venture and be wounded, but always to be connected. In this, we are in the image of a likewise connected and loving God.

Keller's book, *Intercarnations* (2017), explores this theme of entanglement more thoroughly. Again, stating that an understanding of God in which God is "over" or "other than" creation necessitates dominion, she

59. Keller, *On The Mystery*, 80.
60. Keller, *From a Broken Web*, 38.
61. Keller, *From a Broken Web*, 38
62. Keller, *From a Broken Web*, 33–38.
63. Keller, *From a Broken Web*, 19.
64. Keller, *From a Broken Web*, 86.
65. Keller, *From a Broken Web*, 92–93.

expands the concept of the Incarnation of Christ into "Intercarnations." Incarnation is too limited an idea, she explains, and there are ancient Christian traditions (of theosis or theopoesis) that see incarnation as a process that extends outwards into all creation and the purpose of which is to fully embody the divine. Intercarnation "witnesses to the multiplication and entanglement of any and all becoming flesh."[66] This expansion allows Keller to understand God as continually embodied through the whole of creation, rather than entirely focusing on the singular incarnation of Christ. For her, this means that the importance of Creation is elevated, signifying the importance of, particularly, oppressed and marginalized groups. In explaining that God is in relation with the world, she presses that this means "bodies matter"[67]—and this statement must be a claim made within the particularities of the world in which God is embodied. She goes on, "And so, for example, at a particular moment in history—not as exception but precisely as exemplification of a deep history—intercarnation means: black bodies matter."[68] In my continuing focus upon woundedness and with the conviction that the realities of each person's experience must be seen and understood in order to truly be in relation, I see that Keller is also stressing God's particular interaction with the wounds of the world as it is at its ugliest. Furthermore, to see God imaged in those who struggle to state "Black Lives Matter" is to see God risking and participating in the world.

In order to develop her liberative theological approach further, Keller turns to theopoetics, which she describes as "a currently vibrant node of radical theology."[69] She traces the development of theopoetics from "ancient theopoiesis to a modernist and then a current theopoetics."[70] Through this journey, she emphasizes the entangled nature of God and Creation in inextricable relationship. The Incarnation, she believes, "gets radically redistributed as the becoming divine of us all,"[71] and thus theopoetics deals with how we are involved in "Cosmic God-making."[72] This God-making does not mean we are "making God up,"[73] but affirms hu-

---

66. Keller, *Intercarnations*, 2.
67. Keller, *Intercarnations*, 5.
68. Keller, *Intercarnations*, 5.
69. Keller, *Intercarnations*, 106.
70. Keller, *Intercarnations*, 107.
71. Keller, *Intercarnations*, 108.
72. Keller, *Intercarnations*, 110.
73. Keller, *Intercarnations*, 110.

manity participates in the divine making of the world. Keller's thinking here is aligned to process theology, particularly as developed out of the philosophy of Alfred Whitehead, in emphasizing the divine becoming of all creatures. She states, "The image of God is the image of the creature magnified"[74] and the world can thus be imaged as "God's body."[75] In her book *Cloud of the Impossible*, she sees God as intertwined with nature, co-creating with humanity, and embodied by the diversity of creation rather than the singularity of Christ. She says:

> So the alpha and the omega, in this co-incident, fold not into providential predetermination but nonseparable difference. "I am the Alpha and the Omega"—but not necessarily the Origin and the End. And it is that difference which comes before us at any moment—familiar or strange, soft or monstrous, the Other, the Others, the Hyperobject. It mirrors back to ourselves enigmatically. It calls to us in the interplay of question and answer. And it selectively contracts a cosmos in which I am already enfolded.[76]

Because of this view of God-in-Creation, Keller believes we must be more open to the mystery and uncertainty of theology. Theology is not static, since creation is ever growing and evolving, and therefore rather than pursuing a logocentric theology, she prefers theopoetics, a creative and "eventive"[77] exploration of the divine. We are entangled with the Earth, each other, and the divine, and therefore must be concerned with the events of creation in this "cosmic solidarity."[78]

Keller's theopoetics is inspiring and, particularly in light of experiences of trauma, issues a clear call to active concern for the world. Her work, particularly her emphasis on God's essential connection to the world, enables me to see the world as essentially connected to God in turn. As such, it presses upon us the demand to truly encounter others. I will now pursue further the attempt to form a reimaging of the *imago Dei* that stresses God's risky particular and relational participation in the world. The postcolonial theologian Mayra Rivera focuses on issues of gender, race, and postcolonial liberation theology. Like Rhys, her work engages with the intersectional oppressions that constrain identity and also offers

74. Keller, *Intercarnations*, 109.
75. See *Intercarnations* page 113 for exposition on this.
76. Keller, *Cloud of the Impossible*, 287.
77. Keller, *Cloud of the Impossible*, 113.
78. Keller, *Cloud of the Impossible*, 118.

further insights into how human traumas might become sources of theological insight. Particularly significant for my work is her particular focus upon embodiment as the place of encounter between humanity, the world and God which has clear implications for understanding the *imago Dei*. I am also drawn to her because her focus on Latina and Caribbean perspectives resonates with the work of Rhys.

## Rivera: Interaction as Transformation

Rivera's book *The Touch of Transcendence: A Postcolonial Theology of God* begins with a critical interrogation of the concept of God's "otherness." She first discusses Karl Barth's insistence on the ineffability of God. She says that "for Barth [the] reality of God shattered all human cognitive schemes and rendered human understanding of God as ignorance."[79] Though she has some sympathy with Barth's perspective, it leads her to a different conclusion. She agrees that God is "irreducibly Other."[80] However, for her this does not constitute this kind of incomprehensible distance that it implies for Barth. While Barth's theology is systematically formed by a belief that people cannot know God in Godself other than through God's self-revelation, Rivera instead insists that we can identify God's interactions with us in our embodied, everyday reality and thus recognized they can transform us. Rivera's theology more closely aligns with Keller's in this regard and so these interactions and participations in the world are seen as revelatory of God in process within the world.

Though God is transcendent, or in her preferred term, "beyond,"[81] she does not see this in terms of incompatible difference. In looking directly to postcolonial theology, she sees an essential connection in this beyondness. She explains:

> In postcolonial criticism, the beyond (and therefore transcendence, I will argue) becomes inextricable from the witness of oppressed communities . . . In this postcolonial vision, transformation emerges from the encounters with the otherness beyond.[82]

---

79. Rivera, *Touch of Transcendence*, 4.

80. Rivera, *Touch of Transcendence*, 2.

81. Rivera, *Touch of Transcendence*, 13. For Rivera, beyond indicates that while we cannot "grasp" God, we can touch God. This is then a relational "beyond," rather than indicating God as "far away."

82. Rivera, *Touch of Transcendence*, 13.

Transcendence is thus not a distance that cannot be bridged, as Barth argued. It is, instead, experienced in active encounters with others. God's encounters with us are the events that allow us to transform, and it is this transformation that Rivera sees as the key to transcendence. Her view, like Keller's, emphasizes the connection God has to the world in essence. Shelly Rambo says of Rivera's understanding of God's interaction with the world, "The gospel . . . interacts with and transforms in relationship to spirit, body, and bread."[83]

Rivera's understanding of God's presence also draws her to liberation theology, which continues the shaping of her view on trauma. As Rivera explains, liberation theology affirms an "immanent human value,"[84] and this must cause us to revisit the tension between God's transcendence and the idea of immanence. Rather than posing these as oppositional terms she says that "transcendence flows through reality as the sap through the branches of a tree."[85] It does not contradict but rather consolidates our inherent relationship with an Other that is God, but also with all of creation. We are not merely, as she says, "'non-identical repetitions' [quoting Radical Orthodoxy theologian John Milbank] of our relations to the intimate but ineffable God."[86] We are not just a likeness of God, then, but bound to all other creatures in God's living body.

In emphasizing that such integral relations also imply ethical responsibilities, Rivera turns to the work of Emmanuel Levinas and Enrique Dussel to emphasize the importance of relational transformation. Out of their reflections upon the violence of totalizing systems these thinkers developed forms of philosophical ethics which locate transcendence in the world changing encounter with another who is different to myself. She says, "In the face of the Other, they argue, we are encountered by transcendence."[87] She quotes Levinas's warning, "Stop seeing real Jews, and it's easy for people to believe lies. Jews are lazy. Jews are ugly. Jews are evil. Day after day."[88] However, failure to recognize the challenge of transcendence in the other does not only lead to prejudice and violence. The face of the other is what calls us out of our own imminence and into selfhood She continues to use his work to

83. Rambo, Review of *Poetics of the Flesh* by Mayra Rivera, 126.
84. Rivera, *Touch of Transcendence*, 49.
85. Rivera, *Touch of Transcendence*, 53.
86. Rivera, *Touch of Transcendence*, 54.
87. Rivera, *Touch of Transcendence*, 55.
88. Rivera, *Touch of Transcendence*, 57.

argue that it is this openness to the Other through others that enables self-transformation. When we are open, we are allowing the other to affect us and constitute our own becoming. A theme which I have traced repeatedly through my readings of Rhys.

Rivera's exegesis of Jesus's story of the sheep and the goats in Matthew 25 is particularly relevant here. Jesus demanded generosity to those who are hungry and poor, and affirmed that showing kindness to them was showing kindness to him. In Rivera's terms in such acts of solidarity we are practicing our openness to God and encountering transcendence in our midst. In concluding this chapter, she says:

> Taking infinity as our primary metaphor of transcendence, however, we attempt to offer a model that emphasizes the infinite openness and singularity of the other person, within the particularity and complexity of her/his context . . . This notion of relational transcendence should not extract transcendence from the finitude of the person (imagining it as something outside or disguised behind "mere presences"). Instead, it will seek to affirm the "presence" of the "infinite in the finite, the more in the less."[89]

Rivera is demonstrating the *imago Dei* is recognized and practically affirmed in transformative behavior towards the others that is quite literally affirmed as recognizing God through them. This functional movement of transcendence as transformation and transformation as openness to the other can be moved into a focused construction of an active ethic of the *imago Dei* which I find deeply compelling.

In concluding her book Rivera reflects on the "glory of God."[90] God's transcendence means that God's glory is both "hidden and revealed"[91] in creation and is always to be discerned in the midst of life and through our encounters with others and some of these may be deeply wounding. We are all marked by encounters, as Rambo showed Jesus is marked by his encounter with us. Rivera's focus is that our scars, or our marks of encounter, transform us. She says, "As self and Other emerge from the interhuman encounter, as they come forth as new creatures, scars become transfigured in the divine embrace."[92] Therefore, it is in reflecting God that we encounter the other as God would—in love. We also see that

---

89. Rivera, *Touch of Transcendence*, 82.
90. Rivera, *Touch of Transcendence*, 138.
91. Rivera, *Touch of Transcendence*, 139.
92. Rivera, *Touch of Transcendence*, 139.

the other is reflecting God in the encounter and marked by our actions. Rivera says, "We aspire to give and receive that which may open for us new paths for continuous liberation: a love that renounces its consuming impulses while opening itself to be touched by the Other."[93]

This theme is explored further in her more recent book, *Poetics of the Flesh* (2015). In describing her use of poetics here, Rivera utilizes Glissant's *Poetics of Relation*. In his work, as she explains, "poetics refers not only to styles of writing, but also modes of knowing, being, and acting in the world."[94] Glissant sees "gathering the broken pieces" as the poetic work of making new beauty.[95] The transformation Glissant describes, Rivera uses to show that it is not an erasure of wounds but an understanding of the intertwined nature of life and death.[96] She describes the ways in which our flesh is marked by our experiences, our relationships, for both good and ill. However, she refuses to see these markings (even the scarring ones) as depreciating for they are the embodied signs of our relationship with others and with God. She explains:

> We inhabit the same world. This means that the body I experience is tied to the experiences that others have of my body. I can feel empathy for others. I can incarnate the gestures and words of others. I can be wounded by them.[97]

Yet, even as we are affected by and effect the world, there is still for her a focus on love. She continues:

> In Christian texts, God is the initiator and model for such an embrace of flesh. Infusing earth with love, God creates. Becoming flesh, in birth and suffering, God re-creates. Christians are called to remember these stories, to see themselves in the transformations that they depict, to imitate God and be born again.[98]

As Glissant takes broken pieces to make a new creation, Rivera insists that our transformation in relation to God allows us to poetically reconceive our lived experiences. This poetics gives us the ability to "keep us open to others, to sense the entanglements of our carnal relations."[99]

93. Rivera, *Touch of Transcendence*, 140.
94. Rivera, *Poetics of the Flesh*, 2.
95. Rivera, *Poetics of the Flesh*, 3.
96. Rivera, *Poetics of the Flesh*, 24.
97. Rivera, *Poetics of the Flesh*, 145.
98. Rivera, *Poetics of the Flesh*, 154.
99. Rivera, *Poetics of the Flesh*, 158.

Rivera's ability to allow for brokenness is crucial. In Rivera's work I begin to find some answers to the challenges reading Rhys raised for me. Rhys's characters were wounded by the world, as well as being the ones to wound, and these complicated marks on their flesh should not be ignored or erased. However, I am reminded that my reading of Rhys compels me to find the image of God without emphasizing ability. Rivera allows for brokenness, yet in her calls for transformational unity, I am still struck with the requirements placed upon people.

Here, I briefly refer to disability theologian Sharon Betcher, and her work "Flesh of My Flesh." While I cannot devote adequate time to a full exploration of her work, I do believe her critique of Rivera's position is necessary here. As she concludes her article, Betcher notes postcolonialist thinking as a possible resource for disabled peoples. However, she argues that its emphasis on borderland and hybrid identities that multiply and entangle can lead to a refusal to "name the other"[100] which is a failure to see them in their specificity and thus is also an erasure of identity. She argues that both Rivera and Keller adopt the approach of entangling and confusing identities, in increasing forms of multiplicity, out of a desire to increase inclusion by emphasizing that complexity leads to the inevitability of "unknowing"[101]—the blurring of defined boundaries between people. This appears liberative in that it contests against all forms of othering. However, Betcher is concerned about the erasure of specific identities it also entails—particularly those which have become sources of solidarity and strength. She says, "Apophatic unknowing could further suppress that which culture holds abject."[102] In fact, this critique is similar to that I made previously when comparing the perspectives of Jones and Rambo. While the desire for healing and redemption is obvious and important, the need to continue to name the trauma (or, for Betcher, the reality of the individual in their specific context of disability) is vital. Rambo seeks to correct what she sees as Calvin's erasure of the wounds by focusing on the scars that remain and transform. I believe this balance between hope for healing, as with Jones, and sight of the scars, as with Rambo, is the same requirement Betcher calls for in relation to identity as she engages with Rivera's work.

Particularly in light of process theology's insistence on God's existence being in us, I share Betcher's concern about holding a fear of

---

100. Betcher, "Becoming Flesh of My Flesh," 115.
101. Betcher, "Becoming Flesh of My Flesh," 115.
102. Betcher, "Becoming Flesh of My Flesh," 115.

human limitation. As I saw in Rhys, insistence on ability and overcoming places some people outside the possibility of imaging the divine. Betcher's challenge is incredibly important—that I continue avoiding "valorization of ability."[103] Therefore, I must look for the hope of restoration without focus on a kind of active societal or individual transformation. This may mean returning again to questions of transcendence and God's transformative work in creation.

## Remaining Questions

In this chapter I set out to respond to the challenges I had encountered in the work of Rhys to discover ways of imagining the *imago Dei* as present in wounded and damaged people. I was seeking to discern not only how they embodied the divine but also how their very woundedness was incorporated into the transforming presence of God in creation. As I have engaged with the work of theologians who have wrestled with trauma I have realized that my original questions have led me to a new understanding of theological work. As Rambo says:

> The power of these resurrection appearances lie in their ability to offer a vision of wounds that turn us to the world in a particular way. Without an appeal to the seductive pull of promised endings, they can turn to life in the midst of its complexities and uncertainties. This is not weak or ambiguous theology. It is sustaining theology that probes the capacities and readiness of communities to hold pain and to stay with difficult truths.[104]

Like Rhys, Rambo refuses to ignore the complexities and brokenness of life. As I saw with Sasha in *Good Morning, Midnight*, her brokenness allowed her to connect with other broken people, and in the end, she was transformed and changed her view of others. Likewise, Rivera calls for us to be transformed in our brokenness. Yet, as I demonstrated in analyzing Keller, God participates in this transformation. I am reminded of Sasha's analogy of a drowning person. As she states, having "willing and eager friends on the bank" allows you help in being pulled out.[105] As God's connection to the world demonstrates, we in fact have this friend. As Jones stresses, God's transformation of the world is the hope in future

---

103. Betcher, "Becoming Flesh of My Flesh," 108.
104. Rambo, *Resurrecting Wounds*, 150.
105. Rhys, *Good Morning, Midnight*, 177.

redemption. Finally, Rivera points towards an ethics of obligation based on the recognition of God's image in the face of the other that I believe has crucial practical implications. It demands that we put our own safety at risk and try and help those whose life experiences have placed them in such danger. However, while such an ethical stance is hugely important it may divert attention away from another significant preoccupation of this work which is how does the image of God also encourage us to perceive God's transformational reaching out to those in danger of going under in this way—specifically those who appear to be beyond all human reach.

Thus, my explorations of the *imago Dei* are not merely a search for the image of God in people, but also a search for Godself also. Here I must return to the question of transcendence. Can God be broken and wounded, as I have discovered ways of comprehending here, and also the refuge and safe haven for humanity offering forms of hope for those who are so wounded and damaged as to find no help elsewhere?

# 7

# Transcendence Redefined

Kathryn Tanner's Radical, Empowering God

## Introduction

IN PREVIOUS CHAPTERS I have explored various understandings of the *imago Dei* in an attempt to see how God connects with broken humans, particularly the isolated and marginalized in trauma and suffering. I have been challenged by the literature of Rhys to discern how the broken aspects of humanity are included within the *imago Dei*. This then led me to ask if I am really looking to characters like Marya and Sasha as embodying the image of God, what that then reveals of Godself. I thus explored theologies that stressed God's participation in every aspect of created life. The work of Rambo and Rivera, in particular, encouraged me to affirm that this includes God assuming the enduring wounds of trauma. However, I voice my unease as to whether the images of divine imminence and participation in suffering were enough to sustain hope for those who were so completely overwhelmed by circumstances that their selfhood was destroyed. As the doctrine of the *imago Dei* causes us to reassess not only our humanity but also our understanding of Godself, I now continue my efforts to address the challenge of affirming the woundedness of God alongside new visions of enabling transcendence.

## Foundations of Transcendence

As a young person I held a primarily traditional Protestant understanding of God as "distinct from the world metaphysically, intellectually, ethically, emotionally, and existentially."[1] In believing this, I saw God as, essentially, better than me in all these terms. That is: God is smarter, more ethical (or, perhaps, holds to a better set of ethics), perfect in affect, etc. Through theological study I was able to move past this simple comparative distinction. However, the notion of "better" persisted and continued to impact upon my spiritual understanding. Particularly, as I think about the women in Rhys's novels, I still struggle with my previous preconceptions which hinder me from grasping the image of God in those whose lives are full of failures, mistakes, and unfulfilled potential. In order to fully see the *imago Dei* in all of humanity, I must continue to focus on how God is imaged through trauma and wounds, rather than through "perfections."

Clearly there are a lot of weighty precedents for my former understanding of God. Thomas Aquinas, for example, taught that God "contains within himself all the excellencies of perfection."[2] Humanity could only understand God in comparison to ourselves—either as the perfection of good qualities (power, knowledge, etc.) or the opposite of us (immaterial rather than material, eternal rather than mortal, etc.).[3] Similarly, Barth and other neo-orthodox theologians stress God's perfections, particularly God's perfection in freedom and in love.[4]

However, there are many insights still to be distilled from these ideas. As Augustine taught, God's omnipotence does not allow that God can do anything, as God cannot "die, sin, deny himself, etc."[5] Augustine saw God's transcendence and immanence as inextricably linked—God is "above space as the exalted One, immanent in space as the Actuality that fills everything . . . "[6] This Augustinian view of transcendence and immanence deeply influenced the ways in which Paul Tillich developed his theory of the *imago Dei*, which I briefly discussed in chapter 1.[7] Yet,

---

1. Lewis and Demarest, *Integrative Theology*, 239.
2. Lewis and Demarest, *Integrative Theology*, 216.
3. Lewis and Demarest, *Integrative Theology*, 216.
4. Lewis and Demarest, *Integrative Theology*, 218.
5. Lewis and Demarest, *Integrative Theology*, 220.
6. Lewis and Demarest, *Integrative Theology*, 220.
7. Tillich argued that God is "being-itself, not *a* being" (emphasis original).

as I continue to reflect on Tillich's work, I still am struck by a focus on comparison—albeit one not made in terms of gradation which is a notion he firmly rejects. Tillich states:

> As the power of being, God transcends every being and also the totality of beings—the world. Being-itself is beyond finitude and infinity; otherwise it would be conditioned by something other than itself, and the real power of being would lie beyond both it and that which conditioned it. Being-itself infinitely transcends every finite being. There is no proportion of gradation between the finite and the infinite.[8]

This understanding of God as being-itself, in a way like Keller's understanding, sees God as connected to the world in an essential sense. However, it still maintains the "better than" aspects in which God is the perfection of the power we do, or could, have through divine means. Though Tillich sees God as imbuing us with this power, the notion is still one that concerns me. Particularly in light of the theologies of trauma I examined in the previous chapter, I do not think God seeks to reveal Godself so that the image can only be seen in those powerful enough to sustain existential courage. As Rivera observed in her reflections on Matthew 25, Jesus told us that we see him in the hungry and poor.

## The Need to Redefine

For an alternative perspective on how God empowers that embodies a different perspective on human potentiality I briefly turn to the contemporary theologian Jürgen Moltmann. Moltmann has commented extensively on key doctrinal themes and in these has developed a characteristically eschatological approach to Christian theology. His future-oriented methodology is demonstrated in his development of a theology of resurrection, which he calls the "theology of hope."[9] This theology argued that in the face of catastrophe and despair, it is empowering to hope for a real and lived redemption of the suffering world. Moltmann explains that God will bring about this redemption in the world through an "anticipatory consciousness."[10] As I discussed

---

Tillich, *Systematic Theology*, 237.
   8. Tillich, *Systematic Theology*, 237.
   9. Moltmann et al., "Tribute, Hope and Reconciliation."
   10. Moltmann et al., "Tribute, Hope and Reconciliation."

in chapter 2, Black theology emphasized the interaction God has with the world, seeing it as important to bring about positive change. As God actively works toward the end of oppression, so should those who follow God. Therefore, theologian Howard Thurman saw interaction with God as bringing about essential change in humans. As I saw in James Cone's theology, God is represented as actively siding with the oppressed, working toward an end to injustice.[11] Moltmann's theology is similar to the work of these theologians in many respects. In order to demonstrate this hopefulness, in his book *The Trinity and the Kingdom of God*, Moltmann discusses the link between how we understand God and what we desire to see in ourselves. He says:

> The world is God's work, but man is God's image. That means that every human being finds in himself the mirror in which he can perceive God. The knowledge of God in his image is surer than the knowledge of God from his works. So the foundation of true self-knowledge is to be found in God.[12]

He argues that we should understand ourselves through the knowledge we achieve in God's actions. However, the mistake we often make is in looking for God in certain qualities we desire to see in ourselves. Rather than focusing on the work of God in order to see truths about God, we attempt to distil from those works of God qualities humans can acquire—power, might, knowledge, etc. These certainly are characteristics of God, but have we seen those aspects in God inappropriately? Moltmann's stance is that yes, we have wrongly transposed our own desires onto our beliefs about God.

This work to understand how God's characteristics are properly understood and revealed to us is particularly significant when considering God's imaging in traumatized and oppressed people. As I discussed in the previous chapter, many of the theories and debates concerning ability raise serious problems. For example, in order to better understand God's power, Moltmann focuses on how it is in balance with God as love. He argues that God's love means that God cannot be sufficient in Godself, and that this requires participation beyond Godself (with us). He explains:

> Freedom as it truly is, is by no means a matter of power and domination over a piece of property. So total power is by no means identical with absolute freedom. Freedom arrives at its

---

11. See chapter 2.
12. Moltmann, *Trinity and the Kingdom of God*, 14.

divine truth through love. Love is a self-evident, unquestionable 'overflowing of goodness' which is therefore never open to choice at any time. We have to understand true freedom as being the self-communication of the good.[13]

Moltmann here offers us the significant challenge to radically redefine power and freedom. As I redefine God's power, I stop looking to those who are powerful over others as properly bearing God's image. As I expressed in chapter 6, Rhys's challenges require me to understand how my talk of God affects those who are oppressed and those who are traumatized. If I do not appropriately understand what power means in relation to God, I cannot really connect God to those who are powerless. This is why Moltmann's argument for a reconstruction of key characteristics of God, particularly his insistence on redefining God's freedom, love, and power, helps me to reorient my explorations in a more promising direction. Following this, I look now to Kathryn Tanner's radical revisioning of the terms of transcendence to reconstruct my own understanding in the light of the critical challenges I have raised concerning the *imago Dei*.

## A Radical Definition of Transcendence

Tanner's current work is focused largely upon social justice, economic flourishing, and the political contributions of theology. It centers on God's relationship to the world and what economic systems imply for human relations. She is concerned about the manner in which many theological models can add support to hierarchical and oppressive ways of living. As I discussed in the previous chapter, Tanner is thus also seeking a relational model of the Triune God that is empowering and life giving.

The first aspect of Tanner's distinctive approach to transcendence I will examine is her insistence on the need for radical redefinitions of theological categories. Like Moltmann, she asserts that theologies that do not define their terms in relation to God appropriately will always prove inadequate, as they implicitly fall back upon and rely too heavily on flawed human examples to shape their perspectives on the divine. For instance, outlining what she sees as the rules "for speaking of God as transcendent,"[14] she states that traditional definitions of transcendence (such as those I briefly described above), and particularly statements

---

13. Moltmann, *Trinity and the Kingdom of God*, 55.
14. Tanner, *God and Creation in Christian Theology*, 47.

that imply "a simple contrast of divine and non-divine" are "not radical enough."[15] In a significant chapter in the edited collection *Common Goods*, she argues that too often God's transcendence is used to promote exclusion or justify certain beliefs.[16] She states:

> Appeals to a transcendent God become in this way a means of criticizing rather than reinforcing human opinions about right belief and action . . . Seduced by the confident presumption that those standards at least exist, one is tempted, despite God's transcendence, to identify one's own account of truth and goodness with the standards for them that God represents. Specifically religious forms of fanaticism and dogmatism are the result. One dares to speak for or as divinity.[17]

In her novels, Rhys's characters are continually looking to be different than they are, to be in a different class or society, etc. This rejection of themselves predisposes them to see others as hostile (even if this perception is not false), and to believe that the ability to wield power over them evidences the other person(s)'s superiority. With this mindset, it becomes incredibly difficult for the women in Rhys's novels (or any oppressed person) to have hope—"a happy-go-lucky optimism about one's own future prospects is rendered unintelligible by belief in a hostile, perpetually threatening world . . . " as Tanner explains.[18] She goes on to show (from the opposite perspective to Rhys) that those who see themselves in the image of God because of the power they hold to exclude those they do not approve of or relate to, are able to justify their exclusion and subsequent actions on the basis of a self-identification with the divine. Therefore, it is necessary to "radicalize that divine transcendence and thereby prevent identifications of human views with divine ones."[19]

Radical transcendence, then, must be very differently understood. It is too simple, and presents the same dangers, to merely switch the site of identification to a different aspect of God's character or to reframe a divine quality slightly differently. Nor, as previously argued can we rely on a contrastive approach. As she states:

---

15. Tanner, *God and Creation in Christian Theology*, 47.
16. Tanner, "Ambiguities of Transcendence," 92.
17. Tanner, "Ambiguities of Transcendence," 94.
18. Tanner, "Ambiguities of Transcendence," 92.
19. Tanner, "Ambiguities of Transcendence," 95.

A God who genuinely transcends the world must not be characterized, therefore, by a direct contrast with it. A contrastive definition will show its failure to follow through consistently on divine transcendence by inevitably bringing God down to the level of the non-divine to which it is opposed, in the manner outlined earlier.[20]

Whilst this move might appear to be taking us back to the position outlined by Barth, Tanner shifts the insistence that God is Other into a more expansive definition—God is not "other" in terms of our familiar human dualisms. Instead, God is outside our characterizations of difference, our need to compete for stations, or binary (and hierarchical) oppositions such as chaos versus order.

For Tanner, the options Keller sees as leading her logically to process theology and panentheism in order to escape repressive forms of power assume as simplistic a definition of transcendence as Barth's—essentially that transcendence means God is other in an oppositional (and then oppressive) sense, rather than "wholly distinct" in Tanner's vision of transcendence.[21] She argues that the seeming paradox both Barth and Keller address is practically solved through more clearly defining terms in theology which will mean that "what Christians want to say . . . are actually consistent with one another."[22] I will expand on this conviction further through this chapter.

Moreover, in order to explain her move away from "traditional" definitions of otherness or of transcendence, Tanner expands upon her rejection of the comparative model I referred to previously. To do so, she elaborates upon the principles of God's actions and human freedom as necessarily working together. In a similar manner to Moltmann's assertion that God's love actually requires humanity, as God cannot love truly without an outside being to love, Tanner extends this understanding to God's love operative in the world. In a critical assessment of Tanner's contribution to thinking on this matter, Carl S. Hughes states that her rejection of transcendence as a competitive relationship "means to

20. Tanner, *God and Creation in Christian Theology*, 46.

21. It is also important to note that Tanner directly addresses and responds to Keller's theology. She says in her chapter in *Common Goods*, "For the theologians of transcendence [Keller] . . . divinity is itself characterized in terms of a world of becoming . . . I would like to ask: Can one pluralize the sensibility of more traditional Christian claims of divine transcendence to produce allies in the formation of a countermachine? And I would like to answer affirmatively" (92).

22. Hughes, "'Tehomic' Christology?" 261.

exclude all understandings of God as a "supreme being" who occupies one extreme of a continuum of being and who can thus be predicated with the same attributes to which creatures aspire."[23] God is not merely different from creation in God's relationship to it, but instead is beyond such differentiation. As he states:

> The individuating qualities of creatures derive from their differences with one another: a king is a king because he is not a peasant; a prisoner is a prisoner because she is not free. Tanner argues that because God radically transcends the creaturely plane, God is not subject to such oppositionary differentiation. To the contrary, God's transcendence is precisely what enables God's immanence, and God's sovereignty is precisely what enables creaturely freedom.[24]

What is most necessary to take from this approach is Tanner's continual rejection of "otherness" as oppositional. Her redefinition of otherness is more accurately portrayed as a move to say that God is *not* unlike us but rather is defined in terms different to the ones by which we are predicated. To say then, that God is active in the world does not mean we are not ourselves active. Rather God's action far from limiting our free agency enables it, because God's active presence, which is distinctly unlike our abilities, empowers us to freely act. As Tanner states, "God's own agency is transcendent, not just in being outside the world, but in being of a different character from happenings within the world."[25] It is then inappropriate for us to project our forms of work (production, transformative action, fulfilling roles, etc.) onto God's (empowerment, divine creation or love, etc.) or vice versa. The ways these cooperate must also be separated from our human understandings. Instead, as I will further show, God's power allows our agency. If the difference between God and humans is precisely what brings about God's active work in the world, then there is no reduction in human potentiality or creativity due to God's activity. All that humanity does is enabled and empowered by God, yet this does not reduce the significance of our actions. Thus, once again, we must allow our definitions to be shifted in order to break from limiting understandings of both God and ourselves.

---

23. Hughes, "'Tehomic' Christology?" 261.
24. Hughes, "'Tehomic' Christology?" 261.
25. Tanner, "Ambiguities of Transcendence," 98.

In order to understand how God's actions connect and empower ours, I return to the relation model given by Glissant that requires participation, particularly in the "cracks"—those traumas or sufferings that scar us, which Glissant believes then connect us to each other in true relation. As I demonstrated there, Glissant's theory of relation requires identification of wounds and cooperative actions to heal (or redeem) those wounds. As Moltmann also argues, the act of creation began the *self-humiliation* of God. He says, "For God, creation means self-limitation, the withdrawal of himself, that is to say self-humiliation. Creative love is always suffering love as well."[26] This view of love means that God, in participating with humanity fully, is both affecting us and affected by us.

God is then defined by a love that requires, not merely allows, for God to be affected by the world in both suffering and joy. God's suffering then must be seen not as a weakness, for that suffering is the passion of God, integral to the powerful love God possesses. It is this suffering love that allows freedom. Moltmann again explains, "The suffering of God with the world, the suffering of God from the world, and the suffering of God for the world are the highest forms of his creative love . . . "[27] This means God has empowered creation to act, even in actions that wound God.

Therefore, while Tanner sees God as distinct, or indeed over and above creation, there is no need to then believe God is opposed to creation. Here she takes a different position from those offered by process theology that I addressed in the previous chapter. Tanner agrees with the panentheist position that it is important to acknowledge God as implicated within but not limited to the created order. However, for her God is not simply "more than" creation. She offers the reflection that "The Christian theologian needs to radicalize claims about both God's transcendence and involvement with the world if the two are to work for rather than against one another."[28] This radical reframing of transcendence and immanence moves our relationship with God into a perichoresis that mirrors many definitions of the Trinity currently employed in contemporary theology.[29] We are not God, but we are

26. Moltmann, *Trinity and the Kingdom of God*, 59.
27. Moltmann, *Trinity and the Kingdom of God*, 60.
28. Tanner, *God and Creation in Christian Theology*, 46.
29. For a current examination of this, see Graydon Cress, *Perichoresis and Participation*. The thesis examines the language of perichoresis in order to better understand human participation with the divine.
As I also demonstrated, Barth sees the Trinity as three participants in one action (Revelation) demonstrating the cooperative working between the members. Augustine,

186   PART THREE: RECONSTRUCTING A THEORY OF THE IMAGO DEI

essentially linked to God and empowered by God. This relation lessens neither us nor God. As Tanner explains:

> God is different from the world in virtue of the fullness of God's trinitarian life, but it is this very fullness that enables God to overflow in goodness to us. The Father already brings about what is different—the Son and the Spirit—in complete unity with the Father. The triune God is therefore being nothing other than Godself in unity with a world different from God, as that unity and differentiation find their culmination in the human being, Jesus . . .[30]

## The Source of All

As I can now see, through these redefinitions of terms, Tanner's work gives me a foundation upon which to build an understanding God in radically new ways, also shifting understandings of what the image of God could be. While I keep in mind the understanding of presence and participation in the face of trauma that I explored in the previous chapter, I am now able to more coherently combine it with a new understanding of transcendence. As I saw through Rambo, God's participation in the world includes experiencing and taking on the wounds of trauma. In her theological thinking, God's assumption of woundedness (both in taking on our wounds and in the literal wounds of Christ) allows then a transformation of those wounds. By understanding this theory in light of Tanner's illumination of transcendence, I can see that the transformation is not work done by us, as we are the traumatized, but empowerment done by God. It is God who endows us with the *imago Dei*, particularly through our suffering. In looking towards how this speaks to the context of Rhys's women, I see that while Sasha's narrative gives some amount of hope, her story does not transform the stories of the other women. She has not empowered herself, nor does she empower the others. Instead, I can allow the unhappy endings, the "failures" of the other three main characters, to remain as they are and still emphasize the *imago Dei* in them. God is still present with Anna and Marya, even if I cannot see it

---

though a flawed understanding of the Trinity, likens it to love, with the Father being the Lover and the Son being the Loved. In all of these, we see that the Trinity is largely seen through actions, and particularly actions which highlight the distinct importance of each.

30. Tanner, *Jesus, Humanity and the Trinity*, 13.

through active change in them. Instead, as Rambo suggests, God enters into their suffering, "breath[ing] new life" into the room,[31] while not requiring anything of the women.

Because Tanner has rejected a contrastive understanding of God's otherness, it is necessary now to understand what she sees as essential in a theory of transcendence. She takes the work of the Neo-Platonic philosopher Plotinus as enabling a beginning step to a non-contrastive transcendence. As she states, within Hellenistic cosmologies "God transcends the world as a whole in a manner that cannot properly be talked about in terms of a simple opposition within the same universe of discourse."[32] Contrastive language can only be used of things in the world, but because God is not in the world, God also "must transcend that sort of characterization, too."[33] Plotinus expands on this notion, working through different types of terms in order to deal with this difficult conundrum. As Tanner explains he "seems to vacillate . . . between univocal predication and contrastive definition."[34] In discussing the One (God), Plotinus's theory is that:

> the One is not to be identified with any *determinate* particulars or with the *multiple* totality of which it is the source or principle. The one is a simple, undifferentiated unity; as such, it simply *is not* what everything else *specifically is* in virtue of a determinate character . . . Direct contrasts oppose in this way the simplicity of the One to the composite character of what proceeds from it.[35]

In essence, Plotinus argues that while God's transcendence means that God is different to creation, this implies a hierarchy of source rather than value. God is "simply the first in a line of sequentially productive agencies."[36] Tanner is not completely satisfied with this, however, as she notes Plotinus uses contrastive language, which has the danger of appearing to leave God uninterested in the world. Nevertheless, it is a helpful starting point. As she says, "If divinity is to be the source of all, and not just the world's organizing principle, it cannot be properly

---

31. Rambo, *Resurrecting Wounds*, 147.
32. Tanner, *God and Creation in Christian Theology*, 42.
33. Tanner, *God and Creation in Christian Theology*, 42.
34. Tanner, *God and Creation in Christian Theology*, 42.
35. Tanner, *God and Creation in Christian Theology*, 43.
36. Tanner, *God and Creation in Christian Theology*, 43.

characterized in terms of the differences that hold among entities originating in dependence upon it."[37]

If God cannot simply be talked about in terms of difference, even though God is outside the world, then there must be a new way to understand God's transcendence. Tanner then identifies that where Plotinus was unable to fully explain this, "Christian theology takes up the task . . ."[38] She again stresses that the primary rule is to avoid talking of God in "simple contrast" but to understand God's actions alongside God's character. In this she says, "God will become the genuine source of everything that is, *in* all its diversity, multiplicity and particularity, without the need for any indirection."[39] God's actions cannot be removed, since the first action we can discuss is that of creating. If, as Plotinus says, the beginning of understanding God is in seeing God as the source of everything, then God's actions are in fact God.

Tanner argues that Christian theology has wrestled with this understanding for centuries, but she sees it as the essential principle for knowing God at all. In fact, understanding anything about God must begin with understanding that God is creatively connected to everything. She says, "God's nature is clearly not being directly opposed to that of things of this world since God is talked about as being simply identical with what is asserted predicatively of those creatures. If a man is righteous, God is righteousness."[40] God, in creating the world and particularly in creating humanity in God's likeness, has created a world that is a reflection of God. Tanner then shows that if humanity has a characteristic of God like righteousness, then we know that God *is* righteousness.[41] However, she clarifies "God is not, however, what created reality is, because in the creature's cases such terms are only asserted predicatively and not substantively."[42] While humans can display characteristics, God is essentially those characteristics. While humans do actions, God is God's actions (creation, love, etc.). In summation, "God may be other than creatures without differing from them in respect to quality."[43]

---

37. Tanner, *God and Creation in Christian Theology*, 43.
38. Tanner, *God and Creation in Christian Theology*, 47.
39. Tanner, *God and Creation in Christian Theology*, 47–48.
40. Tanner, *God and Creation in Christian Theology*, 58.
41. Tanner, *God and Creation in Christian Theology*, 58.
42. Tanner, *God and Creation in Christian Theology*, 58.
43. Tanner, *God and Creation in Christian Theology*, 58.

She continues to explain this, focusing on positive aspects of both humanity and God. In particular, she says that as many theologians, Barth in particular, have shown, God is love. Yet, again as many say, "one cannot say that love is God."[44] The source of all these things, creation and these particular actions, is God, but yet they are still now not God. I wish to link this more specifically to the work I am doing here, and the notion of participation.

As I demonstrated through my reading of Rhys, an important aspect of a revisioned image of God is participation in the world. And in looking at the theologians in my previous chapter, these participations must often be risky. As Rivera seeks to show, God risked greatly in the Incarnation. Jesus suffered his own traumas, but the triune God suffers still when traumas are inflicted upon those God loves—as I said, behavior toward other people is our behavior toward God. Again, we are marked by our encounters, and similarly God is marked by encountering us. Further, as Rambo demonstrated, Jesus also invited us to not only see his wounds, but to be open with our own. All of this participation is the outpouring of these two important aspects of God which Tanner has shown are essential to God's being. First, creation is the outpouring of God's desire to be both creative and connected to something outside Godself. As 20th century theologian Emil Brunner states, the act of creation was both the first act of love and of revelation.[45] Brunner emphasizes this, saying, "His love to us, to men [sic], is the outflow of His being, of the fact that He is Himself loving, and that He loves."[46] Therefore, God must participate. This leads me to the second important aspect of Tanner's theory of transcendence for my project.

Because God's being requires outward actions (love, creation), God's transcendence cannot essentially separate God from creation. Instead, God's actions connect God to creation. Here is where the redefinition of transcendence must be fully realized.

As I discussed in chapter 6, the traditional theories of transcendence are, for Keller, problematically supportive of hierarchies. Keller believes traditional definitions of omnipotence must be limiting or oppressive. However, while Keller sees abuse of power and an oppressive limiting of human agency and creativity, Tanner sees transcendence and omnipotence as the characteristics that brings about agency and

---

44. Tanner, *God and Creation in Christian Theology*, 59.
45. See Brunner, *Man In Revolt*, 74–76.
46. Brunner, *Man in Revolt*, 75.

creativity in human beings. Humans are not limited because God is omnipotent, but God's omnipotence produces human ability. Tanner's position demonstrates that in its perfection—which she explains is the Incarnation and intervention of Christ—God's interaction with the world means that humans are benefited by God's power. Thus, in her book *Jesus, Humanity and the Trinity*, Tanner states:

> This non-competitive relation between creatures and God is possible, it seems, only if God is the fecund provider of *all* that the creature is in itself; the creature in its giftedness, in its goodness, does not compete with God's gift-fullness and goodness because God is the giver of all that the creature is for the good. This relationship of total giver to total gift is possible, in turn, only if God and creatures are, so to speak, on different levels of being, and different planes of causality—something that God's transcendence implies.[47]

Hughes explains, "it would seem that the more God transcends the world, the less God can be involved with its inner workings. However . . . because God transcends creaturely scales of differentiation entirely, God is able to be immanent at every point within the world."[48] As I earlier said, human characteristics can be reflections of God's being. Humans can love because God is love and has gifted humans with love. I turn quickly again to Brunner, who discusses the importance of God gifting humans with love. He states:

> With this Word [Jesus] God turns to man, imparts Himself to him, and in so doing gives him his life. But He gives it him in such a way that man must receive it. He does not fling it at him—for that would mean that he was a 'finished article'—but He offers it to him through His call . . .[49]

In God's actions (which Brunner is connecting with the Incarnation as the action of love and revelation, as I will discuss further), humans are not left alone, but are gifted by God in a participatory manner. God gives gifts to humans through relationship with humans. Tanner redefines God's power as well, saying, "God's absolute or unconditioned power, in short, is not one of jealously guarded exclusive possession but one of universal, all-comprehensive giving; everything in the world with any causal

---

47. Tanner, *Jesus, Humanity and the Trinity*, 3.
48. Hughes, "'Tehomic' Christology?", 262.
49. Brunner, *Man In Revolt*, 98.

efficacy or agency has that power by virtue of God's own power to give it."[50] God's power is not oppressive, but sustaining of creation's power. Heidler does not image God's power, but instead, by refusing to despise the *commis* and acknowledging some relationship with him, *Good Morning, Midnight's* Sasha is a much closer example.[51]

Similarly, it is important for Tanner to focus also on Christ in understanding God. For Tanner, like Barth, Christ is the perfection of God's gift to Creation. In *Jesus, Humanity and the Trinity*, she states, "In Jesus, unity with God takes a perfect form; here humanity has become God's own."[52] Through the Incarnation, God demonstrates the duality of transcendence and immanence in one act.

This is, again, not a paradox for Tanner. Because God is differentiated from Creation, God is fully able to enact this change. God is not, as we are, enclosed in Godself and can therefore also be "with what is not God."[53] Here, I turn to Amy Plantinga Pauw's assessment of Tanner's work. She explains that, "Gift is the central concept around which Tanner's articulation of the divine life and the incarnation revolves. Gift is also the centre of her understanding of human existence. All that we are—in our creation as in our salvation—is God's gift to us."[54] Because giftingness is key to Tanner's understanding of the Incarnation, and of God's actions since creation, it is important to define this gift correctly. Tanner is not arguing for a gifting that mirrors the "debtor/creditor" relationship but instead as creating "a community of mutual fulfillment."[55]

Seeing God's actions as gifts, and as mutually fulfilling, allows Tanner to also address the ways Christ's Incarnation reconcile humanity and God. Her belief is stated in *Jesus, Humanity and the Trinity*, "The point of incarnation is therefore, as it was for the early Greek Fathers, the perfection of humanity; this is a human-centered Christology just because it is an incarnation-centered one."[56] Jesus perfects the connection God has

---

50. Tanner, "Ambiguities of Transcendence," 100.
51. See chapter 5.
52. Tanner, *Jesus, Humanity and the Trinity*, 9.
53. Tanner, *Jesus, Humanity and the Trinity*, 12.
54. Pauw, "Ecclesiological reflections on Kathryn Tanner's Jesus, Humanity and the Trinity," 222.
55. Pauw, "Ecclesiological reflections on Kathryn Tanner's Jesus, Humanity and the Trinity," 224. This concept, which Pauw critiques as still too vague for us to truly enact in our communities, emphasizes that support of another does not diminish the actor.
56. Tanner, *Jesus, Humanity and the Trinity*, 9.

with humanity, in which the spiritual and the physical are no longer at odds but unified. Again, in connection to the perichoresis of the Trinity, she sees this action as encompassing God's Triune nature. She continues:

> Reinforcing the unity of being between Father and Son by a unity of love and joyful affirmation, the Holy Spirit is the exuberant, ecstatic carrier of the love of Father and Son to us. Borne by the Holy spirit, the love of the Father for the Son is returned to the Father by the Son within the Trinity; so the triune God's manifestation in the world is completed in Christ through the work of the Spirit who enables us to return the love of God shown in Christ through a life lived in gratitude and service to God's cause.[57]

The Triune action of love reinforces the idea that the Incarnation is giftedness out of the transcendent nature of God—God is able to enact this kind of loving action because of the otherness that allows God to extend beyond Godself. In her assessment of Tanner's position, Christine Helmer states that this does not change God but "enables God to assume the other."[58] Likewise, Christ assumes sinners, transforming them while not diminishing in himself. Sinners acquire characteristics of Christ, enabling them to reconcile with God and with humanity and furthermore benefit others. As the hypostatic union of Christ is not seen to diminish his divinity nor his humanity, Tanner argues that God's omnipotence and transcendence should not take away from creation's value or agency. We do not become Christ, but instead are empowered by him.

## Building an *Imago Dei* of Risk

While I have continued to emphasize the participatory nature of God, I believe that it is here that I also can understand the participatory nature of the *imago Dei*. As humanity has now been given, freely, characteristics of God, the display of imaging God is risky participation. As Tanner says, "Such an idea of noncompetitiveness can be generalized . . . to produce a vision of a human community of mutual fulfillment . . ."[59] It is not merely loving those similar to us, as God's transcendence moves God to love outside Godself. We can also not only love safely, as God's participation

---

57. Tanner, *Jesus, Humanity and the Trinity*, 14.
58. Helmer, "Systematic Theological Theory," 216.
59. Tanner, "Ambiguities of Transcendence," 100.

through creation and Christ has demonstrated the great risks God took. In fact, by looking at most of Rhys's female characters, it is evident that even as they remain in their unhealed situations, not being lifted into hopefulness, they are still risking. Even as complicated and broken as they may be, the image is present particularly within their wounds.

Here, it is important to note theologian Sarah Coakley's critical assessment of Tanner's gift-centered theology. In this non-competitive aid, Tanner emphasizes that the Trinity does not lose nor diminish through empowering each other, and that in the Incarnation (and, Coakley points out, Christ's death) there is nothing lost nor sacrificed. In this model, neither should we lose or sacrifice as we empower others. Coakley sees this as a naïve argument in the face of late capitalist problems.[60] While, I believe it is problematic to compare God's transcendence and immanence to the broken order of the world, I would argue alongside Coakley that God did sacrifice and bear loss in incarnational kenosis. Here, I think it is important to distinguish between sacrifice/loss and being diminished. I instead raise a slightly different critique, which I return to Helmer to discuss. She asks, "Does the principle of gift-giving flatten the dynamism in God's own being between, for example, the attributes of mercy and justice?"[61] Is Christ's death not a sacrifice, even momentarily? Is it not a loss, even a temporary one, that God suffered? How do we see God affected by the world if we cannot see God suffer along with us? I look once again to my previous chapter and emphasize Rambo's call to both acknowledge and redeem our wounds. While Christ did not lose divinity, nor did the Triune God diminish because of the Incarnation, it is not true that God did not suffer. The trauma Christ suffered invites us into relation with his wounds, as demonstrated to Thomas, and shows us that in fact the Incarnation did leave God changed. This does not mean God is not powerful, nor does it necessarily negate omnipotence as if it were a quality that could be emptied by degrees when in fact it is the sustaining source of creation. However, if creation is truly empowered, the ability to act upon God must also exist. We see this through both Rambo and Jones, who argue that an aspect of God's empowerment is in the

---

60. "If this strikes one as an essentially bourgeois solution to the dilemmas of global capitalism, I fear that this may be the result of the determined erasure of the motif of 'exchange', and thus of the effective obliteration of distinguishing 'differences' of relation both in God (qua persons of the Trinity) and in us (qua even-ing out difference of resources out of 'our' plenitude)." Coakley, "Why Gift?" 233.

61. Helmer, "Systematic Theological Theory," 217.

kenotic act of redeeming. It is vital, then, to not mistake suffering and woundedness with diminishment. If God can be wounded without being diminished, then our wounds likewise need not diminish us. Again, it is a need to properly understand the terms used, but also to see God's character as it truly is. As Moltmann argued, God's power and freedom are not to be seen as oppressive or negating ours.

This is not wholly out of line with Tanner's work. She also sees hopefulness and stresses active participation in her work *The Politics of God*. Through a vigorous explanation of how traditional systematic theology must constantly progress through critiquing itself, she continues to explain her understanding of God's transcendence and the importance of Christ. Again, her understanding of the indivisible connection God has with creation is displayed:

> As the world God creates and guides and redeems in Jesus Christ, the world is forever God's place no matter how distant it seems from the standards of truth and goodness that God represents. God is at work there for the ends God intends. Indeed, God is at work for those ends in established forms of social relations, no matter how great the effort of human beings to stymie them. Therefore, according to the account of the relation between divine and human working that I have been favoring, one cannot rule out the possibility of human working within such a social sphere to bring human life closer to such ends.[62]

In Tanner's estimation, the brokenness of the world, brought about by creation's pulling away from the will of God, can be empowered as it is. Further, as I saw with Serene Jones the cross shows us God's presence in the brokenness. She believes that community (specifically the Christian Church) must declare God's presence, while acknowledging that people will remain broken. Again, I quote, "we are: God's inevitably broken children, and God's constantly renewed beloved . . . We are not becoming better or worse: we just are these two things, in the juxtaposed tension of our everyday life."[63] That which reveals weakness or brokenness does not need to be forgotten or glossed over, but instead, God can redeem it. This is no naïve belief that wounds will disappear. This is also no obliteration of difference in our present world. Instead, it is a hope that in our brokenness, God is present and active. In the

---

62. Tanner, *Politics of God*, 124.
63. Jones, *Trauma and Grace*, 165.

trauma, God sees us fully and loves us. This hope is for a redemption not of erasure, but of future authentic restoration.

Once the need to erase wounds is left behind, it is possible to begin understanding imaging God within woundedness. Rather than seeking perfections of intellect, actions, or domination, the *imago Dei* can be understood by seeing God in the derided and denigrated aspects of humanity. I think of the work of practical theologian Marcella Althaus-Reid, who discusses the need to understand the lived theology of the oppressed. In her book *Indecent Theology* (2000), she elaborates on the theology of sex workers and others outcast from society. She argues that by thinking primarily of how God (or theology in general) is lived out in these situations, you can more clearly see the longing of God. She describes:

> The excessiveness of our hungry lives: our hunger for food, hunger for the touch of other bodies, for love and for God; a multitude of hungers never satisfied which grow and expand and put us into risky situations and challenge, like a carnival of the poor, the textbooks of the normalisers of life.[64]

Althaus-Reid does not see this excessiveness as something we need to extinguish, but instead as an expression of the connection we were meant to have.[65] God's longing for creation, demonstrated by God's acts of creation, incarnation, revelation, and particularly suffering, should be imaged in our lives. Longing for relationship, joy, etc., all mirrors the longing of God. And the suffering that comes from those risks—rejection, hate, trauma, violence—are also mirrors of the risks of God. The image is seen most clearly in these instances, rather than contexts of ease, power, or elitism.

## Silent Grief: A New Understanding

Belief in this future restoration again focuses on the life and work of Christ. As Christ assumed humanity in the Incarnation, we can see a future restoration of humanity as we see Christ restored to the presence of God.

---

64. Althaus-Reid, *Indecent Theology*, 200.

65. Althaus-Reid is here specifically arguing that we should be comfortable with the desires of people. Arguing that we often only allow poor people to be concerned with food and housing, she maintains that their desires for things like sex and education are as worthy and valid. However, in her discussion, I also see that her connection between desire and God allows us to reject notions that desire is somehow suspect, and that we ought to be more comfortable risking in order to attain certain desires.

Christine Helmer, seeing the restored relationship we can have with God, focuses on the active presence of God in the world. She locates her concern primarily on God's "battle with horrendous evil"[66] and theologians concerns about God's work against evil even in a "self-giving love that costs a life."[67] It does indeed seem too naively positive to assume redemption when those things have not been actualized yet. Though much of Christian theology discusses an "already and not yet" of God's restorative plan, Helmer believes we must remain firm that the actualization of redemption is "still outstanding in the sense of its extensional progress in both individual biography and the church's history (which is related to world history) as a whole."[68] Because of this, we ought to also acknowledge an important aspect of the Incarnation and death of Christ: "the silent grief of which is inscribed into the eternal heart."[69]

This term "silent grief" links me once again to Cannon's work and her development of "silent grace."[70] As I discussed in chapter 2, Cannon sees the silent grace of Black people, particularly Black women, as the announcement that they do not deserve the mistreatment they receive, but are fully embodying the *imago Dei*.[71] In light of this, Helmer's discussion of God's silent grief can say the same. It is a declaration that humanity is not deserving of the evil brought on by broken relationship with God and others, even though humanity assumes some responsibility for these evils. God declares, through the self-giving action of the Incarnation and the suffering God experiences through human violation, that still humanity requires and receives God's love. In the light of this Althaus-Reid says of following God, "We can then say that *to walk with* is an expression of solidarity, a sharing of experience of the 'everyday nature of *Otherness*.'"[72] The redemption God brings is in this solidarity. It is the juxtaposition of wounds and restoration. It is the coming together of the broken pieces of the pottery, which Glissant says connects people in true relationship. This silent grief is the culmination of the redemption hope, in the presence of visible and healing wounds, which God participates in and in solidarity with us transforms us and the world.

66. Helmer, "Systematic Theological Theory," 217.
67. Helmer, "Systematic Theological Theory," 217.
68. Helmer, "Systematic Theological Theory," 219.
69. Helmer, "Systematic Theological Theory," 217.
70. Sporre, *In Search of Human Dignity*, 25.
71. See chapter 2.
72. Althaus-Reid, *From Feminist Theology to Indecent Theology*, 18.

Again, this seems a paradox. However, I see in both Moltmann's redefining of power and Tanner's insistence on God's non-competitive gifting a hopeful redemption of the *imago Dei*, particularly in light of Rhys's challenges to me. There is worthiness in Marya, Anna, and Julia in this silent grief. There is restoring hope in Sasha. Just as God's transcendence enables God's immanence, God's grief and suffering enable God's redemption of our *imago Dei*. It is, as Helmer says, "hope in the face of annihilation."[73] This hope is most clear in relation to the character of Sasha, but in enabling us to approach God in these ways, Rhys's novels all hold out this same fragile hope.

To view God, as I have demonstrated, as defined primarily by love, I must finally declare that God's power is not oppressive nor possessive. Instead, it is a power that is focused outward, empowering those God loves. It is the freedom to interact with the world in love, caring for the world and simultaneously affected by the world. I must refuse to see this self-giving as a weakness, and instead see that being affected by the world is the full demonstration of love for it. Like Tanner, I must instead view separation and oppression as the weaknesses. As she insists, attempts to destroy creation or to deny people the love of God are precisely what God works against, and therefore to be empowered by God is to also work against such destructive forms of power. This understanding leaves us with the hope of Moltmann—a hope that is active in acknowledging the brokenness of the present and yet confident in a redemption within that brokenness. Moltmann is not hoping for a future that is perfect. It is the reconciliation and redemption of the reality of now, much like the redemption Rambo argues for in her theology of suffering, and the radical transcendence of Tanner—this is the space of the "already/not yet" redemption.[74] It is the haunting that Rhys gives us in her characters.

Fundamentally, Tanner's understanding of God's relationship to humanity changes completely the typical issues and questions doctrines of sovereignty and transcendence bring. To believe that God is non-competitively acting in creation allows for both the belief in God's non-oppressive power and also affirms the freedom of the creation. To allow for one need not diminish the other—neither Julia nor Norah need to be in competition, but the fact of their broken relationships simultaneously, and paradoxically, holds hope of the reconciliation of God. This

---

73. Helmer, "Systematic Theological Theory," 220.
74. See my discussion of Rambo, chapter 6.

concept is difficult to grasp, primarily for the reasons Tanner states are fundamental to all attempts to conceptualize God in human terms. To say that God is other means God is not trapped by human understanding of characteristics, and therefore our language and understanding of God must engage with this challenging reality.

Finally, in this understanding, the *imago Dei* simply cannot be understood as reflecting those attributes of God traditionally associated with power over others. It must instead be defined by the woundedness of being affected by the world, by others. It must be seen in the crown of thorns, not an oppressive power of domination. This does not mean the valorization of needless suffering, or practices of self-martyrdom. Instead, this means we must replace our desires to be as God with the desire to act like God, to be in solidarity with others, to empower others, and to embrace the wounds suffered in the process of this. We must recognize the *imago Dei* as another action of love from God—that God has placed us in inextricable relationship with Godself and each other, and to hope that restoration of those relationships will be fulfilled. The *imago Dei* is the silent grief we carry *with God*, essentially and eternally connected to God through the cracks that run through us.

# Epilogue

THERE ARE SEVERAL SIGNIFICANT movements within this research as I have drawn upon the work of a diverse group of theologians, writers and scholars in an attempt to revision an understanding of the *imago Dei* that reflects both the love of God and the deep woundedness of humanity and the created order. I began with the insights of Karl Barth, to which I remain indebted in several points, though not in the way he would have predicted. Firstly, God's purpose is focused on relationship and love—it is precisely this which is passed to humanity, demonstrated through the incarnation and life of Christ, and it is in and through this that we should locate the *imago Dei*. Tillich's work allows me to move toward a more inclusive understanding of God's deep identification with humanity and particularly allowed me to begin understanding a *perichoresis* of relationship. However, his focus upon existential anxiety and its overcoming reflected a universalizing perspective concerning the human condition that did not resonate with many of the urgent concerns of women.

This is particularly well demonstrated through the work of the feminist theologians I considered. By rejecting a theology that did not directly address their real lives, they also rejected the notion of a God who stood apart from human struggles. As Rosemary Radford Ruether explained, God is "beneath and around us as an encompassing source of life and renewal."[1] God participates directly in our yearnings and actions for transformation, and therefore it is vital I understand God in light of this.

---

1. Ruether, *Sexism and God-talk*, 47.

My chapter on Black Theology, Womanism, and particularly the work of Katie Cannon allowed me to understand better how a theology that focuses on resisting oppression can be empowering and liberative. Recognizing the communal support that conveys dignity in the face of horrendous evil, I gained understanding that the *imago Dei* is not an abstract or individualized doctrine but can speak to people who join together in solidarity to seek justice. As Cone and Cannon both advocated, a true understanding of God must be an understanding of God as actively on the side of the oppressed. It is this solidarity with God that allows Cannon to assert the significance of silent grace in communal renewal. However, my attention was then drawn to the situations of those who are so marginalized and traumatized that they are unable to access communal resources.

My thesis question thus became much clearer. How do we understand an *imago Dei* for the truly isolated, oppressed, and broken? How can God be imaged in those who hate themselves? Is God present to them also?

To engage with this question, I turned to literature both in recognition of its power to embody occluded experience but also in its power to provoke affective responses, complexify understanding, enable us to be startled out of conventional theological perspectives and testify to trauma. I found the novels of Jean Rhys's uniquely helpful in their complex portrayals of the kind of isolation and desperation I had wondered about. Far ahead of her time, she sought to give a voice to those who were abused—economically, socially, and personally. Her work in depicting traumas done, through scenes of violent rape and such mundane (but deeply symbolic) action s as dyeing hair, allows the reader to fall. In the words of Anneliese van Heijst, "In both the physical and the psychological senses, falling is losing one's grip and being given up to a movement over which one no longer has any control."[2] Rhys's work challenged me to truly understand how disconnection, oppression, and the subsequent hatred of self occurs. It is through and for the female figures she so powerfully portrays that I could begin to really reconstruct my understanding of the *imago Dei*.

Trauma and suffering should not be erased or forgotten. As I learned from theologians like Rambo and Jones, it is necessary that we enter into that trauma to truly understand people but also God's love

---

2. van Heijst, *Longing for the Fall*, 9.

for people. Jesus's life was filled with isolation, suffering, and a violent death. As the disciple Thomas experienced, Jesus's wounds are displayed for us to see in order that we might understand the woundedness taken up into the heart of God. As our wounds are then connected to God they allow for a restoration hope to begin.

And so, I must understand that God's purpose is not a controlling relationship with humanity. God is not interested in oppressing the creation God loves. I found much of value in the challenge of process and panentheistic theologies that stress God's kenotic abandonment of power and identification with creation. However, they did not resolve for me the challenge of how to hope for and with those who have lost hope and whose wounds remain unhealed. This led me to seek understandings of God that affirm both God's identification with our woundedness and God's power to lovingly transform creation. As Kathryn Tanner explains, God is not in opposition to us, even as God is Other than us. Instead, God's Otherness provides the divine support I have been searching for. Rather than looking to a community to give dignity to the suffering, I see that it is God who declares humanity worthy and made in God's image. God empowers us to then mirror this love to others, as I glimpsed in Sasha's decision to stop hating. Yet there is not a requirement upon us to become better, to achieve more or even to believe ourselves good or worthy of respect. God has already declared all of that by condescending to be with us, in creation and incarnation, in trauma and through wounds.

It is the knowledge that God connects to us through wounds that allows me to see that the *imago Dei* is not a doctrine of perfections, but one of risk and wounds. God has given us this image in order to be in relationship with us, participating in the ugliness of life. We hope for the restoration of these wounds, not their erasure. The *imago Dei* is the silent grief bonding God to us in love.

## The Journey Continues

In the time between when I began this project and now, as I put the final touches on research that has been so integral to my life, the world has gone through significant changes. I had been living in Glasgow, Scotland, when the pandemic began. The COVID-19 pandemic overturned so many lives, mine included. That year, instead of another train journey, I found myself on a nearly empty plane, headed back to Colorado.

When things began shutting down, I was watching the airline websites, trying to ensure I could make it home if needed. When more and more flights were canceled, I made the decision to go home. My parents are elderly, and I could not stop worrying about being unable to return if something were to happen. I booked the last ticket I could, a mere two days away, but with a return ticket for three months later. It was over a year and a half before I returned, to get my remaining things, to finally say goodbye to people who had been my family, and to gratefully attend my graduation—the first the university had held since the shutdown. It was, like so much else then, bittersweet. I am so glad I got to have a graduation, but the trip was marked by the loss.

The pandemic is not the only thing that marked so much loss in the world in the midst of my work on trauma and grief. 2020 brought protests for Black Lives Matter, following George Floyd's murder. When Derek Chauvin was convicted of murdering Floyd, there was a sense of hope that this would mark improvement in policing practices, in treatment of Black people in the US, and yet there was also the feeling that it was really an anomaly. Now, linked with continued protests around the world for various human rights, it seems it was a single step forward in a long journey.

January 6, 2021 brought an unprecedented insurrection upon the United States Capitol. People who had been misled, purposely angered, and driven to extreme measures descended upon the Capitol to stop the legal transition of the presidency to Joe Biden. Against tradition of peaceful electoral transitions, the mob demanded the deaths of politicians, had makeshift gallows set up outside, and attacked police officers and others trying to stop them. While many have been charged with these crimes, the people responsible for manipulating the populace into these actions have still not seen many consequences.

These are only two examples of this growing divisiveness. Within all these events, the almost constant "unprecedented" occurrences marking this time, what has been clear is the ever-growing belief of many in this country, and elsewhere, that there are some people just "not worth saving." Whether it is because of political beliefs, bigotry, or just the growing current of divide and anger, the sentiment of unworthiness penetrates so many areas of culture today. In discussing the idea that God's image is in everyone, even those we dislike or distrust, I find so many people resistant to allow for this. I find myself thinking it more than I care to admit. I mention all of this because it would be inauthentic to end a book dealing with trauma and grief without mentioning the current, complex, and layered traumas and grief we all are undergoing. It is also clear that these events will continue to happen, and that moving forward requires an understanding of trauma that intimately connects us to God, rather than some incorrect belief that things have "returned to normal."

I started this journey hoping I would be affirmed in seeing myself in the image of God. A rather personal, and a bit selfish, goal for theological work! I also wanted to understand the *imago Dei* in terms other than the achievement of certain personal qualities or life outcomes. This was both to relieve the constant pressure I felt and to be able to answer the question of how God could be imaged in those society deems failures. Thinking about how Barth focused the image on Christ, and his belief that we image God through Christ and through behaving like Christ, I realize my academic research journey is much like the journey I've taken these past few years. I left Colorado in pain, fleeing to a new country hoping to heal and to recover who I had previously been. I returned to Colorado realizing that neither things were really the goal, nor should they be. Instead, I carry my wounds openly, allowing them to reshape who I am and how I interact with the world. I can move through this new trauma with restored understanding of how my grief should be. I let myself cry, but also laugh.

In Christian theology imaging God is imaging Christ. Barth was nearly there. However, it is not imaging Christ through works of power in the way Barth saw Christ's reconciling work. Instead, the image of God is revealed in and through the shared wounds we bear. God's reconciliation with the world was traumatic, forever affecting God and Creation. Realizing a theology of the *imago Dei* to include the oppressed, those who suffer and cannot overcome, I had to look differently at how Christ revealed God to us. In this journey, I realized that Christ presents God as desiring, risking, loving, and suffering. God is constantly reaching out to those who reject reconciliation. As Katie Cannon taught me, God's work in the world is in demonstrating value to those who have been denied it.

There is a growing desire to see ourselves as having the answers, of knowing exactly what side is "right" and what side must be defeated. This desire also brings us to see some as undeserving. It dehumanizes the other and justifies it by believing it is because the other has chosen incorrectly. This is not a "both sides" argument. Consequences and justice are right. Erasure and hatred are not. Redemption must be possible for all. Reconciliation must be the goal. This is why I believe the work I have done here is important. It is the denial of the *imago Dei* in people who are called scum, worthless, or worse that has led society to allow their murders with so little care. Rhys demonstrated how easily her women characters were tossed aside—even Anna or Julia's own family did not think them worth helping as they had thrown away their worth. But in fact, Julia is valued and loved by the God who entered fully into our experiences of isolation, shame and trauma. Christ's wounds remain to remind us that God is implicated in the suffering of the world.

As I have learned though this research journey, redemption is not erasure. The wounds are still present. We can still touch them. They have changed us, but they have also connected us. As Glissant argues, these cracks we have connect us to each other in deep ways that constitute true relationship. They connect God to us, and us to each other. Sasha's hope does not come because she or her situation changed. Instead, it is because God is present in the moment of her trauma. The hope is in the silent grief shared by Sasha and God. The paradox of the "already and not yet" of redemption. This silent grief allows us to be present to our trauma while knowing that God is with us.

# Bibliography

Agamben, Giorgio. *Nudities*. Translated by David Kishik and Stefan Pedatella. Meridian: Crossing Aesthetics. Stanford: Stanford University Press, 2011.
Alcoff, Linda, and Elizabeth Potter. *Feminist Epistemologies*. Thinking Gender. London: Routledge, 1993.
Althaus-Reid, Marcella. *From Feminist Theology to Indecent Theology: Readings on Poverty, Sexual Identity and God*. London: SCM, 2004.
———. *Indecent Theology: Theological Perversions in Sex, Gender and Politics*. London: Routledge, 2000.
Angier, Carole. *Jean Rhys: Life and Work*. Boston: Little, Brown, 1990.
Barter, Jane A. "A Theology of Liberation in Barth's Church Dogmatics IV/3." *Scottish Journal of Theology* 53 (2000) 154–76.
Barth, Karl. *Church Dogmatics. I/2 The Doctrine of the Word of God, Part 2*. Edited by Geoffrey W. Bromiley and Thomas F. Torrance. Translated by A. T. Mackay et al. Edinburgh: T. & T. Clark, 1961
———. *Church Dogmatics III/2: The Doctrine of Creation, Part 2*. Edited by Geoffrey W. Bromiley and Thomas F. Torrance. Translated by Harold Knight et al. Edinburgh: T. & T. Clark, 1960.
———. *Church Dogmatics III/3: The Doctrine of Creation, Part 3*. Edited by Geoffrey W. Bromiley and Thomas F. Torrance. Translated by Harold Knight et al. Edinburgh: T. & T. Clark, 1960.
———. *Church Dogmatics. III/4: The Doctrine of Creation, Part 4*. Edited by Geoffrey W. Bromiley and Thomas F. Torrance. Translated by A.T. Mackay et al. Edinburgh: T. & T. Clark, 1961.
———. *Church Dogmatics IV/1: The Doctrine of Reconciliation, Part 1*. Edited by Geoffrey W. Bromiley and Thomas F. Torrance. Translated by A. T. Mackay, et al. Edinburgh: T. & T. Clark, 1961.
Betcher, Sharon V. "Becoming Flesh of My Flesh: Feminist and Disability Theologies on the Edge of Posthumanist Discourse." *Journal of Feminist Studies in Religion* 26 (2010) 107–18.

Brunner, Emil. *Man, in Revolt: A Christian Anthropology*. Translated by Olive Wyon. Philadelphia: Westminster, 1939.

Burrow, Rufus, Jr. *James H. Cone and Black Liberation Theology*. Jefferson, NC: McFarland, 1994.

Cannon, Katie G. *Black Womanist Ethics*. American Academy of Religion Academy Series 60. Atlanta: Scholars, 1988.

———. *Katie's Canon: Womanism and the Soul of the Black Community*. New York: Continuum, 1995.

Carr, Helen. *Jean Rhys*. Devon, UK: Northcote House, 2012.

Chopp, Rebecca S. "Theology and the Poetics of Testimony." In *Converging on Culture: Theologians in Dialogue with Cultural Analysis and Criticism*, edited by Delwin Brown et al., 56–70. Oxford: Oxford University Press, 2001.

Clifford, Anne M. *Introducing Feminist Theology*. Maryknoll, NY: Orbis, 2002.

Coakley, Sarah. "Why Gift? Gift, Gender and Trinitarian Relations in Milbank and Tanner." *Scottish Journal of Theology* 61 (2008) 224–35.

Coblentz, Jessica. "Review of *Resurrecting Wounds: Living in the Afterlife of Trauma*, by Shelly Rambo." *Horizons* 45 (2018) 497–98.

Cone, James H. "The Doctrine of Man in the Theology of Karl Barth." PhD diss., Northwestern University, 1965.

———. *God of the Oppressed*. Maryknoll, NY: Orbis, 1997.

Copeland, M. Shawn. *Enfleshing Freedom: Body, Race, and Being*. Innovations. Minneapolis: Fortress, 2010.

———. "Wading through Many Sorrows: Toward a Theology of Suffering in a Womanist Perspective." In *Womanist Theological Ethics*, edited by Katie Geneva Cannon et al., 135–54. Louisville: Westminster John Knox, 2011.

Cooper-White, Pamela. "The Early 1990s: Whose CWR? Whose Feminism?" In *Feminist Theologies: Legacy and Prospect*, edited by Rosemary Radford Ruether, 16–28. Minneapolis: Fortress, 2007.

Cress, Graydon. "Perichoresis and Participation: Union between the Persons of God and between God and Humanity." PhD diss., St. Andrew's University, 2019.

Daly, Mary. *Beyond God the Father: Toward a Philosophy of Women's Liberation*. Boston: Beacon, 1985.

Earl, Riggins R., Jr. "Black Theology and Human Purpose." In *The Cambridge Companion to Black Theology*, edited by Dwight N Hopkins and Edward P. Antonio, 126–42. Cambridge Companions to Religion. Cambridge: Cambridge University Press, 2012.

Ellmann, Maud. "James Joyce." In *The Cambridge Companion to English Novelists*, edited by Adrian Poole, 326–44. Cambridge Companions to Topics. Cambridge: Cambridge University Press, 2009.

Finstuen, Andrew S. *Original Sin and Everyday Protestants: The Theology of Reinhold Niebuhr, Billy Graham, and Paul Tillich in an Age of Anxiety*. Chapel Hill, NC: University of North Carolina Press, 2009.

Florida, Richard, and Charlotta Mellander. "The Geography of Inequality: Difference and Determinants of Wage and Income Inequality across US Metros." *Regional Studies* 50 (2016) 79–92.

George, Sheldon. *Trauma and Race: A Lacanian Study of African American Racial Identity*. Waco, TX: Baylor University Press, 2016.

Glissant, Édouard. *Poetics of Relation*. Ann Arbor: University of Michigan Press, 1997.

Gouw, Arvin M. "Transcendence and Immanence of the Trinity in Barth and Lossky." *Dialogo Conferences and Journal* 2 (2015) 27–33.
Grenz, Stanley J., and Roger E. Olson. *20th Century Theology: God and the World in a Transitional Age*. Downers Grove, IL: IVP Academic, 1992.
Heijst, Anneleise van. *Longing for the Fall*. Translated by Henry Jansen. Kok Pharos, 1995.
Heller, Tamar. "Affliction in Jean Rhys and Simone Weil." In *The Female Face of Shame*, edited by Patricia Moran and Erica L. Johnson, 166–76. Bloomington: Indiana University Press, 2013.
Helmer, Christine. "A Systematic Theological Theory of Truth in Kathryn Tanner's Jesus, Humanity and the Trinity: A Brief Systematic Theology/Comment/Comment/Reply." *Scottish Journal of Theology* 57 (2004) 203.
Hughes, Carl S. "'Tehomic' Christology? Tanner, Keller, and Kierkegaard on Writing Christ." *Modern Theology* 31 (2015) 257–83.
Hughes, Krista. "Commentary and Study Questions." In *Creating Women's Theology: A Movement Engaging Process Thought*, edited by Monica A Coleman et al., 98–100. Eugene, OR: Pickwick Publications, 2011.
Hunt, Mary E. "Katie Geneva Cannon Incarnate." *Journal of Feminist Studies in Religion* 35 (2019) 109–11.
Johnson, Erica, and Patricia Moran, eds. *Jean Rhys: Twenty-First-Century Approaches*. Edinburgh: Edinburgh University Press, 2015.
Jones, Serene. *Feminist Theory and Christian Theology: Cartographies of Grace*. Minneapolis: Fortress, 2000.
———. *Trauma and Grace: Theology in a Ruptured World*. Louisville: Westminster John Knox, 2009.
Joyce, James. *Ulysses*. 1922. Reprint, Toronto: Everyman's Library, 1997.
Keller, Catherine. *Cloud of the Impossible: Negative Theology and Planetary Entanglement*. New York: Columbia University Press, 2015.
———. *From a Broken Web: Separation, Sexism, and Self*. Boston: Beacon, 1986.
———. *Intercarnations: Exercises in Theological Possibility*. New York: Fordham University Press, 2017.
———. *On the Mystery: Discerning Divinity in Process*. Minneapolis: Fortress, 2008.
Lewis, Gordon R., and Bruce A. Demarest. *Integrative Theology: I*. Grand Rapids: Zondervan, 1996.
Maat, Sekhmet Ra Em Kht. "Looking Back at the Evolution of James Cone's Theological Anthropology: A Brief Commentary." *Religions* 10 (2019) 596.
Moltmann, Jürgen. *The Trinity and the Kingdom: The Doctrine of God*. Translated by Margaret Kohl. London: SCM, 1981.
Moltmann, Jürgen, et al. "Tribute, Hope and Reconciliation." *HTS Teologiese Studies/Theological Studies* 73 (2017) 1–8.
Nebeker, Helen. *Jean Rhys: Woman in Passage*. Montreal: Eden Press Women's Publications, 1981.
Nussbaum, Martha C. *Love's Knowledge: Essays on Philosophy and Literature*. Oxford: Oxford University Press, 1990.
———. *Upheavals of Thought: The Intelligence of Emotions*. Cambridge: Cambridge University Press, 2001.
Pattison, George. *Paul Tillich's Philosophical Theology: A Fifty Year Reappraisal*. New York: Palgrave Pivot, 2015.

Pauw, Amy Plantinga. "Ecclesiological Reflections on Kathryn Tanner's Jesus, Humanity and the Trinity." *Scottish Journal of Theology* 57 (2004) 221–27.

Pinn, Anthony B., and Katie G. Cannon, eds. *The Oxford Handbook of African American Theology*. New York: Oxford University Press, 2014.

Plaskow, Judith. "Lessons from Mary Daly." *Journal of Feminist Studies in Religion* 28 (2012) 100–104.

———. *Sex, Sin and Grace: Women's Experience and the Theologies of Reinhold Niebuhr and Paul Tillich*. New York: University Press of America, 1980.

Rambo, Shelly. *Resurrecting Wounds: Living in the Afterlife of Trauma*. Waco, TX: Baylor University Press, 2017.

———. Review of *Poetics of the Flesh*, by Mayra Rivera. *The Journal of Religion* 99 (2019) 125–26.

Ray, Stephen G., Jr. "Black Sacred Rhetoric: Katie Cannon and the Power of Memory." *Journal of Feminist Studies in Religion* 35 (2019) 127–28. https://link-gale-com.ezproxy.lib.gla.ac.uk/apps/doc/A621894321/EAIM?u=glasuni&sid=EAIM&xid=06d1a98f

Rhys, Jean. *After Leaving Mr. Mackenzie*. New York: Norton 1931.

———. *Good Morning, Midnight*. New York: Norton, 1938.

———. *Quartet*. New York: Norton, 1929.

———. *Smile Please: An Unfinished Autobiography*. London: Deutsch, 1979.

———. *Voyage in the Dark*. New York: Norton, 1982.

Rivera, Mayra. *Poetics of the Flesh*. Durham: Duke University Press, 2015.

———. *The Touch of Transcendence: A Postcolonial Theology of God*. 1st ed. Louisville: Westminster John Knox, 2007.

Roberts, David E. "Tillich's Doctrine of Man." In *The Theology of Paul Tillich*, edited by Charles W. Kegley and Robert W. Bretall, 108–31. New York: Macmillan, 1952.

Ruether, Rosemary Radford. *Disputed Questions: On Being a Christian*. Maryknoll, NY: Orbis, 1989.

———. "Feminist Theology in the Academy." *Christianity and Crisis* 45 (1985) 57–62.

———. "Feminist Theology and Spirituality." In *Christian Feminism: Visions of a New Humanity*, edited by Judith L. Weidman. New York: Harper & Row, 1984.

———. "Retrospective: The Development of My Theology." *Religious Studies Review* 15 (1989) 1–4.

———. *Sexism and God-Talk: Toward a Feminist Theology*. Boston: Beacon, 1983.

Saiving, Valerie. "The Human Situation: A Feminine View." *Journal of Religion* 40 (1960) 100–112.

Savory, Elaine. *Jean Rhys*. New York: Cambridge University Press, 1998.

———, ed. *The Cambridge Introduction to Jean Rhys*. Cambridge Introductions to Literature. New York: Cambridge University Press, 2009.

Schneider, Laurel C. "From New Beginning to Meta-Being: A Critical Analysis of Paul Tillich's Influence on Mary Daly." *Soundings: An Interdisciplinary Journal* 75 (1992) 421–39.

Smith, Aaron T. *A Theology of the Third Article: Karl Barth and the Spirit of the Word*. Minneapolis: Fortress, 2014.

Sporre, Karin. *In Search of Human Dignity: Essays in Theology, Ethics, and Education*. Münster: Waxmann, 2015.

Stephenson, Lisa P. "Directed, Ordered and Related: The Male and Female Interpersonal Relation in Karl Barth's *Church Dogmatics*." *Scottish Journal of Theology* 61 (2008) 435–49.

Tanner, Kathryn. "The Ambiguities of Transcendence." In *Common Goods: Economy, Ecology, and Political Theology*, edited by Melanie Johnson-DeBaufre et al., 91–102. Fordham Scholarship, May 2016.

———. *God and Creation in Christian Theology: Tyranny or Empowerment*. Minneapolis: Fortress, 2005.

———. *Jesus, Humanity and the Trinity: A Brief Systematic Theology*. Edinburgh: T. & T. Clark, 2001.

———. *The Politics of God: Christian Theologies and Social Justice*. Minneapolis: Fortress, 1992.

Tillich, Paul. *The Courage to Be*. 2nd ed. New Haven: Yale University Press, 2000.

———. *Systematic Theology: Three Volumes in One*. London: Nisbet, 1968.

———. "Theology and Symbolism." In *Religious Symbolism*, edited by F. Ernest Johnson, 107–16. New York: Institute for Religious and Social Studies, distributed by Harper, 1955.

Veli-Matti, Kärkkäinen. "The Trinitarian Doctrines of Jurgen Moltmann and Wolfhart Pannenberg in the Context of Contemporary Discussion." In *The Cambridge Companion to The Trinity*, edited by Peter C. Phan, 225. Cambridge: Cambridge University Press, 2011.

Walker, Alice. *In Search of Our Mother's Gardens*. New York: Harcourt, Inc. 1983.

Wallace, Beverly Rose. "'Black Butterfly' Asking the Question, Womanist Reframing, Conscientization, and Generativity A Reminder of the Contributions of Dr Katie Geneva Cannon's Life and Work to Pastoral Theology's Grand Metamorphosis." *Journal of Pastoral Theology* 29 (2019) 169–79.

Walcott, Derek. "The Antilles, Fragments of Epic Memory: The 1992 Nobel Lecture." *World Literature Today* 67 (1993) 261–67.

Wallace, Cynthia R. *Of Women Borne: A Literary Ethics of Suffering*. New York: Columbia University Press, 2016.

Walton, Heather. *Literature, Theology and Feminism*. Manchester, UK: Manchester University Press, 2007.

West, Cornel. *The Cornel West Reader*. New York: Civitas, 1999.

Westenberg, Leonie. "'When She Calls for Help'—Domestic Violence in Christian Families." *Social Sciences* 6 (2017) 71.

Wilmore, Gayraud S., and James H. Cone. Wilmore. *Black Theology: A Documentary History, Volume One: 1966-1979*. Maryknoll, NY: Orbis, 1993.

Wilson, Mary, and Kerry L. Johnson, eds. *Rhys Matters: New Critical Perspectives*. New York: Palgrave Macmillan, 2013.

www.ingramcontent.com/pod-product-compliance
Lightning Source LLC
Chambersburg PA
CBHW070256230426
43664CB00014B/2556